# MUSICAL REVOLUTIONS

# MUSICAL REVOLUTIONS

*How the Sounds of the Western World Changed*

## Stuart Isacoff

 ALFRED A. KNOPF | NEW YORK | 2022

THIS IS A BORZOI BOOK
PUBLISHED BY ALFRED A. KNOPF

Published in the United States by Alfred A. Knopf,
a division of Penguin Random House LLC, New York, and distributed
in Canada by Penguin Random House Canada Limited, Toronto.

www.aaknopf.com

Knopf, Borzoi Books, and the colophon
are registered trademarks of Penguin Random House LLC.

Grateful acknowledgment is made to Concord Music Group for permission
to reprint excerpt from "Adventures Underground" by David Del Tredici and
Lewis Carroll, copyright © 1979 by Boosey & Hawkes, Inc., A Concord Company.
All rights reserved. Reprinted by permission of Concord Music Group.

Library of Congress Cataloging-in-Publication Data
Names: Isacoff, Stuart, author.
Title: Musical revolutions : how the sounds of the Western world changed /
Stuart Isacoff.
Description: First edition. | New York : Alfred A. Knopf, 2022. |
Includes bibliographical references and index.
Identifiers: LCCN 2021045361 (print) | LCCN 2021045362 (ebook) |
ISBN 9780525658634 (hardcover) | ISBN 9780525658641 (ebook)
Subjects: LCSH: Music—History and criticism. | Music and history.
Classification: LCC ML160 .I83 2022 (print) | LCC ML160 (ebook) |
DDC 780.9—dc23
LC record available at https://lccn.loc.gov/2021045361
LC ebook record available at https://lccn.loc.gov/2021045362

Jacket art: *Tout par compas suy composés* by Baude Cordier (1380–1440).
Chantilly Codex
Jacket design by Keenan

Manufactured in the United States of America
First Edition

To Adrienne, still my light

My end is my beginning and my beginning, my end.

—Canon by Guillaume de Machaut (c. 1300–1377)

# Contents

# MUSICAL REVOLUTIONS

# Introduction

THIS IS A BOOK ABOUT MOMENTS in music history when things dramatically changed, a succession of bold leaps in the progress of Western culture. Some of these had a gloriously expansive effect, like the invention of music notation in the eleventh century; the birth of opera in the sixteenth; the time in the early twentieth when American jazz spread its wings and moved to Paris. Others were seriously unsettling, like the tumultuous decision by Austrian composer Arnold Schoenberg and his students to erase the distinction between "consonance" and "dissonance," thereby overthrowing the very pillars of Western harmony; or the determination by John Cage and his followers to craft their music from the indeterminacy of a coin toss. Each one ushered in a new direction—often unexpected, like a planet following an invisible orrery, discernible only after the fact. At times these spurred convulsive reactions against the current trend (as in the swing, during J. S. Bach's lifetime, from clotted complexity to elegant simplicity—a change Bach himself transcended, as his music embodied both).

Still, these changes usually didn't arise in a flash, like an unforeseen volcanic eruption, but instead unfolded as an arc: preceded by earlier hints and models, and encompassing long-term aftereffects. The pattern reflects the definition of "revolution" as suggested by Nicolaus Copernicus in his groundbreaking *On the Revolutions of the Celestial Spheres,* in 1543. "Revolution," in his view, implies cyclic return, as in the elliptical orbits of the planets as they revolve around the sun; or in periodic repetition, per Galileo's explanation of the ocean's tides, based on Copernican theory. The term "revolution," though it conjures images of storming the barricades, is frequently less a cannon shot than a great pendulum swing. And, as J. Bernard Cohen pointed out in *Revolution in Science* (1985), it implies depth, a cumulative impact, a web of contexts.

Even with the disruptive shock of the new, a discernible symmetry can be found within revolutionary change. As Mark Twain pointed out, history may not exactly repeat, but it rhymes: the universe unfolds as a great narrative poem, outlining an endless series of connections. In describing the arc of a particular musical phenomenon, however, the question arises of how far back one should search for its origins. The pursuit could be endless, because there never was a time without music.

Archaeologists have found a flute, at least thirty-five thousand years old, in a cave in southwestern Germany, made from a hollow bone of a griffon vulture, placed in a curated setting, surrounded by cave paintings and carved figures. A conch-shell horn from the Paleolithic period, eighteen thousand years ago, has turned up in southern France; it had been deliberately chipped and punctured to create a musical instrument. Clearly, music and art have always been essential aspects of living.

The list of events in this book is, of course, somewhat arbitrary. No attempt has been made for completeness, since the subject is inexhaustible, and others might well come up with alternate versions—including perspectives more inclusive of world music. There is a great big universe beyond the Western canon, and my narrow focus is simply a result of who I am, and what I have focused on and experienced for most of my life. I don't have the expertise to venture very much beyond the topics presented here.

In fact, I felt compelled to skip even some important facets of Western music, like rock—the stylistic juggernaut that emerged in the 1950s, animated by teenage angst and overheated libidos. It arose from the simmering turmoil at the center of a growing generation gap, with the aim of disrupting the status quo. Like everything else covered here, rock constantly evolved. In the beginning, its transgressions were relatively tame: Elvis Presley stunned a public unaccustomed to artists whose style transcended the Black/white racial divide, and easily sent teen girls into a frenzy with the mere twitch of his hips.

As the years wore on, the festering nihilism at the music's center erupted into outright brutality: pianist Jerry Lee Lewis ("Great Balls of Fire") literally set his instrument ablaze; the Who's Pete Townshend smashed guitars on stage, as the music metaphorically demolished social guardrails. Rock musicians increasingly assumed the role of outcasts and outlaws, though the Beatles, among other groups leading the "British Invasion," brought charm to the mix. The movement's trajectory changed again through increasing levels of sophistication, while diverse currents, from folk-rock and grunge to electronics and hip-hop, influenced the genre in unpredictable ways. If rock is to be written about, it deserves a more knowledgeable observer than myself.

So the scope here is limited. Yet the benchmarks I cite, aspects of a continuing tradition, stand out in my mind as moments of remarkable creativity and daring, though it is unusual to find them compiled into a single volume. They are worth remarking upon, and celebrating.

# CHAPTER 1

# Singing from Symbols

*The music surged in my ears, truth seeped into my heart . . .*
—ST. AUGUSTINE, *Confessions*

STRIKING AN ASCETIC POSE in the church sanctuary, St. Augustine (354–430) knelt for a brief instant, as motionless as one of the chamber's stone columns, while the voices of men and women in the choir gently intermingled in a simple, haunting melody, rising and falling like incense in the musty air. The sound wafted gently along the cathedral's walls, intoxicating, sensuous, even seductive—as wily and dangerous as voluptuous Eve's enticements to a hapless Adam. Flooded with the pleasure of it, Augustine burst into tears. Surrendering to the experience had distracted him from the word of God—a venial sin—and he was gripped with guilt.

For centuries, philosophers had warned of music's ability to manipulate emotions—provoking sadness, igniting fervor, even enfeebling the mind. Augustine was a witness to the danger, and he recorded his experiences in his *Confessions*. Four centuries after he penned them, religious authorities were still grappling with the issue, though no longer warning about the threat of beguilement; instead, they began to consider how the very tones that had led Augustine astray could be harnessed in service of the Church's mission.

In his time, each region under the pope's reign was caught up in its own way of speaking and thinking, including particular approaches to intoning the sacred hymns. "I myself could hardly believe it," noted Notker the Stammerer (c. 840–912), one of the leading literary and musical figures of the early Middle Ages, "how widely the different provinces—nay, not the provinces only but districts and cities—differed in the praise of God, that is to say in their method of chanting." That lack of unity, in the view of religious authorities, robbed the kingdom and the Church of their full power.

They wondered, what if the disparate groups could all be coaxed into singing with a single voice, thereby forging a united people out of a sprawling, polyglot kingdom? It might actually allow the Holy See finally to triumph over a disordered world, though, in fact, putting things in such order seemed a task beyond the abilities of mere mortals.

The job was taken on by Charlemagne (742–814), also known as Charles the Great, the fierce warrior who brought under one rule the individual regions and for his efforts was crowned Holy Roman Emperor by Pope Leo III on Christmas Day in 800. Charles was the son of King Pepin the Short, ruler of the Franks, who purportedly demonstrated his might by piercing a lion's neck and severing a bull's head with just a single blow. According to Notker, Pepin's followers fell to the ground at the sight of this, and instantly declared his authority over all mankind.

Charlemagne inherited his father's grit and succeeded him as Defender of the Faith. He was tall, towering over most of his contemporaries. Whether done up in gold-embroidered robes on feast days or wearing a simple tunic, he would always have a sword by his side, especially a cherished one made with a hilt of gold and a jewel-encrusted scabbard. Standard dress for the Franks included gilt-covered boots with red thongs, a rich linen shirt, and a buckled sword-belt covered in leather and hard, shining wax. A stick of applewood was traditionally carried in the right hand—with "regular knots, strong and terrible," according to one witness. The king's martial skills unfailingly rattled the spirits of foes. Nithard, son of Charlemagne's daughter Bertha, claimed that Charles managed to tame the "wild and iron hearts" of the Franks and barbarians alike through a form of "mild terror." In fact, his name was whispered with such awe that it became part of a well-known magical incantation—the so-called Charlemagne's Prayer—used to invoke Jesus's help in resisting the devil and securing protection against enemies, natural disasters, and illness.

But the idea of compelling everyone in his domain to sing hymns in exactly the same manner faced insurmountable obstacles. Some groups, Notker explained, "torn with envy of the glory of the Franks . . . determined to vary their method of singing so that [Charles's] kingdom and dominion should never have cause to rejoice in unity and agreement." When it came to venerating God through Gregorian chant—named for Pope Gregory I, the sixth-century saint whose identity has been forever linked to the catalog of hymns—the kingdom was a musical Tower of Babel.

In Milan, many clung to a regional style known as Ambrosian chant, which can be heard in some churches there even today. In southern Spain, the inhabitants preserved Mozarabic chant, cultivated under the Visigoths. And the Germans were considered a lost cause, since, as the medieval Church chronicler John the Deacon put it, "their coarse voices, which roar like thunder, cannot execute soft modulations, because their throats are hoarse with too much drinking."

In any case, the dream of teaching everyone to sing in exactly the same manner seemed doomed to failure, because there was simply no good way to make it happen—no means of writing down the melodies so that singers could study them. The most common technique used by teachers at the time involved tedious rote exercise: first locating the pitches of a hymn by playing them on an instrument, such as the single-string monochord, and then asking singers to replicate and remember the result. The process was painstaking. It was also unreliable: as St. Isidore, bishop of Seville (c. 560–636), pointed out, the entire enterprise was built on shaky ground. "Unless sounds are held in the memory by man," he complained, "they perish."

Various historical efforts to remedy the situation had been tried. Small accent marks in ancient Hebrew cantillation placed next to the words—like signs sometimes used to indicate poetic inflection—communicated fixed melodic shapes. Tibetan monks relied on meandering squiggles to guide their throaty incantations, like seismograph printouts tracing the Earth's tremors. Odo, abbot of Cluny, resurrected a Greek method employing alphabetical letters. There were graphic representations of music in such disparate places as China and Syria, where an ancient Hurrian song dating to 1400 BCE was discovered on stone tablets, depicted with what appear to be interval names and number signs. But these were all abstract hints. In any case, it's hard to soar in song while busily attempting to translate theoretical symbols into practice.

The turning point in Europe came about through the efforts of an Italian monk named Guido of Arezzo (990–1050), who as a singing instructor to youngsters daily experienced the difficulties in achieving the alchemy of voices perfectly blended. Guido was studious, devotional, socially awkward, compliant in the face of authority, and extremely frail. Yet he boldly asserted that the usual method of mimicking the sounds of a monochord was "childish," and good only for beginners. After studying the available theoretical treatises on the subject and experimenting on his students, he devised a practical way of connecting notation to the physical act of singing. Success brought him little more than personal grief; his work was received as a provocation, not a cause for celebration.

The man became a victim of his infatuation, a loner pioneering in his limited world, with no real support system. He was, perhaps unintentionally, a revolutionary leader. What qualities did that term convey? The nineteenth-century anarchist Sergey Nechayev declared in his *Catechism of a Revolutionary* that "the revolutionary is a doomed man. He has no private interests, no affairs, sentiments, ties, property nor even a name of his own. His entire being is devoured by one purpose, one thought, one passion." Guido was not spurred by politics or ideology, though his radical solution served a conservative goal (gathering all the flock under the pope's domain). Yet the revolutionary tag seems apt: in breaking through to a new way of seeing music, he had become an insurgent of sorts, leaving convention and common aspects of life behind as a sacrifice to his vision.

He poured his heart out about the situation in a letter to a fellow monk at his monastery in Pomposa, Brother Michael, declaring that other clerics at the monastery had met his achievement with "envy and scorn." Their intense animosity created a "dissipating sadness," he explained, leaving him "dejected and burdened." As his life situation became increasingly intolerable, he left the Pomposa monastery and found refuge at the cathedral school in the nearby town of Arezzo as a singing teacher, with the help of a bishop named Theodaldus.

In his letter to Michael, Guido compared his own victimization to that of "a certain artisan who presented to Augustus Caesar an incomparable treasure, namely, flexible glass. Thinking that because he could do something beyond the power of all others, he deserved a reward beyond all others, he was by the worst of fortunes sentenced to death, lest, if glass could be made as durable as it is marvelous, the entire royal treasure, consisting of various metals, should suddenly become worthless. And so, from that time on, accursed envy has deprived mortals of this boon, as it once deprived them of Eden."

Nevertheless, Guido plunged ahead, wrote his *Micrologus de disciplina artis musicae*, explaining his method, and with Brother Michael's collaboration put out a collection of chants using the notation he had invented. That successful test of his ideas generated unexpected help from the highest places. When Supreme Pontiff John XIX "heard about the fame of our school and how boys could learn chants that they had never heard before," explained Guido, "[he] was most intrigued and sent three emissaries to bring me to him. Thus," he reported, "I went to Rome with revered abbot Dom Grunvald and Dom Peter of Arezzo, provost of the canons of our church, among the most learned men of our time."

When he arrived, the pope and Guido talked about "many things," he recalled, and the pontiff looked through the hymn collection "as if it were a miracle of nature." The pope tried the new method out himself, and found the exorbitant claims—for example, that it was now possible for the first time to "sing an unknown melody" at sight—to be true. Guido's triumph was affirmed.

Every door was now open to the beleaguered monk. But the heat in Rome was bad for his delicate health, and he quickly retreated again to the Tuscan hills. The pope's eager embrace of his work, however, had bolstered Guido's assertion that his new method would make it possible for singers to perfect within five months what used to take ten years. (Perhaps that boast offers a clue as to why he ran into so many difficulties with his jealous colleagues.) The adoption of Guido's innovation was now inevitable.

What was his revelatory new approach? Musicians familiar with modern music notation will recognize its basic elements. He used a staff of four lines, unlike the five lines used today, on which musical note symbols were placed. Like a geographical grid—where crisscrossing arcs of longitude (east-west) and latitude (north-south) are used to illustrate the location of any place on earth—musical staff lines and the spaces formed between them served as a map on which any pitch in a song could be measured in relation to another. The higher the placement, the higher the pitch. Like rungs of an imaginary ladder, on which musical notes could symbolically climb or descend—traversing the musical scale with complete clarity—the lines became perfect guides. Precise rhythm was not indicated, but time flowed from left to right, like the words in a literary narrative.

The method seems perfectly logical and unsurprising today. Yet the idea of regarding pitches as occupying positions in vertical space required a leap of imagination, because the direction we use when signaling a rise in pitch is somewhat arbitrary: on a piano keyboard, higher tones are found by moving the hands

*Manuscript leaf with the martyrdom of St. Peter in an initial P,*
*from a gradual, c. 1270–1280, southern Italian*

to the right; on a cello, fingers over the strings move downward to find a higher tone. However, we do perceive faster vibrations as higher, and once the spatial orientation is set, eyeing the distance between note symbols—represented by dots, hooks, teardrops, and short lines at first, before settling on a rectangle or, in German manuscripts, a diamond or hobnail, as opposed to today's elliptical shapes—allows one to grasp at a glance the exact melodic distances in a hymn to be sung.

Guido used additional markers to help the reader: one of the staff lines was colored red to indicate where F belonged; another, in yellow or green, represented the placement of C. These were crucial markers, because in the common scale derived from the series of white notes, the distance from either C or F to the note immediately below is a half step (with no black note intervening on the keyboard), while for the other scale members that distance is two half steps, or a whole step. Without those color codes, wrote Guido, the notation would "be like a well when it does not have a rope, whose waters, although many, are of no benefit to those seeing them." (The use of colors disappeared in the thirteenth century, replaced in modernity by clefs at the beginning of each line to orient the reader by designating the position of F [in the bass clef], G [in the treble clef], or C.)

Guido gave names to all the musical pitches, using the hymn "Ut queant laxis," a tune in which every half line of text begins one scale degree higher than the previous one:

> **Ut** queant laxīs
> **re**sonāre fibrīs
> **Mī**ra gestōrum
> **fa**mulī tuōrum,
> **Sol**ve pollūtī

labiī reātum,
Sāncte Iōhannēs.

The full gamut of tones became *ut* (in today's parlance, *do*); *re; mi; fa; sol; la.* (The final note of the scale, *si*, was added at the beginning of the seventeenth century; it is now commonly rendered as *ti*.)

Guido's instructions were practical, though his feeling for the subject and its philosophical motivations ran deep. Revealingly, he reiterated an ancient view about the importance to body and spirit of hitting exactly the right tones. "Through the windows of the body the sweetness of apt things enters wondrously into the recesses of the heart," he wrote. "So, it is said that of old a certain madman was recalled from insanity by the music of the physician Asclepiades. Also, that another man was roused by the sound of the cithara [an ancient stringed instrument similar to the lyre] to such lust that, in his madness, he sought to break into the bedchamber of a girl, but, when the cithara player quickly changed the mode, was brought to feel remorse for his libidinousness and to retreat abashed. So, too, David soothed with the cithara the evil spirit of Saul and tamed the savage demon with the potent force and sweetness of this art."

In Guido's day, the musical textures were unfussy: the same exact melody was most often sung by multiple voices. But as musicians built on Guido's ideas, adding over the decades and centuries additional signs to indicate rhythm, dynamics, precisely measured silences, and more, it became increasingly possible for several people, each with his or her own individual musical part, to join together in a complex musical interaction. Even in notation's infancy in the later Middle Ages, music became known as the *ars combinatoria*, the art of combining things, and the evolution of Guido's innovations made this practical in all sorts of interesting, unanticipated ways. Music that couldn't have been performed before the advent of written scores now began to take shape in a brilliant, complex display of human creativity.

By the twelfth century, chant, free-flowing and unmeasured, like free verse, began to adopt the metrical organization of classical poetry. The chief rhythmic trait at first was an overarching feeling of three—like the modern waltz—with melodies built out of variants of poetic feet, such as the trochee (long-short), the iamb (short-long), and the dactyl (long-short-short). In Paris, the Notre Dame school (1170–1250) became famous for employing these springy rhythms, as well as for exploiting ways of adding a second melody to the mix. One approach was simply to mimic the original on a different set of pitches—usually a fifth away (the interval from do to sol)—acting like a luminous reflection. The sound of these simultaneous parallel fifths (or, alternately, fourths—the distance from do to fa) was hollow, haunting, and cavernous, increasing an already palpable sense of mystery that imbued the music. Notre Dame composers introduced more intricate relationships as well, adding a new, elaborate melody above the original chant, to create a florid counterpoint.

Around this time, the relationship between the optical and the aural took on new dimensions. Notation was initially used merely as an aid to performance, a way to capture on paper how sounds are meant to be performed. Now the visual—the look of things—became the door to myriad sonic possibilities, with images spurring new approaches to composition. For example, as church architecture evolved from the heavy, rounded, windowless structures of Romanesque design to the tall, spiky, light-filled cathedrals and intricate interiors of Gothic style, music followed suit.

In Gothic construction the sacred space was divided into three levels: a bottom plane containing large columns, well separated and placed at regular intervals, along the central aisle; on the second floor, an arcade of smaller supports clustered closer together; and above that, on a third level, the pillars were even further reduced in size, and grouped more tightly. Composers replicated this pattern by dividing the choir into multiple layers: on the lowest, pitches moved slowly, in essence acting as drones supporting the melodic elaborations that floated above; in the middle level, tones moved along a bit more swiftly; and on top were the highest, fastest tones, flurries of notes filling out the texture.

By the fourteenth century, the independence of these voices from each other rose to surprisingly absurd levels, especially in multilingual compositions called motets (written for many individual strands of voices). The motet "Dieus! comment porrai laisser la vie / O regina gloriae" was one example: the bottom part was a chant melody; the middle was a hymn that glorified the Virgin Mary; and the highest part, which bore no perceptible relation to the others, intoned a secular declaration about the joys of life in Paris among comrades.

Coordinating a motet's many melodic strands into an organic whole was a feat requiring the kind of detailed, sophisticated assessments being made by painters in the newly emerging world of perspective: another revolutionary change, emerging from a growing awareness of the possibilities inherent in spatial relationships. As in the flowering complexity of music manuscripts, in painting, intricacy begat intricacy. Perspective—projecting the illusion of three-dimensional space onto a canvas—began as an intuitive experiment in the hands of Giotto di Bondone (1267–1337), whose keen eye and artistic sense organized the planes of his canvas so that, in the words of painter Giorgio Vasari, he initiated "the great art of painting as we know it today."

Giotto once painted a fly on a face in a Cimabue painting that was so lifelike, the venerable painter believed it was real and tried to brush it away. His radical approach involved toying with the angles in a painting—skewing the proportions of objects to elicit a special three-dimensional optical effect. Later painters would use advanced mathematical techniques to better achieve those results by calculating precisely the placement of lines and planes as if they all retreated to a vanishing point in a virtual distance.

Over time, musicians toyed with various tunings—shaving or padding the distances between key tones to produce particular sonic flavors—as if replicating the actions of artists adjusting the proportional relationships between subjects on their canvases. The two artistic endeavors, musical tuning and perspectivism, grew together, and each triggered obsessive behavior in adherents. Florentine artist Paolo Uccello (1397–1475) was so enamored of the effect, he spent sleepless nights trying to grasp the exact placement of the vanishing point. Advocates of various tunings are still arguing about the subject to this day.

Meanwhile, musical complexity continued to evolve. Josquin des Prez (c. 1450–1521), perhaps the greatest composer of his age, was cited by Martin Luther as a "master of the notes. They must do as he wills," Luther contended; "as for the other composers, they have to do what the notes will." Josquin's breathtaking skill was on display in the Agnus Dei II section of his *Missa L'homme armé*, where he used the technique of prolation canon, in which the same melody was performed at three different speeds simultaneously. But the possibilities knew no limits. In the baroque era, Johann Sebastian Bach (1685–1750) would craft works in which musical themes ran forward, ran backward, and turned upside down, all the while blending together in meticulous harmony. In his *Art of Fugue*, he even managed to insert his name—B-A-C-H (when tones are used as a theme in German nomenclature, B represents B-flat and H represents B natural).

Symbols in notation continued to proliferate. Huge numbers of musicians could now easily coordinate their efforts. It became possible for Renaissance composer Giovanni Pierluigi da Palestrina (1525–1594) to create a forty-part choral work for eight different choirs singing together; and for Giovanni Gabrieli (1557–1612) to use the cavernous structure of St. Mark's Cathedral in Venice, where two choir lofts stood facing each other, to produce spatial sound effects. Along the way, critics raised many objections to the burgeoning complexity, sometimes likening the extraordinary musical skills displayed to a sort of witchcraft.

Baroque musicians developed a kind of shorthand, placing numbers beneath the bass notes in a piece to indicate what harmonies a keyboardist should draw on to embellish the written score. This "figured bass" notation compressed a great amount of information into a small space on the page. But innovative, intricate music manuscripts continued to flourish, and in some instances crafty notation even took on the luster of artwork. French composer Baude Cordier (1380–1440) penned examples of "eye music": manuscripts like the love song "Belle, bonne, sage," with music written in the shape of a heart, and "Tout par compas suy composés," inscribed as a circle.

*Baude Cordier, "Belle, bonne, sage"*

Johann Theile (1646–1724), known to his contemporaries as "the Father of Contrapuntalists," wrote a ten-part canon positioned on the page in the form of a geometric tree.

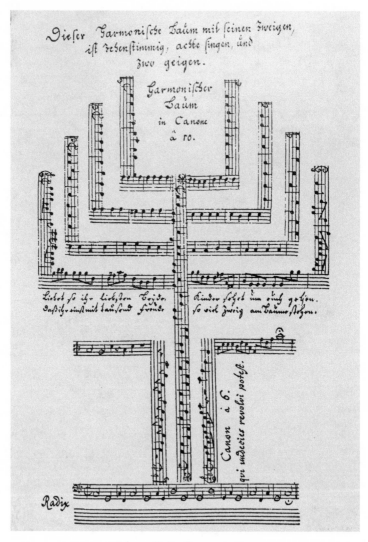

*Johann Theile,* Harmonic Tree

By the twentieth century, composer David Del Tredici, in his *Alice in Wonderland*–themed work *Adventures Underground* (1971), managed to replicate Lewis Carroll's typographic depiction of a mouse's tail (through the curvy arrangement of words on a page in his book) by means of the decorative placement of notes in his orchestral score.

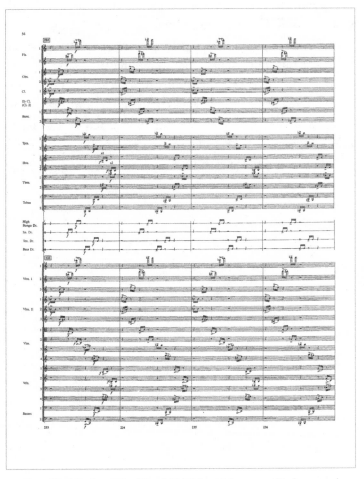

*David Del Tredici, "The Mouse's Tale" from* Adventures Underground

Composer George Crumb created elaborate music manuscripts as well, including one he called "Spiral Galaxy" (1972).

The visual aspect of music performance took on even greater depth in the twenty-first century as choirs added "signing" for the deaf to their execution of intricate works. SING&SIGN, an ensemble formed in Leipzig by soprano Susanne Haupt, brought Bach's *St. John Passion* to the stage complete with gestures using German Sign Language, conveying the music's texture and emotional tone through sweeping arm gestures, balletic hand movements, and communicative facial expressions. Even for those with perfect hearing, these movements introduced an enhanced level of clarity to the work's structure, bringing a tangible presence to the music, and producing an effect as gripping as that of any modern-dance work. It came very close to being a sort of living notation.

# CHAPTER 2

# Tones Like Coiling Vines

When music sounds, gone is the earth I know,
And all her lovely things even lovelier grow;
Her flowers in vision flame, her forest trees
Lift burdened branches, stilled with ecstasies.

—WALTER DE LA MARE, *"Music"*

G UIDO'S INNOVATIONS helped transform nebulous melodic contours into clear, graphic structures. His notation enables us to picture tones clearly as they rise and fall, stall, reach at times for jaunty heights, or plummet toward stable ground. Of course, the essence of all sound is turbulence—a frenetic stirring of air, stimulating the membranes and bones in our ears, and thereafter our minds and emotions. Within that din, discrete musical steps can be discerned—differentiated pitches that form melodies, suggesting a soft linear geometry, like the particular shapes favored by medieval musicians: curves over spikes—rounded edges mimicking nature's gentle spirals in sunflower blooms or cauliflower florets, or the concentric ripples in a pond aroused by a tossed pebble. Medieval dance followed these same patterns, often taking on a circular shape, as when men and women, holding hands, formed lines around a tree, while moving to lyrics like "Love me, my sweet blonde, love me, and I shall not love anyone but you." Such line dances were especially popular at court.

The vaporous strains of Gregorian chant most often settled similarly into an arc or oblong shape, the melodies gently rising and falling in long stretches. Hildegard of Bingen (1098–1179), the Benedictine composer known for her divine visions, produced tunes that traced such eloquent reliefs in air; softly climbing up the musical scale, executing gracefully inflected turns, then looping back down—in phrases free of sharp angles or wide leaps—before finally coming to a rest. By Hildegard's time, music had taken on a rhythmic lilt, like the metrical accents found in poetry. Performers executed these tunes as one: no matter how many people were singing, all voiced the exact same notes together (either in unison or an octave apart).

Music in this age served clear social purposes: there were narratives about knightly valor or courtly love (especially under the rule of Eleanor of Aquitaine [c. 1122–1204]), or tales of folk heroes like Robin and Marian, and of the legendary Arthurian character Lancelot. These themes pervaded the songs of the troubadours (their heartsick laments could also be confessional, as in the popular "I must sing of that which I would rather not"), following the same musical paradigm of soft curves as chant. But by this time something new was also beginning to take hold—a change in the music that dramatically distinguished it from that of many other cultures: multiple voices singing simultaneously in independent lines or tiers.

Music all over the world makes use of melody and rhythm—Indian raga pairs inventive vocal skills over a constant instrumental drone; West African drumming explores far-reaching, intricate rhythms. But the art of combining independent voices (a practice known as polyphony)—each one following its own individual musical path while also blending into a concordant whole—was fairly unique to the West.

There were exceptions: the songs of the Central African Pygmy people, as demonstrated by the Banda Linda, can involve eighteen separate interlocking parts—an outgrowth of the rhythmic complexity of African drumming ensembles. The music of Guria, in western Georgia, can embrace a rich polyphonic intricacy, merging into unexpected, unsettled tone combinations. The latter can perhaps be understood as an outgrowth of distinct societal forces: the linguistic root of "Guria"—a word that means "restlessness," as in "the land of restlessness"—suggesting a rugged independence of spirit in the Gurian character, perhaps leading to the musical impulse toward simultaneous independent expressions rather than a blend. Nevertheless, for the most part, world music is essentially monophonic, based around a single melody. The framing is simplicity itself.

Melding multiple, independent melodies together into a unified tapestry turned music in an entirely new direction. Like many such watersheds, this development was likely not so much a proactive choice, but rather a result of experiments unfolding over time.

History often records dramatic shifts as taking place in lurches rather than in protracted stages. Indeed, such changes can be spurred by a lucky mishap. Alexander Fleming's revolutionary discovery of penicillin saved countless lives and transformed medicine, but it was made possible by an accident: inadvertently leaving a petri dish of bacteria next to an open window before leaving for vacation. When he returned home,

Fleming discovered that a green mold had appeared, and that it had stopped the bacteria's growth.

However, even when progress reveals itself slowly, when what has been happening all the while at a snail's pace finally comes fully into consciousness, it will be seen as a revolutionary moment. As the new idea is pushed forward, often in the heat of battle against naysayers—just as Galileo clashed with and temporarily succumbed to the leaders of the Inquisition, who declared his observations foolish and heretical—heroes appear.

In the case of the technique of performing multiple simultaneous melodies, we can find pathbreaking proponents in several sources. The practice was described early on by a twelfth-century Welsh churchman writing under the name Giraldus Cambrensis (Gerald of Wales), who reported on his fellow countrymen: "They sing their tunes not in unison, but in parts with many simultaneous modes and phrases. Therefore, in a group of singers you will hear as many melodies as there you will see heads, yet they all accord in one consonant and properly constituted composition."

Ways of handling these individual strands, corralling them together into a pleasant mix, were first described in the *Musica enchiriadis* (Handbook of Music), the Frankish treatise thought to date from between 860 and 900, and in its companion volume, *Scolica enchiriadis,* a handbook of commentary on it. Musical composition had become a technically tricky endeavor: how could several independent melodies sung at once all manage to coexist successfully?

The issue of melding them was fraught. Pythagoras, the ancient Greek philosopher, mathematician, and spiritual leader, addressed the topic, recognizing that not all tones found agreement together. He realized that when two tones dance together in the air, they form a new identity, a sonic compound with its own properties, whether smooth or rough, irritating or enticing. Pythagoras discovered by experiment which ones coalesced nicely, which ones didn't, and determined that a set of simple mathematical ratios produced the best outcome. The serene, most beauteous harmonies created as tones melded together were produced only through certain specific proportions, and these became known as music's consonances.

His interest was more than a passing curiosity: for Pythagoras, as later for Renaissance polymath Leonardo da Vinci, the bonds between art and the natural world were revelatory, a key to the mysteries of God's creation. The relationship seemed especially evident when it came to vibration. Strike a table with a hammer, reported Leonardo, and small clumps of dust will gather into tiny dunes. That, he concluded, was how particles of the earth gave rise to hills, just as "waves of sand carried by the wind" created the mountains in present-day Libya. The material world is alive, declared Leonardo; the "earth's soil is a kind of flesh . . . the rocks which form the mountains are its bones . . . and the waters its blood. . . . The ebb and flow of the ocean is its breathing. . . ."

Harmony, the way separate tones melded together, was also a measure of nature's vital signs, and Pythagoras's calculations provided new insights into the role of resonating bodies. He found that when one tone oscillated at twice the rate of another (a correlation that corresponded to the relative lengths of the vibrating strings), the two formed an octave (the interval of one *do* to another in the major scale). The constituents of octaves sound so alike that together they seem like a single pitch.

A number of other harmonic proportions seemed less like a mirror reflection of just one image and more like a collection of pleasant marriages. The ratio of three to two, for example, with the higher tone vibrating three times for every two vibrations of the lower one, created a perfect fifth (in the major scale, do to sol); and when the ratio was four to three, the outcome was a perfect fourth (do to fa)—providing, in both cases, a haunting, hollow-sounding congruence. Other, far more complex ratios would yield only grating, unpleasant auditory collisions. Since the strongest congruence arose from the ratio of 2:1, it is little surprise that the earliest performance style employing more than one voice involved merely doubling the melody, either in unison or at the octave. (As it turns out, vibrating objects, like strings, naturally subdivide as they oscillate, and very softly emit all the basic tones Pythagoras described, and more; these overtones accompany the main, or "fundamental," tone as harmonic shadows, and help create the particular sonorities of different instruments.)

Using unisons and octaves to harmonize a chant was therefore a safe bet at the start. Early treatises also proposed more adventurous options, such as keeping the final note of a piece as a sustained drone throughout the performance—a technique still employed in the Byzantine chant of the Eastern Orthodox Church. Another technique involved mimicking the melody at a distance of a fifth, or a fourth, rather than at the octave—creating an independent parallel line, like the formation of ski tracks in the snow. These combined voices—called "organum"—could also merge together on the final tone of the chant, by approaching it stepwise from opposite directions (the top voice moving down, the bottom one moving up), thus introducing a degree of freedom and variety into the texture. (There were dangers to be assiduously avoided when creating such parallel tracks: when fourths or fifths are used consistently to harmonize the notes of a major scale, because the members of that scale are not all equally distant, the twin tracks will inevitably reach a moment when the interval between the two voices comprises three whole steps [such as in F to B], a discord known as "diabolus in musica"—the devil's interval.)

These various techniques blossomed in Winchester, England, in the tenth century, and at Chartres, France, in the eleventh century. But they famously flowered in radically new ways in the twelfth century in Paris, at Notre-Dame Cathedral, where two composers led the way to classical music's future. Léonin and Pérotin were both born in France in the mid-1100s. We learn of them through an English medieval musical theorist now known as Anonymous IV, who credited Léonin with the development of the *Magnus liber organi*—the Great Book of Organum. Léonin's approach involved employing a Gregorian chant as the foundation of a piece (the cantus firmus, or fixed melody), using it as a tune upon which an entirely new work could be built.

One way to undertake this involved stretching out the initial chant melody—creating in effect a "slow-motion" version of the tune—while faster-moving ornamental filigree was added above it, with multiple notes placed on each syllable of the text (a musical technique known as melisma). The slow cantus firmus, like a garden stake, provided a ground of support for those additional tones, which coiled around it like climbing vines. (Today, gospel and pop singers are renowned for adding melismatic flourishes to a tune.) Another approach—faster-paced, with the singers conjoining in a rhythmically insistent "note-against-note" style—was the jubilant manner most favored by Pérotin, who cultivated dense textures with three or four simultaneous voices.

Soon complications abounded. There were objections to the busy textures. Bishop Guillaume Durand (1230–1296) justifiably branded the emerging motets "disorganized music," and Pope John XXII in 1324 condemned polyphony altogether, complaining that innovating composers "chop up the melodies . . . so that these rush around ceaselessly, intoxicating the ear without quieting it, and disturbing devotion instead of evoking it." The fiery Renaissance preacher Girolamo Savonarola (1452–1498) charged that intricate counterpoint, the art of combining melodies, was "invented by Satan," and his influence in the matter caused the musical style to be forbidden in the cathedral and the baptistery in Florence in 1493.

However, advances in polyphonic techniques opened up ever more prospects in expressing the human drama. Johannes de Grocheio's *Ars musicae*, around 1300, provided a survey of repertoire "which men in Paris use," including epic songs "for old men, working citizens, and average people so that, having heard the miseries and calamities of others, they may more easily bear up under their own, and go about their tasks more gladly." It was all fodder for the composers, even though superimposing many disparate elements in a single work created serious challenges, as in one motet where in addition to an Easter hymn that formed the fixed melody, singers intoned such lines as "The other day at morn / down by a valley / at break of day / I spied a shepherdess / and watched her awhile." Musicians were embracing a greater range of human emotion and intricacy in their tone paintings, and adherents quickly proliferated; as the troubadour Folquet de Marseille put it: "A poem without music is a mill without water." And this was only the beginning.

.  .  .

Throughout history, cycles of simplicity have alternated with phases of complexity—just as straightforward plainchant eventually led to melismatic organum and the motet—and the fourteenth century ushered in ever-new complications. The name "*ars nova*" (new art), taken from the writings of composer Philippe de Vitry (1291–1361), was later applied to this period, a time when rhythmic dislocations (bucking against the usual pattern of stresses) and unusually labyrinthine melodies flourished. The new landscape seemed untidy at times, yet it was based consistently on mathematical principles.

Connections between those two disciplines, music and math, were strengthened through devices like isorhythm, in which two patterns—one a rhythmic configuration, the other an extended melody—were both stated repeatedly, yet never perfectly lined up. Because they were of different lengths, the pitches took on a different rhythmic emphasis at each appearance, making a connection to the original material barely recognizable. Isorhythmic motets grew in popularity and became a mainstay of the repertoire.

Such practices gave rise to musical puzzles and canons (in which a theme begins over and over through successive entrances, even as the rest of it continues, as in "Row, Row, Row Your Boat"). These inventions could get quite tricky, as in the famous piece by Guillaume de Machaut (c. 1300–77) "My end is my beginning and my beginning my end." Written initially for two voices, Machaut's music also contained indications for the introduction of a third: the highest part was to be sung from beginning to end; the lower voice to render the music backwards; and the third to sing just half the piece before doubling back to the beginning.

Such hidden schemes were resonant with the growing complexity of sacred architecture, as reflected in the Gothic cathedral, the design of which now permeated the landscape. And church interiors, once populated with simple floral motives, now featured a proliferation of ornamental twigs, flowers, fruit, and the full cornucopia of nature, along with statuary of zoological and imaginary creatures.

The secret musical agendas aligned with a particularly medieval worldview, in which much of life remained a mystery—where did fire go when it was extinguished? how did the Earth, in all its density, remain afloat in space?—while it was thought that an invisible hand was actually behind it all. The musical mazes framed the composer as ultimate creator, secretly shaping all aspects of the tonal universe, even if some were beyond the ken of the rational mind. Often, this meant investing a work with deep symbolism.

Such was the case with the famous motet "Nuper rosarum flores," written by Guillaume Dufay to consecrate the great dome of Florence's cathedral, Santa Maria del Fiore, in 1436. He based the work's rhythms on the biblical proportions of Solomon's temple, the iconic symbol of the spiritual sanctuary. The church had been under construction since 1294, and a gaping 138-foot span at its top remained an unhealed wound—a blight seemingly impossible to remedy—for half a century, until architect Filippo Brunelleschi (1377–1446) won a contest for a solution to the dilemma. He and fellow artist Donatello searched among the artifacts of Rome and discovered some answers in the Pantheon, which was secretly constructed in two layers. Brunelleschi subsequently also developed brilliant innovations that made possible the construction of the church's crown.

Dufay had been in Florence as a singer in the papal choir when Pope Eugene IV commissioned him for the great reveal.

The composer took the circumstances to heart, basing the music on a fourteen-note chant melody, above which a new composition is built, "Awesome is this place." He took note of the description of the great temple in Jerusalem in the biblical first book of Kings, which used the proportions 1:1, 1:2, 2:3, and 3:4—Pythagoras's universal harmonies, translating them into rhythmic schemes. According to the Bible (at least in Kings, which differed from accounts of the temple in other sections), the inner sanctum was forty cubits from the doors, and the feast of dedication lasted "seven days and seven days, that is, fourteen days." Dufay's rhythms followed the temple's proportions, 60:40:20:30, reduced to 6:4:2:3; and the length of the melody corresponded to the dedicatory feast, 7 + 7 = 14 notes.

Florentine scholar Giannozzo Manetti witnessed the ceremony at the cathedral's consecration: "All the places of the Temple resounded with the sounds of harmonious symphonies," he recounted, ". . . so that it seemed not without reason that the angels and the sounds and singing of divine paradise had been sent from heaven to us on earth to insinuate in our ears a certain incredible divine sweetness, wherefore at that moment I was so possessed by ecstasy that I seemed to enjoy the life of the Blessed here on earth." Dufay, and Brunelleschi, in their zeal, had led the way with a revolutionary spirit. Naturally, the fourteen condemned prisoners who were released in honor of the pope on the occasion were also quite moved.

Music's coiling vines, the melodic strands that gave a sense of direction while exerting a flowery charm, continued to be central to the art. But over the years, styles continued to evolve, and in the thirteenth century musical tones were made to obey entirely new rules, as the very definition of which ones fit together shifted.

The Pythagorean ratios had become sanctified as divine law, and Augustine even declared 2:1, 3:2, and 4:3 to be the dimensions of the ideal church. But over time other harmonic relationships began to dawn on musicians, especially among the English, who developed a sensibility much closer to that of modern listeners. Today, to contemporary ears, the harmony of a fourth—from do to fa—sounds as an unresolved dissonance, producing a tension that finds relief by moving that fa downward to the mi below it, thereby settling the harmony into a stable-sounding major third (the combination of do and mi). This is the exact opposite of what we find in medieval theory, where the harmony of a fourth can happily stand alone, but a third is considered unsettled.

By the thirteenth century, Anonymous IV reported that the English considered the third as the "best consonance" of all. It conveys something soft and beautiful, something very "human." (It's possible that astute medieval listeners, hearing the reverberations of chant melody in the vibrant acoustical setting of a spacious cathedral, detected the faint harmonic natural overtones that included the third, and came to embrace it.) Soon thereafter, composers began to regard the interval of a fourth as a harmony in "suspension," in search of more stable ground.

One of the earliest musical pieces to feature harmonies of thirds was "Sumer is icumen in"—also known as the "Summer Canon" and the "Cuckoo Song": "Summer is a-coming in / Loudly sing cuckoo! / Groweth seed and bloweth mead / And blossoms the woodland now: Sing cuckoo!" A copy of the manuscript is displayed in stone relief on the wall of a ruined chapter house in Reading Abbey. The work is a round, and the accompanying instructions indicate that it should not be sung by fewer than three: "This is how it is sung. While all the others are silent, one person begins. . . . And when he comes to the first note [after the end of the first two bars], another singer is to begin and thus for the others." When the singers are all fully engaged, the music becomes filled with major chords— containing the root, the third, and the fifth of the harmony (as in a C-major chord, spelled C-E-G). That triad, which became a prominent feature of Western music going forward, is still familiar today as a mainstay of pop music.

There was no turning back. In the fifteenth century, the Duke of Bedford, fighting the French, included in his entourage composer John Dunstable (c. 1390–1453), a revolutionary music leader who brought an English musical sensibility to the Continent. Soon, reported one witness, a generation of French composers had "taken to the English guise and followed Dunstable, which has made their song marvelously pleasing, distinguished, and delightful." The music took on an unprecedented sensuousness. Pieces began to incorporate chains of thirds, in a style known as "fauxbourdon."

The changing understanding about what constitutes consonance and dissonance also spurred new compositional procedures, solidified in the sixteenth century and modeled by composer Giovanni Pierluigi da Palestrina, who artfully wove the separate melodic strands of his music into a seamless, placid texture, like threads in a tightly knit fabric. His style was later codified by Johann Joseph Fux (c. 1660–1741). For generations since, Fux's *Gradus ad Parnassum* (Steps to Parnassus, 1725) became a theoretical and practical guide for students of musical composition to hone their skills at handling multiple voices.

Palestrina's historical importance was bolstered by the Church's Council of Trent (1545–1563), convened as part of the Counter-Reformation, to respond to the arguments of the Protestant movement.

Though the council, as an official body, never actually banned any particular musical approach, many attendees found in Palestrina's examples an ideal, and over the centuries claims were made that the composer singlehandedly saved polyphony as it was on the brink of being outlawed. This was an exaggeration, but barely. Palestrina's *Missa Papae Marcelli* was performed in the presence of the pontiff in 1565. Its dissonances were so carefully controlled—leading consistently to flawless, mellow resolutions and polished surfaces—that Palestrina's techniques have been a model for tonal music ever since.

These changes swept through the art world as well. The smoothness of Palestrina's music, its calming effect and avoidance of anything that would ruffle the emotions, comported with the council's decrees to avoid lasciviousness in art, to contain nothing "disorderly, or that is unbecoming or confusedly arranged." For the moment, art, whether in music or in painting, was being purged of any ripple of emotional agitation. Yet lurking even in the hearts of the faithful was a craving for theatrical experience.

· CHAPTER 3 ·

# The Birth of Opera

I hear the train'd soprano (what work with hers is this?)
The orchestra whirls me wider than Uranus flies,
It wrenches such ardors from me I did not know I
    possess'd them . . .

        —WALT WHITMAN, *Song of Myself 26*


PALESTRINA'S ART and its pervasive influence bolstered the Church's prescription for emotional restraint. Yet a contrary current flowed in many quarters. Resistance against pious curbs was at the very root of opera, which delivered flamboyant spectacle, enticing music, and engaging theater—a revolutionary reversal of the precepts of the Council of Trent, whose placid ideal was upended by advocates of freewheeling emotion and carnal desire. The form blossomed in a Venice struggling to burst free of the Church's spiritual manacles, a city populated by carnival revelers, aristocratic glitterati, and antipapal agitators.

In the words of seventeenth-century French social critic Jean de La Bruyère, opera was designed to distract (the very aspect of music that so concerned St. Augustine). It aimed, he said,

*The auditorium and stage of Bernardo Buontalenti's Uffizi theater,*
*decor by Giulio Parigi for the first intermezzo of Marco da Gagliano's*
La liberazione di Tirreno e d'Arnea *(1617)*

"to keep the mind, eyes, and ears in a constant state of enchantment," a description that would still resonate with modern fans. In short, it was a sensual celebration.

Birthed in conflict amid a swirl of colliding cultural forces, opera served the needs of wealthy aristocrats yearning for extravagant diversions, which commonly included masques—a combination of music, dancing, and acting, with elaborate set designs—and *intermedii*, music and dance numbers performed between the acts of plays. It all ran up against the ambitions of Church authorities, for whom theatrical display was anathema (despite the bleeding self-flagellants and penitents who regularly engaged in ritual exorcism during Holy Week processions). In 1577, the Venetian state in a burst of puritanism even expelled all actors from its territory. (Such decrees were not really the final word, however: when Pope Pius IV ordered the expulsion of prostitutes from the Papal States, businessmen complained that it would depopulate the city, and so accommodations were made. The ban on actors also failed to hold. Despite pressure from the Church, popular diversions thrived in the private courts.)

In the end, however, the drive to create the first operas arose not so much from insurgent impulses or from the lure of libertinism, but out of something more rarefied: the academic program created by a band of intellectuals known as the Florentine Camerata, humanists who met regularly at the home of Count Giovanni de' Bardi, beginning in 1573, to explore the cultural foundations of ancient Greece. (Bardi's son, Pietro, somewhat defensively described it as an innocent amusement, "a delightful virtual continuous academy," avowing that its upstanding members kept "vice and every sort of gambling in particular at a distance.")

In the Renaissance imagination, the Greeks had managed to achieve the pinnacle of civilized culture, and Count Bardi—who was praised at his induction into the Accademia degli Alterati for a command of mathematics, astrology, cosmography, and poetry—was particularly interested in how the ancients made music. "It is no wonder," declared the Accademia members, that Bardi, "altogether well-proportioned in his soul and body, has always had the greatest affection for the sweet and delightful harmony of music, the art of the ancient Greeks, among whom all the noble arts and virtues flourished to such a degree that whoever was not expert and practiced in it was reputed to be uncouth and worthless." That conviction became a credo for members of his entourage.

One of them, Vincenzo Galilei (1520–1591), Galileo's father, scrupulously explored the subject of Greek music (with Bardi's support) under the tutelage of Girolamo Mei (1519–1594), a Florentine considered the leading expert. The Greeks had purportedly harnessed music's miraculous powers in ways now lost, and Mei, who compiled his research in an unpublished treatise, *De modis musicis antiquorum*, asserted that they accomplished this through a unique performance style contrary to what was currently in vogue.

The approach was based on the ancient theory that each scale resonates in a particular way with the human soul; the Greeks had in fact carefully fashioned their music to trigger specific reactions in the listener. The "marvelous effects of the music of the ancients in moving affections," Mei concluded, were achieved because their intentions were so different from those of contemporary musicians, who seem interested merely in "the delectation of the sense of hearing"—the sheer enjoyment of sound. The effect for the moderns was too broadly aimed. In contrast, he claimed, the ancient composers had focused more narrowly on leading others to experience specifically "the same affections as one's own."

Modern musical practice, claimed Mei, had a serious weakness: interweaving simultaneous melodic lines of different types cluttered up the musical texture; thus composers diluted and confused the core emotional message. Any effect stirred up by a particular scale would be neutralized by a competing scale. Like the din of a social gathering where all the guests are talking at once, the result was muddle. What was needed to recapture the lost magic, Mei claimed, was a return to simplicity through the practice of monody, an uncomplicated style consisting of a single simple melody and straightforward accompaniment. In sixteenth-century Florence, this musical ideal became realized as recitative—singing that adheres to the inflections of everyday speech, with little additional melodic shaping. Today's operas still employ moments of recitative as a quick way to advance the plot.

Recitative's declamatory style was the prominent feature of the very first opera, which was based, not surprisingly, on an ancient Greek myth—the story of Daphne, daughter of the river god Peneus, who becomes the object of Apollo's unwanted affections and ultimately is turned into a laurel tree. The opera, *Dafne,* created by Camerata members Ottavio Rinuccini (librettist) and Jacopo Peri (composer), was first performed during Carnival in 1598 at the palazzo of Jacopo Corsi.

That novice attempt was successful enough to encourage the Medici family to commission Rinuccini and Peri, along with composer Giulio Caccini, to write another opera, *Euridice,* for the wedding of King Henry IV of France to Maria de' Medici in Florence in 1600. Most of *Dafne* has now been lost, so

*Euridice*—based on books 9 and 11 of Ovid's *Metamorphoses*, about the musical enchanter, Orpheus, who follows his love, Euridice, into Hades in an attempt to rescue her—remains the oldest extant opera.

The story is an allegory about the glory of musical power and the tragedy of fateful love. Orpheus, son of Apollo and the muse Calliope, purportedly had the ability to tame wild beasts and even to uproot trees with his lyre playing. In the course of trying to save his beloved, he seduces even the creatures of Hades with his musical gifts. In the end, however, his weakness of character ultimately brings disaster down on the pair.

After the Medicis' wedding guests arrived, they had to wait a full day to experience the new opera, but in the meantime there was plenty to occupy them. Following the nuptials on October 5, a banquet in the great hall of the Palazzo Vecchio featured a "winter landscape" of desserts, including a snowy forest populated with animals and hunters, all made from icing. A musical interlude, *La contesa fra Giunone e Minerva*, by Emilio de' Cavalieri, was staged in an enthralling setting. At one end of the hall stood two grottoes, from which luminous clouds emerged and slowly opened. On one was Juno in her chariot, drawn by peacocks. On the other sat the goddess of war in a car pulled by a unicorn. The two deities then engaged in godlike behavior: battling for superiority. Juno expressed her displeasure at the mere presence of the warrior goddess, and the two argued strenuously, finally coming to agree on just one thing: that valor was the principal quality to be found in the newlyweds. Then, satisfied with the outcome, each returned to Olympus.

The next day, *Euridice* was staged at the Pitti Palace. The opera opened with a prologue, sung by the character of Tragedy. Six separate scenes followed, featuring spectacular scenery: there were three-dimensional "magnificent forests," and an underworld of forbidding rocks, defoliated trees, and the burning city of Dis, its flames leaping under a glowing copper sky. The visual spectacle was merely a backdrop for the music, of course, where all stops were pulled.

Though in many cities women were not welcome on stage, in this case, Euridice was played by Vittoria Archilei, the prima donna of the court of the Grand Duke de' Medici. Her performance thrilled Peri: "Not only has she embellished my music with trills [ornaments of quickly alternating notes] and long simple and double runs [rapid scale passages]," he later declared, "but she also adorned it with those graceful and charming turns which no amount of notation can express and which, if written down, cannot be learned from writing." Peri himself assumed the role of Orfeo, and Marco da Gagliano, who eventually created fourteen of his own operas, was in the audience: "One cannot grasp the charm and power of [Peri's] music without having heard him sing it himself," he declared. "For he endows it with such consummate grace that he is able to convey the total emotional content of the words to the listeners, swaying them at his will to feel joy or lamentation."

The music for *Euridice*, adhering to the formulaic ideals expressed by Mei, feels a bit hollow today—emotionally distant, like a mirror held up to a fire, offering a fair depiction but failing to convey any heat. It is music for a select audience, more to be admired than felt. The more visceral sort of musical writing familiar to contemporary aficionados would soon make an appearance, however, through the pen of the supremely gifted composer Claudio Monteverdi.

But *Euridice* was just the start of an explosive trend. On October 9, the theater in the Uffizi became the site of another impressive production as part of the Medici festivities: *Il rapimento di Cefalo* (The Abduction of Cephalus), an opera with music mostly by Giulio Caccini and a libretto by Gabriello Chiabrera. Renowned stage designer Bernardo Buontalenti (who was credited with inventing gelato as well as enhancing opera stagecraft) created a fantastic setting for an audience of three thousand men and eight hundred women. His scenery included a twenty-three-meter-high mountain covered with trees and bushes; a waterfall trickling down a slope; a winged horse; and Apollo and his nine Muses. With that backdrop, the character of Poetry sang the praises of the newly married couple. Other scenes depicted plains, caverns, floating clouds, a whale, and a chariot drawn by four horses.

The story of Orpheus and Euridice soon became a pervasive theme in opera, eventually bearing such fruit as the exquisite rendering of the story in 1762 by Christoph Willibald Gluck— and the trend was still in evidence in 2020, when composer Matthew Aucoin's *Eurydice* was premiered by the Los Angeles Opera, while a Broadway musical version of the tale, *Hadestown*, was running in New York. Monteverdi adapted it as *L'Orfeo* in 1607, and his innovative genius gave rise to yet another musical revolution. Though he was denounced in some quarters for "licentious modulations" and "illegal progressions"—theorist Giovanni Artusi even accused him of "mountainous collections of cacophonies"—Monteverdi would soon reign as one of the greatest originators in the art. In *L'Orfeo*'s second act, spotlighting Euridice's death and Orpheus's brokenhearted response, the audience heard something entirely new: a fusion of intense drama, ecstatic music, and erotic fervor that remains at the heart of opera as we now know it.

*L'Orfeo*'s premiere excited interest even before it took place, when a Mantuan court official announced that "tomorrow evening the Most Serene Lord the Prince is to sponsor a [play]. . . . It should be most unusual, as all the actors are to sing their parts." The audience found that the composer had managed to integrate recitative, arias, choruses, dances, and musical interludes—merging old and new forms in an inspired, unique way.

Monteverdi himself described what he was doing as a "second practice," in which the words became "the mistress of the music and not the servant." The previous "first practice," he explained, was a style "chiefly concerned with the perfection of the harmony"—that is, focused merely on the behavior of the notes rather than on the expression of ideas. In embracing the new way, elevating textual meaning, wrote the composer's brother, Giulio Cesare, Monteverdi was following "the principles taught by Plato . . . and those who have followed him in modern times."

In 1612 Monteverdi moved to Venice as *maestro di cappella* (music master) at the magnificent St. Mark's Cathedral. That city would soon become the new center for opera, opening the first-ever public opera house in Europe, the Teatro di San Cassiano, in 1637, for a production of the opera *L'Andromeda* by a traveling troupe led by Francesco Manelli and Benedetto Ferrari. Monteverdi's own *Adone* (now lost) ran in that very same house from 1639 until the Carnival of 1640. By then, the experience of going to the opera had taken on new dimensions.

Venetian audiences were particularly receptive to grander, emotionally richer productions, because they were already accustomed to a life of pageantry and drama. In the annual Carnival season, the population of Venice, around fifty thousand during most of the seventeenth century, grew to nearly twice that number; social barriers were temporarily dropped, and the town embraced fireworks, ballet, masquerades, bull chases, and fights. Who could reasonably resist?

New theaters became staging areas for the hedonists and rabble-rousers. Wealthy libertines who financed the opera productions often disguised their identities when in public (it was easy to do when Carnival masks were a common practice). Theaters were designed to help facilitate such secrets, offering privacy for the clandestine encounters that took place in box seats, where patrons often engaged in notoriously indecent behavior. The Florentine ambassador to Venice reported: "The Jesuit priests have complained a great deal, that in the boxes that have been erected . . . many wicked acts take place, creating scandal." But you can't fight human nature. After a papal interdict punished Venetians for their conduct by withholding fundamental sacraments in 1606, retaliation was swift: the Jesuits were exiled from the Venetian territory and not allowed to return for half a century.

One hundred and fifty years later, when young Wolfgang Amadeus Mozart was performing throughout Italy, the opera house was still a center of immoral behavior, especially at Carnival time. As one observer described it: "Every lady's box is the scene of tea, cards, cavaliers, servants, lapdogs, abbes, scandal, and assignations; attention to the action of the piece, to the scenes or even to the actors, male or female, is but a secondary affair. If there be some actor, or actress, whose merit, or good fortune, happens to demand universal homage of fashion, there are pauses of silence. . . . But without this cause, or the presence of the sovereign, all is noise, hubbub, and confusion."

An important antipapal group was the "Incogniti"—the Unknowns—highbrow opera enthusiasts (and influential provocateurs) who inspired the construction in 1640 of the Teatro Novissimo, the fourth opera house in Venice. In 1641 they produced perhaps the greatest operatic hit of the century, *La finta pazza* (The Fake Madwoman). The company of traveling musicians that first introduced opera to Venice in 1637 had arrived there from Padua, home to Cesare Cremonini, the intellectual godfather of the Incogniti, who had riled the Inquisition by preaching the value of physical pleasure, claiming that the mortal soul was bound up with bodily sensations, and that therefore sexual drives should not be suppressed but expressed. Cremonini's influence was widespread; among his disciples was Giovanni Francesco Loredan (1607–1661), who founded the Accademia degli Incogniti in 1630.

Loredan's literary work *Bizzarrie accademiche* (1654) was a free-for-all of intellectual and ethical provocations. It included discourses on whether blushing was a sign of virtue or vice; whether card games were immoral; why physicians had long beards; and why Pythagoras prohibited the ingestion of fava beans. Loredan helped to get published the novella *Alcibiade fanciullo a scola* (Alcibiades the Schoolboy), a tale of pederastic seduction attributed to Cremonini's student (and Incogniti member) Antonio Rocco, a priest who was brought to Venice to teach moral philosophy, then refused to say Mass, declaring himself an atheist. His rebellious example set a tone for the times. Little wonder that in Monteverdi's final opera, *L'incoronazione di Poppea* (1643), Emperor Nero repudiates his legitimate wife and crowns his mistress Poppea. (The librettist, Giovanni Busenello, was a member of the Incogniti.) It was scandalous—and the public couldn't get enough.

By now, Monteverdi's style had evolved considerably from his earlier efforts, like *L'Orfeo*, intensifying in dramatic effects. In his *Combattimento di Tancredi e Clorinda* (1638), for example—an operatic scena in which the hero, Tancredi, has mortal combat with a soldier who turns out to be his love, Clorinda, in disguise—the composer's "agitated style" came to the fore, with rhythms that convey hoofbeats, the clashing of swords, and other signs of battle.

Opera now began truly to thrive. After the success of *L'Andromeda* in 1637, another Venetian opera quickly appeared in 1638, followed by three more in 1639, five in 1640, and seven in 1641 (with more theaters added each year). By 1678, nine theaters had been adapted or built for opera in Venice, and audiences saw as many as 150 productions all told, by some twenty composers and twice that many librettists. The stages became filled with lustful satyrs and scheming gods, duplicitous servants and unfaithful counts. And along with the productions there developed such now-familiar phenomena as publicity campaigns, season tickets, sold-out performances, and a city packed with unruly tourists.

While some observers of the phenomenon demurred—Voltaire decried the opera house as a "public gathering place where one meets on certain days without quite knowing why"—for the most part the Venetian fans were exhilarated, though legitimate criticisms of opera also abounded. The seventeenth-century French writer and moralist Charles de Saint-Evremond (1613–1703) found the fact that in opera the whole work is generally sung as exceedingly strange. "Can one imagine that a master sings when calling his servant or when giving him an order?" he asked. "That a friend confides a secret to another musically? That deliberations in a council of state are sung? That commands are chanted, and that people are killed melodiously in battle?" Those criticisms would continue. German philosopher Friedrich Schelling (1775–1854) asserted that opera was the lowest caricature of the highest form of art (that of Greek drama), and Russian novelist Leo Tolstoy (1828–1910) labeled it "a complete nonsense and regrettable waste of time and money."

The proliferation of opera also raised issues of social concern. In part because of the reluctance to invite women to the stage in some regions, composers turned to castrati—boys surgically adjusted to prevent their voices from changing—to cover their vocal range. The resulting sound was of unearthly beauty, and the lure of fame and riches induced many parents to offer up their male children for the honor. But the consequences of this surgery most often included a failed career and lives that were left desolate, with bodies permanently diminished, though they were often prized by royalty and clergy as playthings and sexual toys. Casanova's *Mémoires* contains scenes of an orgy that included "seven or eight girls, all of them pretty, three or four castratos . . . and five or six abbes."

Still, a few major stars emerged from the practice—internationally famous, wealthy, and living lavish lifestyles. Among them, the most celebrated was Farinelli, born Carlo Broschi (1705–1782). Perhaps the last great castrato was Giovanni Battista Velluti (1780–1861), who notoriously pursued women all over Europe and Russia, and lived for a while with a grand duchess. The attraction of these stars—with heavenly voices in combination with unmatched physical endurance—is difficult to overstate. According to one critic, the Abbé Raguenot, in 1709: "These pipes of theirs resemble the nightingale; their long-winded throats draw you so to speak out of your depth and make you lose your breath; they will execute passages of I know not how many bars together; they will have echoes on the same passages and swellings of a prodigious length, and then with a chuckle in the throat exactly like that of a nightingale they'll conclude with a cadence of an equal length, and all of this in the same breath."

Farinelli debuted in Naples at fifteen. Arriving in London in 1734, he was engaged by the Opera of the Nobility, a rival to Handel's own opera company. Reported Abbé Prévost: "This man is idolized, adored; it is a consuming passion." He was a wonderful musician, and his phenomenal range extended to a high E! Hired by the wife of Philip V of Spain in 1737 to help alleviate the king's melancholia, Farinelli sang the same four songs to him every night for ten years. The two men bonded, and soon Farinelli directed the royal chapel, redesigned the opera house, staged operas, imported Hungarian horses, worked with engineers to redirect the Tagus River, and helped the king in matters of state.

But it was his singing above all that remained legendary. Music historian Charles Burney (1726–1814) recounted a challenge between Farinelli and a trumpet player: "During the run of an opera, there was a struggle every night between him and a famous player on the trumpet, in a song accompaniment by that instrument; this, at first, seemed amicable and merely sportive, till the audience began to interest themselves in the contest, and to take different sides. . . ." They tried to rival each other in brilliancy and force, until "both seemed to be exhausted, and, in fact, the trumpeter, wholly spent, gave it up, thinking, however, his antagonist as much tired as himself, and that it would be a drawn battle; when Farinelli with a smile on his countenance, showing he had only been sporting with him all this time, broke out all at once in the same breath, with fresh vigor, and not only swelled and shook the note, but ran the most rapid and difficult divisions [embellishments], and was at last silenced only by the acclamations of the audience. From that period may be dated that superiority which he ever maintained over his contemporaries."

Following Philip's death in 1746, the singer worked for his son Ferdinand VI, but on Ferdinand's demise thirteen years later he retired to his luxurious villa in Bologna, a legend.

After opera's start in Florence, Venice became the fount of all things operatic. Despite King Henry IV's firsthand experience of opera at his own wedding, in the decade that intervened between that event and his assassination, neither he nor his bride showed any interest in bringing the art form to France. Of course, the French had their own popular performance tradition—ballet—which had taken root in Paris by the mid-1500s. It, too, could be quite spectacular.

For example, there was the six-hour entertainment at the wedding of Henry III's favorite the Duc de Joyeuse to Marguerite de Vaudémont, the queen's half-sister, in 1581. That *Ballet comique de la Reine*, based on the story of the sorceress Circe, was skillfully choreographed with dancers forming allegorical patterns, enhanced by stage machinery. The elaborate and lavish production is sometimes described as the first ballet. (As in opera, women performers in dance were at first often unwelcome, at least until the late seventeenth century. That was not true here.) However, in certain respects, French ballet simply could not measure up to Italian opera. When Pierre Corneille, the leading French playwright, wrote *Andromède* in 1650, he felt compelled to apologize for the music, saying it was there "only to satisfy the ear while the eyes are looking at the machines."

Then along came Lully. Though born Giovanni Battista Lulli in Italy in 1632, this violinist and dancer became France's answer to Italian opera. Early on he danced in a ballet with Louis XIV, who in 1661 named him *surintendant* of the king's chamber music. That same year, Louis also founded Europe's first official dance school, the Académie Royale de Danse. But Lully's Terpsichorean gifts were not celebrated nearly so much as his music, especially his extensive collaborations with the celebrated playwright Molière, Together, the two excelled at a new form, the *comédie-ballet*, which combined theater, comedy, and ballet with interludes of instrumental music. When the pair split up, Lully's subsequent collaborations with librettist Philippe Quinault in a series of *tragédies lyriques*—that is, dramatic operas—finally put French opera on the map. Initially, Lully had considered the French language not as suited as mellifluous Italian to his projects, but his early success in Paris convinced him otherwise. And he planted the roots there for a new tradition.

Strangely, both Molière and Lully died while performing: Molière collapsed while acting on stage at the end of the fourth performance of his *Le Malade imaginaire* in 1673. Lully received his own mortal blow in 1687, while rehearsing his Te Deum, which was to be sung as part of the celebrations marking Louis XIV's recovery after surgery. In keeping with the conducting tradition of his era, Lully simply beat time by pounding a long stick on the stage floor, and in the process accidentally struck his foot. The wound developed gangrene, and he refused to allow doctors to amputate, since it would end his dancing career. Instead, the injury put an end to everything.

The opera phenomenon continued to spread across the globe. In England, the afterpiece, an often-scandalous entertainment performed at the end of a play (in the manner of a French masque), evolved into an operatic form. In 1656, dramatist Sir William Davenant invited composers to set sections of his play *The Siege of Rhodes* to music, since his theater was not licensed to offer drama, and thus created the first English opera. By 1689, England's Henry Purcell had produced the great opera *Dido and Aeneas*, based on Virgil's *Aeneid*, with a libretto by Nahum Tate, in which the action was propelled by Italian-style recitative.

England celebrated a watershed in 1728 with *The Beggar's Opera* by John Gay and Johann Christoph Pepusch, based on popular ballads—lampooning Italian models and elevating ordinary folk. The work was initially sparked by satirist Jonathan Swift, who had asked Alexander Pope what he thought of the idea of a work that would focus on "thieves and whores." Few in attendance would have missed the satire directed against the prime minister, Sir Robert Walpole, his wife, and his mistress. In 1928, two hundred years after its premiere, Bertolt Brecht and Kurt Weill created a new adaptation of *The Beggar's Opera*—the wildly successful and still-popular *Threepenny Opera*. Weill, who had studied with Engelbert Humperdinck and Ferruccio Busoni, managed to embrace both high art and unpretentious, lowbrow earthiness in his music. Busoni asked him if he aspired to be a "Verdi of the poor," to which Weill responded, "Is that so bad?"

Even in the eighteenth century, the controversy over the nature of opera was unceasing. In 1752, factions in Paris warred over whether French or Italian style was superior. The battle was set off when an Italian troupe made its debut on the stage of the Académie Royale de Musique in Paris, presenting Giovanni Battista Pergolesi's *La serva padrona*. "Paris was divided into two parties, more violently opposed than if it had been a matter of religion or of an affair of State," wrote Jean-Jacques Rousseau in his *Confessions*. "One . . . the great, the wealthy and the ladies, supported French music; the other, more lively, proud and enthusiastic, was composed of real connoisseurs, persons of talent and men of genius." The French language, argued Rousseau, with its poor prosody, and lacking clarity in the proportion of long and short syllables, was incapable of producing either good rhythm or good melody. French music, he complained, is filled with burdensome ornaments and congested harmony, with the piling up of one voice upon another. Italian music, he explained, used simple and pure harmony, lively and brilliant accompaniments, was well defined in measure and rhythm, and featured moving modulations from key to key.

It's not difficult to imagine what fate befell Rousseau in the City of Light: "Although my liberty was not attacked," he reported, "I was unsparingly insulted, and even my life was in danger. The Opéra orchestra entered into an honorable conspiracy to assassinate me when I left the theater."

When Pergolesi's opera was performed as an intermezzo between the acts of Lully's *Acis et Galatée*, the contrast between old and emerging styles could hardly have been greater. Lully's opera was filled with pagan deities and traditional mythological characters—the old style. Pergolesi's intermezzo portrayed in realistic terms the characters and scenes of a bourgeois home: a wealthy but stingy old bachelor and a winsome young servant girl who tricks him into marrying her. Meanwhile, a comic male servant was constantly buffeted around without ever opening his mouth. This was opera that exploited common societal stereotypes in place of outsized mythical ones, and sympathized with their plights.

Pergolesi's approach set the stage for a work Napoleon described as the first shot in the French Revolution: *The Marriage of Figaro.* Written by Pierre-Augustin Caron de Beaumarchais, the play was a farce that unmercifully skewered the ruling class—telling the story of servants Figaro and Suzanne, who manage to marry, foiling the efforts of their unscrupulous employer, Count Almaviva, who is intent on seducing Suzanne, and teaching him a lesson. Joseph II had it banned in Vienna. Meanwhile, the life of its irrepressible author had the makings of an extravagant entertainment: married three times, he was accused by enemies of murdering his first two wives. When Mozart turned the play into a successful opera (with some revisions to soften its political impact), his librettist was Lorenzo da Ponte—as scandalous a figure as Beaumarchais. Da Ponte, who spent time in jail, was an unrepentant seducer who got his just rewards when a dentist he had cuckolded treated an abscess he had developed with a potion that contained nitric acid; it removed most of his teeth. *Figaro,* however, retained its bite.

Mozart's operatic daring continued with *Don Giovanni* (1787), described by a Berlin critic as a story that "will make honest maidens blush for shame." Once again, the plot revolved around a shameless seducer. Yet, as always, the creative skills Mozart evinced were on display: "Never, indeed never before, was the greatness of the human spirit so tangible," asserted the reviewer, "and never has the art of composition been raised to such heights! Melodies that an angel might have invented are here accompanied by celestial harmonies, and anyone whose soul is the least bit receptive to the truly beautiful will surely pardon my saying our ears are enchanted." Mozart's special gift was the ability to use common forms and yet fill them with innovative surprises at every turn. As he related it to his father, his trick was thus managing to appeal to both the uneducated listener and those with sophisticated knowledge.

The impetus behind *The Beggar's Opera* emerged again robustly in the vehicle of German singspiel—combining music and entertaining sketches, often focusing on the lives of thieves and lowlifes—as the mainstream tradition settled into two principal approaches: opera seria and opera buffa. "There shouldn't be anything playful in an opera seria, which should rather be learned and sensible," wrote Mozart in a letter, "just as an opera buffa should be less learned and more playful and amusing." Of course, being Mozart, he still managed to dissolve those boundaries.

As the years advanced, composers created a glut of forgettable operas and a handful of masterful ones, each reflecting the particular era in which it was created: there were ephemeral bonbons, but also Rossini's brilliant lyrical comedic spirit in *The Barber of Seville;* the Italianate lyricism of Verdi in *La traviata* and Puccini in *La Bohème;* the silky impressionism of Debussy in *Pelléas et Mélisande* and Ravel in *L'Enfant et les sortilèges;* and the modernist sounds of Bartók (in the harrowing *Bluebeard's Castle*), Strauss (with gorgeous harmonies and a shocking plot in his setting of Oscar Wilde's *Salome*), Shostakovich (whose boisterous *Lady Macbeth of the Mtsensk District* got banned by Stalin), and tonally transgressive Schoenberg and Berg, along with American contributions by bluesy Gershwin (the unforgettable gem *Porgy and Bess*), hymnal-like Virgil Thomson (in his nonsensical collaborations with librettist Gertrude Stein),

Samuel Barber, Gian Carlo Menotti, and Leonard Bernstein, among others.

Along the way, Germany's Richard Wagner (1813–1883) designed a wooden opera house at Bayreuth, which opened in 1876 (and described by Igor Stravinsky as like "a crematorium, and a very old-fashioned one at that"). It became the fanatical operagoer's mecca—a musical temple where, noted Mark Twain, "you seem to sit with the dead in the gloom of a tomb." Bayreuth became so popular that Karl Marx could not get a hotel room there, complaining that the Wagnerians occupied every bed; he was forced to pass the night on a hard bench at the railroad station.

Wagner festivals in Bayreuth, like the operas themselves, became saturated with ritual. During the hour-long pause between each of Wagner's acts, reported Nobel Prize–winner Romain Rolland, "The French flirt, the Germans drink beer and the English read the libretto." Wagner's craft—an all-encompassing approach governing every aspect of the production, from the musical tones to the costumes and stage props, all meticulously tailored to the drama—often stirred the audience into a kind of religious catharsis. No wonder Clara Schumann, wife of composer Robert and a formidable musician herself, said that Wagner's output, dripping with overwrought emotion, was not so much music as it was a kind of sickness—and this was long before the composer became an icon of the Nazis.

Expressing the natural antipathy between German and French musical worlds, twentieth-century French composer Darius Milhaud similarly complained that Wagner's music sickened him "by its pretentious vulgarity." Those were minority opinions, however. Alma Mahler (wife of composer Gustav), surrendering to Wagner's hypnotic allure, justified the social appeal of his works (inadvertently touching on their dangers): "Our century, our race, our outlook on life, our blood, our heart—everything is decadent! That's why people prefer operas in which the music whips up every feeling and tears us apart like a whirlwind. We need madness—not dainty pastorals—to refresh the heart and mind."

The enthusiasm of fans continued to propel the careers of great singers, and the rise of the celebrated opera diva ushered in a host of female stars. There was Giuditta Pasta (1797–1865): when the famous contralto Pauline Viardot heard Pasta's final appearance, she burst into tears, saying, "It is like *The Last Supper* of da Vinci at Milan—a wreck of a picture, but the picture is the greatest in the world." There was Pasta's rival Maria Malibran (1808–1836), Viardot's sister: when Vincenzo Bellini heard her sing his opera *Norma*, he said, "I believed myself in Paradise." And later in the century there was the notoriously self-indulgent Adelina Patti (1843–1919), an expert at self-promotion. Rumor had it that Patti's pet parrot was trained to say "Cash! Cash!" when her manager entered her dressing room. She was less impressive, though, when it came to musical taste; Rossini heard her sing an aria from one of his operas and asked, "Who wrote that?" But each of these singers managed to touch audiences in profound ways.

Modern opera singers have sustained the art brilliantly, with contributions by a long line of immortals: Marian Anderson, Cecilia Bartoli, Montserrat Caballé, Maria Callas, Enrico Caruso, Feodor Chaliapin, Plácido Domingo, Renée Fleming, Jonas Kaufmann, Anna Netrebko, Luciano Pavarotti, Leontyne Price, Paul Robeson, Beverly Sills, Joan Sutherland, Renata Tebaldi, and countless others—singers of a myriad variety of color, gender, and national background.

Today, contemporary composers, from Philip Glass and John Adams to Thomas Adès, continue to add to the repertoire. In the twenty-first century, the Metropolitan Opera in New York presented an opera by a Black composer for the first time in its 138-year history. Award-winning jazz trumpeter and film composer Terence Blanchard wrote the music for *Fire Shut Up in My Bones,* which was based on a memoir by columnist Charles Blow. It had premiered two years earlier by the Opera Theatre of St. Louis.

The Met also began to transmit to movie theaters around the world, extending opera's reach to ever greater numbers of patrons as live performances were temporarily halted during the Covid-19 pandemic. At the same time, streaming also proliferated. But live music will never wear out its welcome, and as life began to return to normal, audiences again flocked to myriad concert venues. As they did, one classical composer who remained a mainstay of season programs around the globe continued to be recognized for his importance and extraordinary skill.

# CHAPTER 4

# Out of the Bachs

Sebastian Bach at length acquired such a high degree of facility and, we may almost say, unlimited power over his instrument in all the keys that difficulties almost ceased to exist for him.

—JOHANN NIKOLAUS FORKEL,
*Johann Sebastian Bach: His Life, Art, and Work* (1802)

O PERA'S COMPOSERS and performers revealed the power of musical enchantment to overcome social obstacles. In like manner, a family of societal underlings named Bach transcended their station in life through sheer talent, rising over time to the status of "musical royalty." The line's founder, Veit Bach (c. 1550–1619), from Pozsony (now Bratislava), Hungary, moved to the village of Wechmar in Thuringia (the land of Martin Luther) in the sixteenth century in order to escape the Counter-Reformation. "Simple old Veit," as composer Carl Philipp Emanuel Bach would later call him, was a baker whose leisure time was spent playing the cittern, a mandolin-like instrument; he passed those musical proclivities on to two sons, who in turn bestowed them on their own offspring, spreading musical seeds throughout the family tree.

*1746 portrait of J. S. Bach holding his "Riddle Canon," BWV 1076,
painted by Elias Gottlob Haussmann. To solve the puzzle of this six-voice
perpetual canon, one must read the three parts that are presented,
then complete the piece by picturing the music upside down
and played in reverse (using different clefs), as if seeing the page
from the painted composer's perspective.*

According to one of Johann Sebastian Bach's biographers, Johann Nikolaus Forkel, from those beginnings a large clan emerged, "all the branches of which were not only musical but made music their chief business." Over time, the hardworking, humble Bachs became renowned as cantors, instrumentalists, and organists, so that the very name Bach came to be synonymous with "musician." The next in line after Veit, Johannes Bach (c. 1580–1626), first took up his father's trade, then became a musician. Veit's grandson Christoph (1613–1661) and his great-grandson Johann Ambrosius (1645–1695) both made substantial musical marks. Johann Ambrosius assumed the post of organist in Eisenach, Germany, and was heralded as a master of harmony.

But a single member of the lineage, one of Johann Ambrosius's eight children, emerged as perhaps the greatest musical talent who ever lived. Johann Sebastian Bach (1685–1750)—stunningly gifted, cantankerous, and constantly beset by quarrels—rose inexorably to the pantheon of musical greats, becoming a pivotal figure in the history of Western music. Orphaned at age ten, his professional life included a long record of pleas, gripes, and heartbreaking disappointments. Yet posterity chronicles the deep and lasting impact his music made on Western culture.

J. S. Bach is an unlikely candidate to be called a revolutionary, however. His path was one of rigorous distillation rather than of a single breakthrough, extracting the essential elements from the wide array of extant musical styles in his day—adopting the rhythmic jauntiness of the French, the rigor of the Germans, the lyricism of the Italians, the intricacy of the Netherlanders—and engaging with each in a thoroughly original way. The French component in his music, for example, reflected the composer's exposure at court to French dance masters, whose combination of the stately and the nonchalant characterized early ballet—a template that Bach readily adopted, along with a fitting rhythmic quirkiness in his rendering of the French overture. Bach was a sponge, and a thinking one. The entire musical world flowed through his pen, and at the same time he set a new, unmatched standard for mastery.

As Albert Schweitzer wrote in his biography of the composer: "All the artistic endeavors, desires, creations, aspirations and errors of his own and of previous generations are concentrated and worked out to their conclusion in him." Bach also forged the disparate strands in compelling new directions. In that respect, his work was both a summing-up of traditions and a radical recontextualizing of their components: he offered through his creative efforts a heightened way of viewing the commonplace.

His output, like the phenomenal compilation of preludes and fugues called *The Well-Tempered Clavier*—a collection Romantic composer Robert Schumann advised musicians not to go a day without practicing—revealed extraordinary technical skill: in the various fugues in all the keys, melodic strands are taken up in one register of the instrument, then in another, tossed back and forth or staggered so that an individual entrance interrupts what another has already begun. And, amazingly, in Bach's hands all of the autonomous musical lines blend into the most thrilling harmonies. Once heard, many of the themes in his extensive catalog remained forever etched in the hearts and minds of listeners—examples include heartbreaking beauties such as the alto aria "Erbarme dich" from the *St. Matthew*

*Passion* and the spiritually animated perpetual-motion chorale "Jesu, Joy of Man's Desiring."

Inherent in this composer's music are the qualities cited by his contemporary the philosopher Immanuel Kant as necessary to great art—such as "formal completeness" and "lawlike coherence." But, filled with joy and anguish, and marked by the intangible shadings of a thoroughly human spirit, the end result is always so much more than mere logic. That's why, over 250 years later, his work still has the power to inspire.

Bach seems, in fact, to touch the whole range of mortal experience, from suffering to beauty, and he makes it easier to live with all of it. Nobel Prize–winning author J. M. Coetzee wrote about the stunning moment when, as a fifteen-year-old boy in Cape Town, South Africa, he heard *The Well-Tempered Clavier* emanating from a neighbor's house. That afternoon in his garden, he explained, "everything changed." And the eminent philosopher Martin Buber, facing a crisis of faith in his youth, was considering suicide when he had a sudden insight into the fragile possibility of a just (ethical) human existence. How? "Bach helped me," he said.

One might imagine that the solace triggered by Bach's unfailing mastery arose from a sense in his work that a clockmaker God still ran an orderly universe. However, Buber obliquely suggested another explanation in a passage from his philosophical masterpiece *I and Thou*. The creation of great art, he stated, involves both a sacrifice and a risk. What is sacrificed is endless possibility, now offered up on the altar of form: like a prophet, the artist labors to bring down to earth the beauty of eternal, unseen worlds, reducing the limitless to something easily graspable. The risk Buber referred to rests in the fact that true artistic expression must be uttered by the whole self, with no protective buffer against the world. In Bach, we perceive the generosity inherent in both.

Nevertheless, as an aspiring musician he repeatedly ran into headwinds. Personal conflicts began early on. According to official accounts, when Bach commenced his career as a young organist and teacher in Arnstadt, Germany, he baffled the congregation with elaborate accompaniments during services; he was accused of inviting a young girl to the choir loft and "allowing her to make music there" (women were forbidden to do so in church); and he overstayed his permission to visit the town of Lübeck—where the great organist Dietrich Buxtehude was in residence—remaining for three months in 1705 although he had been granted leave for just one, thus missing his obligations as organist during the Christmas season. (He likely had his sights set on Buxtehude's job, but when Bach learned that one requirement for succeeding the veteran organist was to marry his daughter, the aspirant made a quick retreat. Handel had come to the same panicked conclusion when his opportunity arose.)

Other violations of decorum in the official reports were even more alarming. A bassoon student named J. H. Geyersbach went after him with a stick, claiming that Bach had called him a "nanny goat bassoonist." During the tussle, Bach attempted to draw his dagger, which he carried for protection, fell into his foe's arms, and the two tumbled around before being separated by other students. Geyersbach even demonstrated puncture holes in his vest as a result of the encounter, but little came of the incident—other than remonstrations to the composer that he had to learn to accept imperfections in people.

Throughout his life, musical contemporaries and those in powerful positions often failed to appreciate Bach's enormous talent and artistic leadership. He was hired in 1708 as court organist for the city of Weimar, but in 1716, when he was passed over for the post of kapellmeister, he attempted to move on to a position in Anhalt-Köthen. For the audacity of believing he had a right to choose his own employer, the stubbornly unrepentant musician was thrown in jail. When, in mid-career, Bach applied for the post of cantor in Leipzig—it would be the last in a line of significant positions he obtained in his lifetime—the town council there lamented (astoundingly) that since they were unable to hire the best for the job, they had to settle for the mediocre. In 1737, even after Augustus III, Elector of Saxony and King of Poland, had appointed him court composer, the critical onslaught continued: influential theorist Johann Adolf Scheibe described Bach's music as "turgid and confused" and suffering from "an excess of art"—that is, of too much complexity. By the end of his life, musical tastes had changed sharply in favor of classical simplicity over baroque convolution.

Largely self-taught as a composer—determinedly copying scores by hand from an early age, sometimes by moonlight—Johann Sebastian spent most of his life within a very small geographical area, making only short journeys to hear other organists within walking distance, or to inspect church instruments. Yet he knew the music of important Italians like Girolamo Frescobaldi, Arcangelo Corelli, Tomaso Albinoni, and Antonio Vivaldi; the work of Jean-Baptiste Lully and François Couperin from France; and also Germany's esteemed Johann Jakob Froberger and Johann Caspar Ferdinand Fischer, whose *Ariadne musica* furnished Bach with themes for his own musical "inventions."

In fact, he seemed to know intimately the music of every significant musician across the cultural landscape. And he topped them all. In the intricate dance of its comingling melodies, Bach's music, said Goethe, sounded "as if the eternal harmony conversed with itself." To later generations he became, in Claude Debussy's portrayal, nothing less than "a benevolent god."

His skill was simply astounding. When listening to a many-voiced fugue, reported his son Carl Philipp Emanuel, "he could soon say, after the first entries of the subjects, what [compositional] devices it would be possible to apply, and which of them the composer by rights ought to apply, and on such occasions, when I was standing next to him, and he had voiced his surmises to me, he would joyfully nudge me when his expectations were fulfilled." Yet he was anything but doctrinaire. As C.P.E. later told Forkel about his late father, "the departed was, like myself or any true musician, no lover of dry mathematical stuff."

Indeed, influential composer and critic Friedrich Wilhelm Marpurg (1718–1795) recounted a discussion he had with Bach in Leipzig about the art of writing a fugue, revealing the master's view of the limits of technical expertise: "I myself heard him pronounce the works of an old and hard-working contrapuntist dry and wooden, and certain fugues by a more modern and no less great contrapuntist, pedantic; the first because the composer stuck continuously to his principal subject, without any change; the second because, at least in the fugues under discussion, he had not shown enough fire to reanimate the theme by interludes."

Of fire and animation, Bach had no shortage. His creative resources came to bear in majestic dramatic works like the *St.*

*John Passion,* the *St. Matthew Passion,* and the Mass in B Minor, as well as in elegant concertos, sonatas, cantatas, keyboard collections, and more. *The Well-Tempered Clavier,* in two volumes exploring all the keys (1722 and 1742), unusual in his time, was considered so essential by pianist/conductor Hans von Bülow that he dubbed it "music's Old Testament," with the gravity of a holy document. (It remained unpublished in Bach's lifetime, but was often hand-copied and was deeply influential on such luminaries as Mozart and Beethoven.)

The idea of exploiting all the keys had some predecessors, including Fischer's *Ariadne musica* (1702, reissued 1715)—with twenty pairs of preludes and fugues—as well as works by Johann Mattheson, Christoph Graupner (who was briefly preferred as a candidate for the Leipzig job before Bach landed it), and Johann Pachelbel. But executing such far-ranging music on an instrument with fixed pitches required overcoming serious technical hurdles. Traditionally, a keyboard's strings were tuned using perfect fifths (whose frequencies form the proportion 3:2) as a standard measure—thereby establishing the correct intervals from do to sol, from sol to re, and so on. Yet the notes of the scale generated by stacking such perfect fifths are different from the ones created when using a series of beauteous, pure thirds (equally important, but based on the serene-sounding proportion 5:4)—the two versions clash. Of course, the music of Bach's time can demand both. Thus early tunings generated sporadic dissonances in certain keys (a painful circumstance that is successfully dodged in modern equal temperament, which slightly alters the ratios that create those revered consonances, allowing them to blend and avoiding the collisions that occur when attempts are made to fit them all into a single keyboard). Because of this, Bach's pursuit has created endless speculation about the tuning he preferred.

A tuning system devised by Andreas Werckmeister in the late seventeenth century made all the keys usable; however, some sounded harsh or sour (lending the music a particular personality, reinforcing one idea in common circulation that each key should have its own "character"). Equal temperament, which divides the octave into twelve equal parts, could traverse the full range of keys with no such noticeable changes, yet it was at a fledgling stage in Bach's day and was challenging to achieve (yet not unheard of—among many manuals in the mid-1700s explaining how to accomplish it, one of the most popular was even dedicated to Bach's son C.P.E.). Equal temperament has its own drawback, however, as it robs the music of the luminous luster bestowed by pure, natural resonance. Many of the proposed answers to the question of Bach's preference—like those that have attempted to interpret the ornamental squiggles on Bach's title page of *The Well-Tempered Clavier* as a secret code—are tea leaves that lead nowhere.

Bach's association with the piano was another aspect of his forward thinking, though it has also been a contentious subject. Some musicians today claim that the modern piano, with its enhanced expressive abilities, is unsuitable for the performance of Bach's works. Yet his dealings with Gottfried Silbermann, one of the earliest piano makers, reveal the importance of the early piano in Bach's life.

Silbermann had been constructing giant hammered dulcimers for Pantaleon Hebenstreit—whose unique performances on the gargantuan contraption captured the imagination of Louis XIV—when he switched to building versions of the piano, which had been invented around 1700 by instrument technician Bartolomeo Cristofori in Florence. The piano offered a performer the unusual ability to control the music's dynamics by varying the force exerted on the keys, since it employed hammers to strike the strings, rather than plucking them at a constant volume, as on the harpsichord. When Silbermann presented his instrument to Bach, though, the master was displeased, and he offered criticisms, especially in regard to its clunky touch, complaints that Silbermann apparently took to heart. In time, though, Bach approved of the improved Silbermann piano sufficiently to serve as an agent in the sale of one to Count Branitzky of Bialystock.

But the most famous example of Bach's relationship with the piano occurred in 1747, when the composer visited the Potsdam residence of Frederick the Great, who had employed his son C. P. E. Bach as a court keyboard musician. Frederick had a collection of Silbermann pianos, and he invited the elder Bach to try them out. (The king was a flutist of some reputation, though Bach's son was clearly unimpressed by his sense of time. When an admirer praised Frederick's performance with the comment "What rhythm!" C.P.E. responded, "You mean, what rhythms!") Wilhelm Friedemann Bach, another of Johann Sebastian's sons, accompanied his father on the Potsdam visit, and left an account.

"Gentlemen, old Bach is come," announced Frederick, who quickly took the composer to different locations in which the pianos had been placed. "The musicians went with him from room to room, and Bach was invited to play extemporaneously upon them. After he had gone on for some time, he asked the king to give him a subject [a musical theme] for a fugue in order to execute it immediately, without any preparation."

Fugues are complex: they state an initial theme, and then, while it is still unfolding, begin it again in another voice, and then in another, until the texture is dense with segments of the melody all sounding against one another—sometimes combined with other themes as well—in intricate, harmonious counterpoint. "The king admired the skillful manner in which his subject was developed," continued Wilhelm Friedemann, "and, probably to see how far such art could be carried, expressed a wish to hear also a fugue with six obbligato [indispensable] parts." That's where J. S. Bach stumbled: the task was too difficult to perform on the spot. Instead, "Bach chose [a melody] himself and immediately executed [developed] it to the astonishment of all present in the same magnificent and learned manner he had done that of the king."

Once he arrived back at home, however, Bach was determined to finish the task with the king's theme, creating a piece with six imitative voices, and adding additional settings, some in encrypted form as riddles (like the canon in which tones become longer as the music progresses, which Bach inscribed with the words "May the fortunes of the king increase like the length of the notes"). He named the collection *A Musical Offering* and dedicated it to the royal tune giver.

Carl Philipp Emanuel (1714–1788) was one of seven children Bach had with his first wife, his second cousin Maria Barbara Bach, of which only three survived him, including composer Wilhelm Friedemann. After Maria's death, he married again, this time to Anna Magdalena Wilcken, and together they had thirteen more children, among which were such significant musicians as Johann Christoph Friedrich and Johann Christian (1735–1782), his youngest. "He is the father, we are the children," declared Mozart of C. P. E. Bach, though the two composers largely pursued very different paths.

In fact, C.P.E. and J.C. became revolutionary leaders on their own terms, creating stunningly opposite trends in the history of classical music. Their contrasting sensibilities continued to resonate long beyond their own era. In some ways, their differences reflected the divergent approaches in modern art represented by Henri Matisse (1869–1954) and Pablo Picasso (1881–1973). Matisse told his students, "One must always search for the desire of the line, where it wishes to enter, where to die away." His hand flowed effortlessly, elegantly, organically, like the music of Johann Christian Bach. Picasso's shapes, on the other hand, were assembled through sheer will, insistent and startling, like the efforts of Carl Philipp Emanuel.

Willfulness is a pervasive character of C.P.E.'s music: often explosive, shifting moods on a moment's whim, its musical lines scampering and stalling, simmering and bursting, transitioning from one thought to another unpredictably. This became known as the *empfindsamer* (sensitive) style, in keeping with a parallel movement in the literary world known as Sturm und Drang (storm and stress), which elevated qualities like emotional turmoil, psychological struggle, and hopeless love. The iconic model was Goethe's *Sorrows of Young Werther* (1774); an epistolary novel in which the protagonist ends his own life, it sparked a popular movement of young men attempting to emulate him.

Related tendencies, often accentuating melodrama and dread, appeared in striking paintings—like Henry Fuseli's *Horseman Attacked by a Giant Snake* (1800)—and were also linked to a late-eighteenth-century style of gardening in England known as the "picturesque," in which cultivated designs were placed alongside scenes of natural unruliness. William Gilpin (1724–1804), "the Father of the Picturesque," described the aesthetic as a kind of artistic vandalism: picture an elegant piece of architecture by Palladio, he suggested; to give it picturesque beauty, "beat down one half of it, deface the other, and throw the mutilated members around in heaps." C.P.E.'s music elicited the sense of surprise and chaos stimulated by such juxtapositions, which in turn inspired several foundational composers, such as Haydn, and Beethoven, to emphasize quirkiness, novelty, and whimsy in their own works, creating in effect a celebration of the unexpected. While J. S. Bach's music often rings with heavenly certitude, that of his son C. P. E. Bach (and of Beethoven) radiates human struggle. And this show of effort became a centerpiece of the Romantic tradition. In a sense, C. P. E. Bach was Beethoven's spiritual model.

The influence of the tumultuous quality at the heart of Beethoven's art extended well beyond the world of music. Aldous Huxley mused in his novel *Point Counter Point* about how writers could emulate the techniques of that towering musical figure: "Meditate on Beethoven. The changes of moods, the abrupt transitions. . . . More interesting still, the modulations, not merely from one key to another, but from mood to mood. A theme is stated, then developed, pushed out of shape, imperceptibly deformed, until, though still recognizably the same, it has become quite different. . . . Get this into a novel. How? The abrupt transitions are easy enough. All you need is a sufficiency of characters and parallel, contrapuntal plots. While Jones is murdering a wife, Smith is wheeling the perambulator in the park. You alternate the themes."

It sounds simple. Perhaps that's why many of Beethoven's sonatas are found in the repertoire of young pianists. But Beethoven's biographer Wilhelm von Lenz pleaded: "Don't listen to the charming child, her hair in spiral curls, serve you up the *Pathétique* [Sonata] with barley sugar." Many of his sonatas are technically daunting, at a new level that spawned yet another important change in performance history. Scholar and pianist

Charles Rosen believed that the challenges in Beethoven's piano sonatas led to the transition of music making from the home parlor to the concert hall. He cited the time Beethoven's student Carl Czerny informed him of a lady in Vienna "who has been practicing your B Flat Sonata for a month, and she still can't play the beginning." It is no surprise that she couldn't. Even his trendily popular works required more skill than many at first suspected. The last piano sonatas, of which the one in B-flat referenced by Czerny, op. 106—the *Hammerklavier*—is a trial by fire even for professionals, brought the art of piano playing to the very pinnacle of difficulty.

Beethoven, though leading directly from C. P. E. Bach, is nonetheless perhaps the musical figure who comes most readily to mind when the term "revolutionary" is uttered. He was a tragic figure: perhaps the greatest musical genius of his age, who slowly went deaf, reduced to using conversation notebooks (devices like ear trumpets did little good). Beleaguered, short-tempered, unlucky in love, and often misunderstood, especially when critics typically accused him of subordinating beauty to the "powerful, violent, and intoxicating," he revealed a wish to commit suicide, and said he resisted only because his talent obligated him to carry on.

Frequently losing his footing, he would champion heroes, like Napoleon, then turn against them when they disappointed. He could stand defiantly against the norms of the social order, as when he was out walking with Goethe (who described him as an "utterly untamed personality") and refused to step aside when an imperial party came along (Goethe moved out of the way and bowed deeply). And yet he could demonstrate the greatest tenderness, as when his pupil the pianist Dorothea von Ertmann was unable to weep after the death of her three-year-old son. According to composer Felix Mendelssohn, Beethoven visited her and, sitting at the piano, announced, "We will now talk to each other in tones." She later reported, "I felt as if I were listening to choirs of angels celebrating the entrance of my poor child into the world of light."

His music, like his personality, encompassed extremes (a close observer of his compositions during his lifetime described him as harboring together "doves and crocodiles"). His technically knotty, radical shifts of mood were one of Beethoven's core trademarks. And the result could indeed seem violent. When Mendelssohn played the opening of the Fifth Symphony on the piano for Goethe, the poet called it "absolutely mad. It makes me almost fear that the house will collapse. And supposing the whole of mankind played it at once!"

His nine symphonies—especially the Third, Fifth, Seventh, and Ninth (a monumental, trailblazing effort that included a radical finale with full chorus and vocal soloists, featuring his unforgettable setting of the "Ode to Joy" by Friedrich Schiller, pleading for universal brotherhood)—each broke the mold. As E. T. A. Hoffmann exclaimed in 1810: "Beethoven's music sets in motion the machinery of awe, of fear, of terror, of pain, and awakens that infinite yearning which is the essence of Romanticism." And it did so in both large and small settings. The delicate Cavatina of his String Quartet op. 130, for example, conveys in a profoundly quiet way the experience of deep grief: "He really wrote it with tears of sadness in his eyes," reported Beethoven's secretary Karl Holz.

Yet his music is also filled at times with playfulness, along with startling innovations, often foreshadowing modern devices. There is the surprising "Tico Tico"–like Latin rhythm in the Rondo of his First Piano Concerto, for instance, and the "Charleston"-sounding section of the last piano sonata, op. III, as if the spirit of the Roaring Twenties suddenly appeared, like a harbinger of future speakeasies and raggy pandemonium.

There is astounding rhythmic play in the second movement of Beethoven's final string quartet, op. 135, where insistent, repeated figures tumble on in a kind of unending freefall. As their gripping, galloping energy builds into organized commotion, like the roar of a whitewater rapid, the composer suddenly shifts into an odd, lopsided rhythm that leaves the listener feeling startled and off-balance. But aside from these small, isolated examples, what the composer harnessed in his last string quartet was less a matter simply of rhythmic vitality than of the expressive potential inherent in the play of elements of musical structure—the drama that emerges from the collision of a work's tectonic plates, its structural foundations. With Beethoven, even amid the charm of a particular moment, there is always a larger game afoot. Carl Philipp Emanuel led the way.

Bach's other most influential son, Johann Christian Bach (1735–1782), became a leader of the very opposite trend in music—exemplified by Mozart—known as *galant* style, an elegant and courtly approach, the term sometimes used to describe architectural decoration filled with curved arabesques. This marked the birth of the classical era—valuing symmetry, clarity, and grace over complexity and emotional extravagance.

Johann Christian developed his deep strain of lyricism as he trained in Italy. Known as "the English Bach," he wrote some of the earliest piano concertos—a chief medium for Mozart, who fell under Johann Christian's influence in London—joining the ranks of others who turned out showcases for the newly popular instrument, like composers James Hook and Philip Hayes (otherwise known as "the fattest man in England"). The child Mozart, when on tour in London, was even given personal attention by Johann Christian. According to Mozart's sister, Maria Anna ("Nannerl"), the two appeared together at court, Bach seated at the harpsichord and Mozart placed between his knees; the two actually improvised together, sounding as one, reported Nannerl, while venturing into exotic harmonies and sophisticated musical wanderings.

Despite his son's protestation that J. S. Bach was not interested in mere mathematics, his music abounds in calculated play. He delighted in musical puzzles, and left us several. In his final work, *The Art of Fugue*, which was still incomplete at the moment he died, Bach inserted his name as a melody, as I mentioned earlier. In his monumental *Goldberg Variations*—an aria and thirty variations named after its first performer, the young harpsichord virtuoso Johann Gottlieb Goldberg—the variations are built on the bass line rather than on a singable solo melody, and are organized in divisions of three: every third in the series is a canon, and in each one the distance between the tones in the counterpoint increases progressively. Other examples abound. Musicologist Helga Thoene proposed that Bach's famous Chaconne for violin (the final movement of his Partita no. 2 in D minor) was created using gematria—number symbolism based on giving values to members of the alphabet—along with assembled bits of melodies from various sacred chorales. Like the music of the fictitious Edmund Pfühl in Thomas Mann's *Buddenbrooks,* we find in Bach "technique as an ascetic religion . . . holy in and of itself."

Unfortunately, in Bach's time such a master of arcane musical practices tended to sow distrust and fear. Court musician Johann Beer's novel *Das Narrenspital* (1681) featured a lunatic asylum with a wing set aside just for musical theorists who have "driven themselves insane by studying and meditating upon . . . the numbering of the tones." In fact, musicians in the seventeenth century, like shepherds, bailiffs, hangmen, skinners, and linen weavers, were often regarded as dishonorable. When composer Georg Philipp Telemann ((1681–1767) wrote a school opera, his mother and other "enemies of music," he reported, prophesied that "I would become a juggler, tightrope walker, itinerant musician or monkey-trainer, unless music was taken away from me." Even brilliant musicians who achieved a high level of success were often secretly held in contempt: composer Johann Kuhnau, Bach's predecessor in Leipzig, wrote a satiric novel, *The Musical Charlatan* (1700), in which a man named Caraffa, a German musician, pretended to be a visiting Italian virtuoso. After ducking out of various opportunities to be tested (claiming, for example, that his hand was injured by a mugger), this incompetent character finally had to flee from patrons, pupils, and village musicians to avoid discovery. The message was clear: beware musical stars, especially those with high aspirations.

Bach's output transcends easy categorization: it was both serious and light, holy and profane—while searching the heavens for inspiration, he was often very down-to-earth. In 1729, during his tenure in Leipzig, Bach became director of the Collegium Musicum, a group of professional musicians, competent amateurs, and music lovers, founded by Telemann in 1704. The group met every week (twice a week during the Leipzig trade fairs in the spring and fall) at Zimmermann's coffee house, which gave him the opportunity to create entertaining secular pieces, like the *Coffee Cantata*—in effect, a comic opera in which a young girl, addicted to coffee, sings lines like "If I couldn't, three times a day, be allowed to drink my little cup of coffee, in my anguish I will turn into a shriveled-up roast goat." There are many other examples of his humor, like an early keyboard canon that imitated a chicken and a cuckoo, and the combination of two amusing folk songs in the final movement (the Quodlibet) of the *Goldberg Variations:* "It Has Been So Long Since I Was with You"—in anticipation of the reappearance of the opening aria—and "Cabbages and Turnips Have Driven Me Away." Still, the music is never less than eloquent: even when Bach was slumming, he managed to elevate the neighborhood.

By the end of his life, he was regarded by many as old-fashioned, fussy, and academic. Much of his work was quickly forgotten, but not among the most astute consumers of musical art, and despite the bad rap he continued to influence the direction of classical music. Mozart, for example, was unaware of the elder Bach until he started attending the Sunday musicales at the home of Baron Gottfried van Swieten (1733–1803) in Vienna. The baron had been an ambassador to Berlin, beginning in 1770, and studied music with Johann Kirnberger, a former student of J. S. Bach; he had heard reports about Bach even earlier from Frederick the Great, who whistled the theme of *A Musical Offering* to him while praising the composer as even greater than his son Carl Philipp Emanuel. When van Swieten returned to Vienna in 1778, he was recognized as an influential musical expert.

By 1782, Mozart was soaking up the music of Handel and Bach at van Swieten's, and he quickly became enamored of intricate fugues (as did his wife, Constanze). It changed his composing style dramatically, culminating in works like the Little Gigue, K. 574—written during his visit to Leipzig, which in its jazzy ebullience could almost have come from the pen of Duke Ellington—and the masterful *Jupiter* Symphony, K. 551, with its multithemed fugal finale, about which encyclopedist Sir George Grove commented: "Mozart has reserved [here] all the resources of his science, and all the power, which no one seems to have possessed to the same degree . . . making it the vehicle for music as pleasing as it is learned. Nowhere has he achieved more."

Bach was resurrected and celebrated like never before in the nineteenth century through the efforts of composer Felix Mendelssohn (1809–1847). As a child, Mendelssohn had stunned Goethe by playing a Mozart autograph at sight and performing from a nearly illegible manuscript by Beethoven. He developed into an astounding craftsman (his Octet, composed at the age of sixteen, remains an undisputed masterpiece). And his reverence for Bach was limitless; once, when Robert Schumann told him about the existence of a large telescope, and suggested that if it were aimed at us by inhabitants of the sun, we would look like "worms in a cheese," Felix replied, "Yes, but *The Well-Tempered Clavier* would still command their respect."

Mendelssohn's great-aunt Sara Itzig Levy (1761–1854), who had studied harpsichord with Bach's eldest son, Wilhelm Friedemann, and also commissioned works from Carl Philipp Emanuel, joined the Singakademie chorus, which was later led by Carl Friedrich Zelter (1758–1832), a pedagogue who unearthed important Bach works, like the monumental Mass in B Minor. Zelter eventually became music tutor to both Felix and his sister Fanny. The family connections to Bach ran deep in other ways, too: Mendelssohn's maternal grandmother, Bella Salomon, gifted him with a copy of a manuscript of Bach's extraordinary *St. Matthew Passion*. To Felix, this music became a revelation.

At the age of twenty, in 1829, Mendelssohn staged a performance of that important work, which launched a full-scale Bach revival that lasted throughout the century. Mendelssohn later prepared an edition of Bach's organ works. And Bach's keyboard music took on new prominence in the twentieth century, as eminent harpsichordist Wanda Landowska and pianist Rosalyn Tureck each made it a specialty.

Bach was now performed on modern instruments, on historical instruments, on electronic instruments (such as on the groundbreaking Moog synthesizer recording by Wendy [formerly Walter] Carlos, *Switched-On Bach*, one of the best-selling classical recordings of all time), and with odd combinations of instruments that the composer had never even imagined. In 1955, Canadian pianist Glenn Gould burst onto the music scene with a jaw-dropping recording of Bach's then-obscure *Goldberg Variations,* rendering the once-austere work into something spellbinding, dramatic, and kaleidoscopic. The piece, no longer the province of academics, soon became a revered part of the standard repertoire, and it continues to make its way onto recordings and concert programs to this day, even in unexpected versions for guitar, harmonica, string trio, and "prepared piano," in which various objects, such as screws and bolts, are inserted between the instrument's strings, converting its mellow sonorities into a clanging, thumping percussion orchestra.

In his very last year, J. S. Bach continued to work as an artistic creator and a battling crusader on behalf of the musical values to which he had devoted his many efforts. Having lost none of his bluntness, he accused Johann Gottlieb Biedermann, a minister in Freiburg who advocated Latin studies over musical training, of having a *Dreckohr*—a filthy ear. The accusatory language was so scandalous that fellow composer Johann Mattheson explained that it was "a base and disgusting expression, unworthy of a kapellmeister, a poor allusion to the word 'rector.'" Once again, J. S. Bach had given offense. But the intent was noble, a blow struck in defense of the highest ideals, for which he continued to serve as a model. To paraphrase what Mozart said of C. P. E. Bach, Johann Sebastian is, in many ways, still the father of us all.

# CHAPTER 5

# The Show-offs

In art as in lovemaking, heartfelt ineptitude
has its appeal and so does heartless skill,
but what you want is passionate virtuosity.

—JOHN BARTH

*Im Concertsaale!*

*Nineteenth-century drawing of Franz Liszt driving an audience
(especially the women) into a frenzy*

THE BACHS WERE VIRTUOSOS before the advent of the Romantic heartthrobs who mesmerized audiences with fiery technique—artists such as violinist Niccolò Paganini and pianist Franz Liszt, who, leaving audiences gasping in awe, were at times regarded as unearthly conjurers. The purity of Bach's vision, the modesty of his spirit, his dedication to the art of placing tones in their rightful order, all served as a foil to the exhibitionists of the next revolution. They were the egomaniacs, the daredevils, the tricksters who captured the hearts and minds of music lovers through sheer physical abilities.

The term "virtuoso," from the Italian root *virtù* ("individual initiative" or "power"), was first applied not to performers, but to composers who demonstrated superior theoretical skills. Their artistry could astonish with intricate tonal tapestries, as when Josquin des Prez crafted the same melody to be performed at three different speeds simultaneously. Indeed, as composer Johann Kuhnau explained, the physical exploits of the "performer virtuoso"—those who had "nothing more than practical facility," as opposed to intellectual mastery—were at first little celebrated.

On the other hand, the overwhelming cerebral talent of a Josquin was often regarded not just with awe but with suspicion. Polyphony—the art of combining melodies in intricate juxtapositions, so that all the disparate parts in the texture fit together like pieces of a complex puzzle—was sometimes likened to the mythical "philosopher's stone," as something touched by the divine, yet with an unholy tinge.

That dark vision also pervaded the nineteenth-century tradition of musical showmanship. Musicians in the time of J. S.

Bach retreated from view behind the works themselves, happily lending credit for their creations to patrons, or to the Holy Spirit. But as the Romantic period wore on, the era of the musical egotist—the soaring superstar—arose. It was the age of the show-off.

Paganini (1782–1840) was the model. He threw off such sparks when he played that nearly everyone who heard him believed he was possessed. "I had played the variations entitled *Le streghe* [The Witches]," Paganini recalled of a concert in Vienna, "and they produced some effect. One individual, who was . . . of sallow complexion, melancholy air, and bright eye, affirmed that he saw nothing surprising in my performance, for he had distinctly seen, while I was playing my variations, the devil at my elbow, directing my arm and guiding my bow." This was a particularly popular hallucination, helped along by the demeanor of the violinist, who looked like something from another world. Composer Hector Berlioz described Paganini as "a man with long hair, piercing eyes, and a strange, ravaged countenance." Everyone agreed that there was something demonic in his appearance. Mary Shelley, author of *Frankenstein*, confessed that he threw her into hysterics.

One London critic who attended a Paganini concert could hardly believe his eyes: "A vampire in an orchestra is not an everyday sight," he wrote. Paganini's doctor provided a harrowing physical description of the man: "His thinness and his lack of teeth, which gives him a sunken mouth and more prominent chin," made him seem older than he was. "His large head, held up by a long, thick neck, appears at first glance to be rather strongly out of proportion to his delicate limbs. The left shoulder is an inch higher than the right."

But the deepest impression was surely made by the astounding proficiency he displayed. In truth, some of it was cheap trickery. For example, he practiced breaking a string on his violin (in his day something easily accomplished. since strings were made with catgut) in order to continue the piece as if nothing had gone amiss—a feat made possible by working out alternate fingerings ahead of time. But whenever it happened, audiences were convinced that something unnatural was afoot.

At performances of his Violin Concerto no. 1, fans gasped at the technical brilliance—especially the double stops (playing more than one string at a time) and the use of harmonics (eerie, high-pitched notes achieved by placing the fingers lightly at crucial points along the strings to bring out hidden members of the natural harmonic series that were quietly resonating). Paganini placed the orchestra parts in E-flat, but wrote the solo violin part in D, with instructions to tune the instrument a half-step higher than usual. That retuning made it possible to achieve certain effects, as in the opening of the third movement, where the violinist plays a downward scale, both bowed and played pizzicato (plucked) at the same time. (This would be impossible to achieve on an instrument tuned normally, because the passage can only be played on an open [unstopped] string.)

Paganini stirred shock waves in other ways as well. As a biographer of his, François-Joseph Fétis, reported, "His moral education had been grossly neglected." He was accused of obsessive womanizing, compulsive gambling, murder, and more. It was said that his advanced musicianship resulted from hours of practice while in prison. That story arose from his illicit liaison with twenty-year-old Angelina Cavanna, whom he had been accused of abducting in 1815. Her father, an "impecunious tailor," according to a later biographer, Geraldine De Courcy, falsely testified against him at trial. Years later, wrote De Courcy, another accusation arose: John Watson, a man Paganini had repeatedly bailed out of jail, tried to frame the violinist in connection with his daughter, Charlotte.

Nevertheless, the violin star was irrepressible. The singer Antonia Bianchi—"an untamed, passionate creature, consumed by a jealousy that knew no peace," claimed De Courcy—gave birth to his son, Achille, in 1825. Perhaps his many affairs lent his compositions some of the earthy emotional depth that touched his listeners. In Lucca, Paganini reported, he played on a violin with only two strings. "The first was to express the sentiments of a young girl, the other was to express the passionate language of a lover," he explained. "I had composed a kind of dialogue in which the most tender accents followed the outbursts of jealousy. . . . The Princess Eliza lauded me to the skies and said to me in the most gracious manner possible, 'You have just performed impossibilities; would not a single string suffice for your talent?' I promised to make the attempt. . . . My predilection for the G string dates from this period."

The specific aspects of his playing that made it so special, wrote Fétis, could be found in "the diversity of sounds—the different methods of tuning his instrument—the frequent employment of double and single harmonic notes—the simultaneous pizzicato and bow passages—the various staccato [short articulations]—the use of double and even triple notes—a prodigious facility in executing wide intervals [leaps across the scale] with unerring precision, joined to an extraordinary number of various styles of bowing—such were the principal features of Paganini's talent."

Yet the weaknesses in his character—particularly the egomania—were also reflected in his performances. "There was fullness and grandeur in his phrasing—but there was no tenderness in his accents," observed Fétis. After all, there is more to music than fireworks and adrenaline. Yet Paganini's example spurred a generation of eager followers, galvanizing the era into an apotheosis of the brilliant exhibitionist, and they drew big crowds.

There had been earlier musical stars who didn't quite reach the same level of notoriety. Some, like pianists Muzio Clementi (1752–1832) and Mozart, nearly did. The two went head to head in a musical duel at the court of Emperor Joseph in Vienna in 1781, where each did his utmost to outdo the other. Neither had known what was in store when Joseph offered them separate invitations to visit. At the event, they were forced to take turns improvising on a theme selected by the emperor's sister-in-law, the Grand Duchess Maria Luisa. Mozart complained that his piano was "out of tune and three of the keys were stuck," but the emperor dismissed his griping with a wave of the hand. Both men pulled out all their best tricks. Clementi's included scales played in harmony, rapid repeating notes, melodies executed in broken octaves (alternating the notes with their octave equivalents), and more. The competitive spirit brought out Clementi's most impressive displays of imagination and athletic prowess.

Mozart's artistry had the deeper dimension, however. It reflected the qualities poet Friedrich Schlegel defined in 1798 as "Romantic"—Romantic works, he stated, should sail freely on the wings of poetic reflection, be animated with wit, and embrace everything in life. Mozart conceded afterward that Clementi had a good right hand—but, he wrote in a letter to his father, "not a kreuzer's worth of taste or feeling." He was a "robot . . . a charlatan, like all Italians." Clementi was kinder to his rival: "Until then I had never heard anyone play with so much spirit and grace." Yet Joseph declared the contest a draw.

The fiery Beethoven fared better in 1800 against challenger Daniel Steibelt (1765–1823), a man known for depicting storms at the keyboard by means of broad tremolos (quivering chordal effects executed with a rapid rotation of the wrists). Steibelt went first, tossing a page of his music aside with a dramatic flourish. When it was Beethoven's turn, he simply picked up Steibelt's discarded sheet, turned it upside down, and proceeded to improvise variations on the overturned manuscript while picking apart Steibelt's music in a totally humiliating way. The challenger hurriedly left, vowing never to return to Vienna as long as Beethoven was still there.

But the mantle of the larger-than-life musical virtuoso—the conquering giant capable of superhuman feats, in the mode of Paganini—fell to a pianist who consciously sought to take over that violinist's reins. Franz Liszt (1811–1886) attended Paganini's Paris debut in 1831 and, at nineteen, resolved on the spot to match the older man's accomplishments, thereafter transforming himself from the "pale, delicate" figure that pianist Carl Czerny had auditioned as a talented youngster into one that the musician-poet Heinrich Heine called "the Attila, the scourge of God."

"What a man, what a violin, what an artist!" he wrote in response to Paganini. "Heavens! What sufferings, what misery, what tortures in those four strings!" From that time on, for Liszt, "virtuosity [was] not an outgrowth, but an indispensable element of music."

Much of what Liszt, Mozart, and Beethoven accomplished was ushered in by the revolutionary invention of the piano. The instrument's distinguishing feature was the ability to vary volume in reaction to the amount of force exerted by a player's fingers. With the emergence of the piano, keyboardists could impart nuanced emotional content to the music—offering a wide range of sounds, depicting growls and whispers, fanfares and sighs—and as the instrument evolved, its range and technical responsiveness continued to expand. (The diminutive clavichord—a musical instrument that consisted of a rectangular box small enough to fit on a tabletop, with metal "tangents" that struck strings inside when any of the levers on the keyboard were depressed—had the same ability, but its volume was so restricted that it wasn't useful in performing situations.) By the nineteenth century the piano's popularity had exploded to the point that no middle-class home could be without one. And the best musicians, like Liszt, learned to take full advantage of its potential.

Caroline Boissier, the mother of Liszt's student Valérie, described the nature of the great virtuoso's pianism: "Stormy moments are followed by a soft abandonment, a melancholy full of grace and feeling," she recounted. "One no longer hears the piano—but storms, prayers, songs of triumph, transports of joy, heart-rending despair." Determined to enthrall, Liszt injected extramusical drama into his presentations as well. There were, for example, the green gloves he wore to the stage and ceremoniously peeled from his hands before tossing them on the ground. (Women in the audience would dive after them, often tearing them to bits in a frenzy.)

When at the piano, Liszt himself was, reported pianist Charles Hallé, "in perpetual motion: now he stamps with his feet, now waves his arms in the air, now he does this, now that." More recently, we have had the similar examples of pianist Lang Lang and conductor-pianist Leonard Bernstein. But the virtuoso pianist in perpetual animation has been a common trope, no matter the stylistic category. Writer Eudora Welty paid tribute to jazz artist Thomas "Fats" Waller (1904–1943) in *Powerhouse* by portraying him as "in motion every moment."

Then there was Liszt's practice of energetically reducing pianos to splinters. Friedrich Wieck, Clara Schumann's father and piano teacher, reported on a Liszt performance he attended in 1838. "He played the Fantasy on a C. Graf [Conrad Graf piano], burst two bass strings, personally fetched a second C. Graf in walnut wood from the corner and played his Etude. After breaking yet another two strings he loudly informed the public that since it didn't satisfy him, he would play it again [on a third piano]. As he began, he vehemently threw his gloves and handkerchief on the floor." (His assault on the pianos was a theatrical device rediscovered in the 1960s by rock musicians like Pete Townshend and Jimi Hendrix, who routinely destroyed their guitars on stage.) Heinrich Heine coined the term "Lisztomania" to describe the frenzy he created. "When formerly I heard of the fainting spells which broke out in Germany and especially in Berlin, when Liszt showed himself there," wrote Heine, "I shrugged my shoulders. . . . And yet, how convulsively his mere appearance affected them! How boisterous was the applause, which rang to meet him. . . . A veritable insanity."

Echoing Louis XIV's assertion that he was the state, Liszt, who called his recitals *monologues pianistiques*, haughtily announced, "Le concert, c'est moi." He wasn't exaggerating the importance of his persona. Pianist Ignaz Moscheles (1794–1870) had already inaugurated the solo recital as a legitimate vehicle (violating the previous norm of a variety-show format featuring multiple acts) in a series he called "Classical Piano Soirées." And

Czech pianist Jan Ladislav Dussek (1760–1812) had established the practice of sitting with his side to the audience, in order to show his profile. But when it came to entertaining spectacles, Liszt was hard to beat. And like Paganini's, his social reputation became a part of the draw.

He had intimate relationships with a gallery of notorious women: Carolyne zu Sayn-Wittgenstein, the cigar-smoking princess; Marie d'Agoult, who described herself as "six inches of snow covering twenty feet of lava"; Countess Marie von Mouchanoff, portrayed by Heine as "a Pantheon in which so many great men lie buried"; and Countess Olga Janina, who threatened Liszt with a poisoned dagger and a pistol and sent scandalous articles about him to the pope.

And yet the pianist had another, pious side—taking minor religious vows and assuming the title of abbé toward the end of his life. The Metropolitan Museum of Art in New York has a piano in storage that was used by Liszt at the Villa d'Este in Italy, and it contains two revealing remnants: a set of rosary beads and a cognac stain. Taken together, they form a perfect portrait of the man.

He was, in a word, human, with all the vibrancy and fragility that implies. The soul of his art was that humanity. Though he was the first to play recitals from memory, and to offer audiences the full range of the piano repertoire (even the term "recital" was his), Liszt was never a mere technician. To a student playing Chopin's Polonaise in A-flat Major, op. 53, he offered a reprimand: "I don't want to hear how fast you can play octaves. What I wish to hear is the canter of the horses of the Polish cavalry before they gather force and destroy the enemy!" When pianist Arthur Friedheim was studying one of Liszt's *Transcendental Études,* "Harmonies du soir," the composer took him to the window. It was late autumn and the sun was about to set over the Italian mountains. "Play *that*," Liszt said. "There are your evening harmonies." His message was akin to Schlegel's prescription for achieving a Romantic sensibility: embrace all of life. Insisting that the "cult of personality" was less harmful to music than the "cult of anonymity," Liszt declared that for the formation of the artist, the first prerequisite was "the improvement of the human being." Perhaps this, most of all, explained his ability to touch people.

Hans Christian Andersen attended a Liszt recital in 1842 and described his demeanor. "The first impression of his personality was derived from the appearance of strong passions in his wan face," he wrote, "so that he seemed to me a demon nailed fast to the instrument whence the tones streamed forth—they came from his blood, from his thoughts. . . . His blood flowed and his nerves trembled; but as he continued to play, so the demon vanished. I saw that pale face assume a nobler and brighter expression; the divine soul shone from his eyes, from every feature; he became as beauteous as only spirit and enthusiasm can make their worshippers."

All these qualities could be discerned in his playing. In 1837, a decade after Beethoven had died, a gathering of friends in the salon of writer Ernest Legouvé included Liszt, who sat at the piano; Hector Berlioz was there. The room had been lit by a single candle, whose flame went out. In the darkness, wrote Legouvé, the pianist "began the funereal and heart-rending adagio of [Beethoven's] Sonata in C-sharp Minor [the *Moonlight*]. The rest of us remained rooted to the spot where we happened to be, no one attempting to move. . . . I had dropped into an armchair, and above my head heard stifled sobs and moans. It was Berlioz."

. . .

The emotional wallop delivered by flying fingers remained ever potent as the nineteenth century wore on, even when performance standards were questionable. For Liszt, a virtuoso was obligated to maintain the integrity of the work of art: "If he trifles and toys with this, he casts his honor away. He is the intermediary of the artistic idea." Many other musicians showed little concern for such ideals, particularly when it came to performing in America, where, it was believed, the streets were paved with gold.

Once that idea proliferated, Europeans scurried to cash in, often with the subtlety of a three-ring circus. There was corpulent pianist Leopold de Meyer (he was "himself a grand piano," commented one critic), who traveled with an extra-large instrument, performing variations on "Hail, Columbia" and "Yankee Doodle." And there was pianist Henri Herz, of whom it was said that "de Meyer may break a piano, but Herz can break a heart." His "monster concerts" featured four pianos on stage (one patron complained when he failed to play all four at once), and he drew criticism for his "Thousand Candles Concert" when it was discovered there were only 998 lights. But Herz's major success was in performing for miners in the California Gold Rush, especially with his variations on the song "Oh! Susanna."

Anton Rubinstein (1829–1894) swept listeners off their feet with hurricanes of emotion and untold wrong notes (once, when he played a nearly perfect concert, pianist Moriz Rosenthal commented, "Poor Rubinstein must be losing his vision"). Ignacy Jan Paderewski (1860–1941), the longhaired, charismatic pianist, created such a rage—James Huneker in the *Musical*

*Courier* called it "Paddymania"—that Charles F. Tretbar, head of the concert and artist department at Steinway & Sons, arranged an American tour of eighty concerts, beginning in 1891, for a guaranteed $30,000. Audience reaction was so overwhelming that more dates were quickly added. In the end, Paderewski netted $95,000 for his efforts—and a bad case of exhaustion. Noting that no one could live up to all the hoopla, Rosenthal wryly commented, "Yes, he plays well, I suppose, but he's no Paderewski."

In the end, the tour was beset with problems. Accommodations were dreadful—those hotels that were actually free of cockroaches and mice wouldn't allow Paderewski to practice in his room—and the stress of performing 107 times in 117 days took its toll. The worst experience of the trip came toward the end, at the Chicago World's Fair (officially known as the World's Columbian Exposition, in celebration of the four hundredth anniversary of the discovery of America) in May 1893, where a war broke out between rival piano makers. It nearly scuttled Paderewski's performance, since he was a Steinway Artist. In the end, he gave his concert, but then canceled his last New York appearances because of fatigue. It drained him even more than his role as Poland's prime minister, beginning in 1919.

Instrumentalists and singers of every stripe joined in the virtuoso craze: sopranos Jenny Lind (1820–1887), "the Swedish Nightingale," and Nellie Melba (1861–1931); violinists Joseph Joachim (1831–1907), a close associate of Brahms, and Jascha Heifetz (1901–1997) ("flawless," agreed many of his contemporaries); and in the twentieth century and beyond, breathtaking keyboard artists who equaled in impact even the originators of the trend. On the jazz scene, pianist Art Tatum (1909–1956) outshone such formidable rivals as Thomas "Fats" Waller

(1904–1943), James P. Johnson (1894–1955), and Willie "the Lion" Smith (1893–1973)—giants of the Harlem "stride" school, befriended by George Gershwin, who introduced them to his high society friends. Once, when Tatum was in the audience at a Waller performance, the irrepressible Waller strode to the front of the stage and announced, "Ladies and gentlemen, I play the piano, but God is in the house tonight."

In the classical world, the Russians assumed the forefront for a while, with near-universal celebrity attaching to such names as Sergei Rachmaninoff (1873–1943) and Vladimir Horowitz (1903–1989). The two met only when each had eventually gravitated to the United States. From that moment on, however, their fates were intimately tied. They were very different types. In Rachmaninoff's hands, said composer Nikolai Medtner, "the simplest scale, the simplest cadence," acquired "its primary meaning." What made his performances especially beautiful was the sense of inevitability he brought to an interpretation, the way he shaped a phrase with finesse and authority. Horowitz, on the other hand, was a firebrand: an emissary of the unexpected, often accused of ignoring the composer's intentions in pursuit of added excitement.

A good example was Horowitz's American debut at Carnegie Hall, featuring the Tchaikovsky First Piano Concerto with Thomas Beecham conducting. Beecham, who was also making his American debut that night, had a different conception of the work, one that was, in Horowitz's view, too self-absorbed. At the event, feeling that time was running out, Horowitz took off in the last movement like a thoroughbred in the final stretch of a race. "I wanted to eat the public alive," said Horowitz, "to drive them completely crazy." According to *The New York Times*, "The piano smoked at the keys." The conductor fought to keep up, but he had been taken by surprise, and the situation quickly became hopeless. Horowitz later quipped, "We ended almost together." His American career was assured.

Theodor Leschetizky (1830–1915), co-founder with Anton Rubinstein of the St. Petersburg Conservatory, claimed there were three indispensables to becoming a virtuoso pianist: one had to be Slavic, Jewish, and a child prodigy. This was an odd assertion, especially since Leschetizky was a Catholic, but the statement was no stranger than Horowitz's pronouncement that there were only three kinds of pianists: Jewish, gay, and bad. Horowitz himself fit all three categories, the last only occasionally. He remains the very picture of the virtuoso.

Horowitz had been attracted to Rachmaninoff's formidable, intense, and technically daunting Third Piano Concerto, a work he was already playing on tour. So when he received an invitation from Rachmaninoff to meet, the day after arriving in New York, he was thrilled.

They wasted no time. Rachmaninoff began by playing music by Medtner for Horowitz; then, off they went to the basement of Steinway Hall, where they had a run-through of Rachmaninoff's Third. The composer played the orchestra part on one piano, while Horowitz played the solo part on another. "He swallowed it whole," said Rachmaninoff. "He had the courage, the intensity, and daring that make for greatness."

Neither Horowitz nor Rachmaninoff had been a child prodigy, but countless other virtuosos began their careers as young children with gifts that astonished. It is a phenomenon that was often applauded. But the term's Latin root, *prodigium*, meaning "omen" or "monster," gives pause. Prodigies have at times been treated as freaks, and history records countless cases of prodigious talents rising swiftly but coming to a bad end, as if cursed. Examples include violinist Thomas Linley (1756–1778), who gave a public concert when he was just seven, played with Mozart (another wildly talented prodigy) when both boys were fourteen, and subsequently met his demise in a boating accident. Carl Filtsch (1830–1845), Chopin's favorite pupil—about whom Liszt said, "When this little one begins to tour, I will have to close up shop"—fell ill and died in Venice before his fifteenth birthday.

Of course, not all prodigies had their lives cut so short. Felix Mendelssohn so impressed Goethe when he was only twelve—improvising on a theme, reading a Mozart musical autograph at sight, and deciphering the nearly illegible scrawl of a Beethoven autograph—that the poet likened his demonstration to the conversation of adults in comparison to the childlike "prattle" of the precocious Mozart. Mendelssohn later enjoyed great success, until Richard Wagner's anti-Semitic putdown began to chip away at his reputation.

Renowned prodigies in modern times have included such successful artists as pianists Claudio Arrau, Daniel Barenboim, Martha Argerich, and Evgeny Kissin. But many others started splendidly and fared less well. Violinist Michael Rabin (1936–1972) made his professional appearance at age ten with the Havana Philharmonic under Artur Rodzinski and debuted at Carnegie Hall in New York at thirteen, when *The New York Times* declared him "already an accomplished artist." Conductor Dimitri Mitropoulos christened him "the genius violinist of tomorrow." Yet Rabin suffered from emotional instability as well as chronic drug use, and after one mishap when he lost balance, he developed a fear of falling off the stage. It all became overwhelming. He died from a fall in his apartment.

The secret torment of being a musical prodigy was the subject of pianist Ruth Slenczynska's autobiography, *Forbidden Childhood*. "All that comes back is the stinging misery—Father's sullen mood, the mute pain on Mother's face, the closed keyboard, the crying and crying," she wrote. "No dolls, no skipping rope, no pets, no tricycles, no marbles, nothing except the grinding routine of nine hours a day at the keyboard and lessons in reading and writing and geography in between."

She was subject to constant physical punishment. "Every time I made a mistake, [my father] leaned over and, very methodically, without a word, slapped me across the face." He warned her that people went to concerts with bags full of rotten eggs and vegetables, "and if you hit a wrong note, these rotten eggs and vegetables, particularly tomatoes, would come flying at you." And he didn't confine the psychological torture to his daughter alone. "[I shared a program] with a boy violinist only a few years older than I," she recalled. "Father took one look at his hands and flatly told him he would never be a violinist. The boy stood there crushed and speechless. He was Isaac Stern." Stern would, of course, become America's highest-paid violinist, and almost single-handedly save Carnegie Hall from the wrecking ball.

Despite some major achievements, in the end, Slenczynska's performing career was erratic. "The worst of the reviews said I was a burned-out candle," the pianist shared, "an example of the prodigy who had blazed for a while and subsided into mediocrity."

Young "monsters" come and go. But the era of the artful show-off never faded. In the twentieth century, audiences were mesmerized by an endless stream of great artists, including such pianists as Russians Sviatoslav Richter, Emil Gilels, and Grigory Sokolov; Italians Arturo Benedetti Michelangeli and Maurizio

Pollini; Polish-American Arthur Rubinstein; Canadian Glenn Gould; and American Van Cliburn, who captured the world's imagination by winning the first-ever Tchaikovsky Piano Competition in Moscow in 1958, at the height of the Cold War.

The tradition continues today with several Chinese artists, including pianists Lang Lang (b. 1982) and Yuja Wang (b. 1987). Exquisite musicality and jaw-dropping control exemplify the pianism of the Russian-German Igor Levit (b. 1987) and Russian Daniil Trifonov (b. 1991). The musician as ground-shaking powerhouse lives on in artists like Yefim Bronfman (b. 1958), the Russian-Israeli-American pianist who was described by Philip Roth in his novel *The Human Stain* as "Bronfman the brontosaur! Mr. Fortissimo." Roth's account of a Bronfman performance suggests the kind of rapturous response that Liszt himself once elicited:

> Enter Bronfman to play Prokofiev at such a pace and with such bravado as to knock my morbidity clear out of the ring. . . . When he's finished, I thought, they'll have to throw the thing out. He crushes it. He doesn't let that piano conceal a thing. Whatever's in there is going to come out, and come out with its hands in the air.

Brilliant athleticism was one way to grip an audience. Another was through the captivating resonances of what Debussy called "harmonic chemistry"—sounds that captured the ears and hearts of listeners through a potent sensuality. As the nineteenth century moved into the twentieth, that quality more and more pervaded musical practices.

# CHAPTER 6

# The Alchemy of Sound

As long-drawn echoes heard far-off and dim
Mingle to one deep sound and fade away;
Vast as the night and brilliant as the day,
Color and sound and perfume speak to him.

—CHARLES BAUDELAIRE,
*"Correspondences,"* translated by James Huneker

A RT IS INEFFABLE—and never more so than in the period that gave rise to French impressionism, when one artistic medium smoothly coalesced into another. In painting, colors now seemed to swirl and dance; in music, harmonies no longer followed inexorable paths leading from one point to another, but instead became glistening, independent bodies of sound—like constituents of an audible sculpture garden. Seen through impressionist eyes, all the world was mutable.

"I was born on a sound wave," declared the early symbolist painter Odilon Redon. "Every recollection of my early youth is mingled with music. . . . It has entered the folds of my soul." Music, the artist declared, "promotes an acute sensibility more powerful than passion itself."

In attempting to harness that creative force, composer

*The Eiffel Tower at night during the Paris Exposition, 1889*

Claude Debussy (1862–1918) abandoned music's traditional structures. His aim, wrote critic Émile Vuillermoz, was "to pursue an onrush of reflection, fluencies, shimmerings, iridescences, glimmerings, ripplings, and shudderings." The result, less like a static picture and more like a living entity, could be found in such Debussy works as his orchestral evocation of the sea, *La Mer*, with its shifting waves of sound and unabashed eroticism. Many found this approach untenable. The piece "was not so long," wryly recounted Louis Elson of the *Boston Daily Advertiser*, "but it was terrible while it lasted." *The New York Times* found it "persistently ugly . . . prosaic in its reiteration of inert formulas"—a "barnyard cackle." Today, audiences find it ravishing.

Aesthetic standards were in flux across the board. The linear purity of neoclassicism in painting, for example, gave way to murky "impressions," as artists reveled in hazy atmospherics. Thus, when artist Camille Pissarro painted a small freighter floating on a river, he emphasized neither the boat nor the water but the emissions of the vessel's smokestack. Edgar Allan Poe, a master of the dark regions of the human psyche, became a shadowy inspiration to many artists through what D. H. Lawrence called his "horrible underground passages of the human soul." "I spend my existence in the House of Usher," said Debussy.

Painterly techniques found their way into many musical pieces, like Debussy's piano miniature "Gardens in the Rain," where rapid, repeated notes emulate the tiny dots of color that proved so effective in portraits like Georges Seurat's *Sunday Afternoon on the Island of La Grande Jatte*. The impressionist movement was based on such blurrings; it gained its appellation when critic Louis Leroy reviewed Claude Monet's indistinct painting of the port of Le Havre, *Impression, Sunrise*, in

1874. Asked to provide a name of his work for the exhibition's catalog, Monet had simply replied, "Put 'Impression.'" Thus, an official school was launched.

Supporters of the trend congregated at a bookshop named L'Art Indépendant, where patrons included symbolist poet Stéphane Mallarmé (whose "The Afternoon of a Faun" was the basis for Debussy's orchestral tone poem *Prelude to the Afternoon of a Faun,* a work the composer described as "undulating, cradle-rocking music, abounding in curved lines") and Gustave Moreau, Debussy's favorite painter. Their common bond was the search for an artistic language liberated from conventional techniques, and, in the words of Baudelaire, "intensely aware of mystery." As a young student, Debussy was criticized by school officials for his tendency toward strangeness; in response he asserted that he was not interested in "the science of the beaver"—that is, in using music's basic building blocks in predictable ways—but, rather, in "the alchemy of sound." (Paul Cézanne similarly rejected traditional works that revealed too much of "the influence of the academies.")

Just as the mythical alchemists converted base metals into precious ones, Debussy sought to convert musical sounds into agents of transcendence. Such transformations could be found, impressionist artists believed, in "hidden correspondences"— connections formed in the dream state described by an opium-intoxicated Edgar Allan Poe, where "sounds ring out as in music, where colors speak, where perfumes tell us of the world of ideas." French tradition had long embraced the kind of entrancing beauty Poe was after, where particular tones intermingled like swirling fragrances. The effect could be found early on in the music of baroque composers François Couperin and Jean-Philippe Rameau, later to be highlighted in Franz Liszt's experimental piano works, like *Les Jeux d'deaux à la Villa d'Este* (Fountains of the Villa d'Este), where sparkling waterfalls are conjured—the kind of music Debussy appreciated as supple enough "to adapt itself to the lyrical impulses of the soul and to the whims of reverie."

Composers drew on special techniques to achieve their aims. Liszt's *Gray Clouds,* a misty, lugubrious piece, evoked musical rootlessness through its unusual harmonies, based on the whole-tone scale (which, unlike the major scale, with its clear beginning and end, arranges its tones in strictly equal distances, projecting a free-floating feeling, with no clear sense of direction). That particular scale became an impressionist trademark, its oddness a valued commodity.

The movement wasn't confined to France alone. In Russia, a cadre of homegrown symbolists included poet Konstantin Balmont (author of *Poetry as Magic*) and composer Alexander Scriabin (1872–1915). Balmont, who could never be accused of understatement, described Scriabin's music as "the singing of a falling moon. Starlight in music. A flame's movement. A burst of sunlight. The cry of soul to soul." Scriabin's art was fueled by his mystical pursuits, and by the synesthesia that caused him to perceive musical tones in specific colors: C, as intense red; E, as sky blue; and so on. The score of his orchestral work *Prometheus: Poem of Fire* (1910) includes a part for "color organ," a lighting device designed to project different parts of the color spectrum. The prototype, built by his friend Alexander Mozer, still sits in the composer's last Moscow apartment, which has become a museum in his honor.

At the time of his death, Scriabin was hard at work on a project called *The Mysterium,* a multimedia opus intended to be unveiled in the Himalayan Mountains to include such fanciful notions as bells suspended from clouds and pillars of incense surrounding the singers, dancers, and instrumentalists, whose performance would usher in the Messianic Age. His "Prometheus chord" is still studied by music students and often exploited by jazz musicians.

Such unusual harmonies became a special draw at the 1889 World's Fair (Exposition Universelle) in Paris, where Debussy and fellow French composer Maurice Ravel first encountered the sounds of Indonesian gamelan. It bolstered their interest in writing music with little or no harmonic direction. "Do you not remember the Javanese music . . . where tonic and dominant became naught but vain ghosts for the use of unruly children?" wrote Debussy to poet Pierre Louÿs in 1895, pointing to the Indonesians' practice of neutralizing the usual gravitational force found in Western music, in which the harmony built on the fifth degree of the scale (known as the dominant) naturally led to the one built on the first degree (known as the tonic).

The bell-like sonorities of the gamelan were produced mostly by various metallophones—tuned metal bars and gongs, struck by mallets or activated by friction. These instruments, with their overtone-rich reverberations, produced quivering, indistinct pitches. And to further enhance their tremulous quality, they were sometimes placed slightly out of tune with one another. The resulting musical fog was in some ways akin to the blur of impressionist painting. (Ironically, the French impressionist painters themselves were actually excluded from the exposition. Paul Gauguin and his colleagues had to exhibit their works instead at Volpini's Café des Arts, on the Champ-de-Mars, during the summer of 1889. They billed themselves as "the Impressionist and Synthetist Group.") Another musical element the French absorbed from gamelan was the pentatonic (five-note) scale, as found on the black keys of the piano—a neutral frame on which several tones may sound together without generating any sense of dissonance.

That 1889 fair marked a moment of great cultural change. Featuring 62,722 exhibitors and attracting thirty million visitors, it was a walled city unto itself, with displays and artists imported from Japan, India, Persia, Mexico, Siam, Morocco, Greece, Argentina, and more. Music was everywhere, declared *L'Art musical*, "raging with equal violence at the bandstand of the gypsies, under the tents of the Arabs, in the picturesque shacks of Morocco and Egypt." Among the exhibits, Thomas Edison's new phonograph vied for attention with Marie Antoinette's piano and the latest keyboard produced by Érard (demonstrated by Paderewski).

There was a *village nègre*, populated with four hundred indigenous people; a Palace of Machines and another of Fine Arts and Liberal Arts; the newly created Eiffel Tower, which served as one of the entranceways; and a "Street of Cairo" with a minaret, two mosques, myriad Egyptian musicians, belly dancers, and craftsmen—all dressed in authentic costume.

A fascination with "otherness" saturated the atmosphere, though in certain quarters it also held the seeds of revulsion. "How vulgar," announced *La Vie parisienne* in describing the music accompanying the Egyptian belly dancers. Foreign cultures hit some observers like the unpleasant slap of a cold shower, raising moral alarms, even in bawdy Paris. "How unlike the descriptions of writers or the striking images of the painters are these obscene calls of girls moving rhythmically to a barbaric motive, the precise opposite of those accents that our

Western musical language applies to express the infinite volup-tuousness of the flesh. . . ."

The Javanese, in contrast, could elicit more positive reviews. The teenage dancers that accompanied the gamelan ensemble caused writer Catulle Mendès to wax poetic:

> Moving their small, boneless bodies
> Following a rite of fateful laws,
> In the way waters slither
> And rattlesnakes undulate
> They dance, sacerdotally.

The music was, reported an audience member, "nothing but a long, mourning sound, growing and fading." Yet poet Judith Gautier found within that din the core of earthly life: "Whis-perings, murmurs, the rustling of a tree in the wind, rain-drops . . . nothing but the sounds of nature, and a melody that is always beyond reach." To composer Camille Saint-Saëns it was "a dream music which had truly hypnotized some people." No wonder it drew the attention of the musical impressionists.

Naturally, controversies brewed at every level of the fair from the start. Among the seven hundred proposals submitted for the event's signature image, one was to be "in the form of a guillotine—to honor the victims of the Terror." However, not many savored the thought of constructing that grim reminder of the French Revolution. The ultimate winner, Gustave Eiffel's tower, created such a critical backlash that a committee of three hundred (one for each meter of the proposed Eiffel structure) was formed to protest. It included some of the most illustrious names in French arts and letters, including Guy de Maupassant, Romain Rolland, Jules Massenet, and Charles Gounod. ("Even the commercial Americans would not want this Eiffel tower," they proclaimed.)

In the end, the tower turned out to be a thrilling attraction, especially when illuminated with Thomas Edison's powerful incandescent bulbs. "Hundreds of thousands of visitors . . . waited long hours and bore every inconvenience of weather to see them," gushed William B. Franklin, the United States commissioner general for the exposition. Paris had a history of street lighting—during the revolution, oil lamps were suspended by pylons and overhead wires, replaced by gas lamps in the mid-1800s—and the first electric candles were actually used in 1878 to light the Avenue de l'Opéra, but they sputtered and wavered. Edison's invention was a vast improvement.

Along with the exhibits, multiple concerts, dances, and theatrical productions took place. When the fair was over, some of the acts lingered. Javanese dancers stayed on in Paris and became a permanent part of the cultural scene, and French audiences quickly became accustomed to encounter the Indonesian gamelan ensembles.

The Indonesian influences absorbed in Paris went beyond even the harmonic realm, however. A gamelan rhythmic cycle known as the "great gong" underlies Debussy's oriental piano piece "Pagodes." Ravel's beautiful Trio bases one of its movements on an Indonesian poetic form, the pantun. And there remained for the impressionist a heightened fascination with instrumental "color"—writing parts so skillfully that individual timbres might emerge like glimmers of sunlight playing on the ocean's rippling surface. The idea of basing a piece entirely on shifting sonorities—with no other changes—occurred to

Arnold Schoenberg in 1909, when he wrote his Five Pieces for Orchestra. The third movement, "Colors: Summer Morning by a Lake," features a five-part chord played first by flutes, clarinet, bassoon, and solo viola. The instrumentation then changes, with English horn, French horn, and trumpet taking over. "The chords must change so gently that no emphasis can be perceived at the instrumental entries," wrote Schoenberg. He named this concept of timbral melody *Klangfarbenmelodie*—a new way of creating music using sonority instead of pitch—it was a term that permanently entered the lexicon.

The sensibility grew and spread, even across the ocean. American composer Henry Cowell (1897–1965) eventually built on impressionism's expanding palette, creating the concept of "string piano," in which a performer reaches inside the instrument to pluck, scrape, and stroke the strings, resulting in works like *Aeolian Harp* (1923) and *The Banshee* (1925), a groaning, ghostlike evocation of the title's mythological demon. A decade later, his student John Cage, encouraged by Cowell's example, would come up with the idea of the "prepared piano," its clanging sounds bridging the divide between the piano and the gamelan ensemble.

Debussy's extensive tonal palette was also expanded even further by other composers working in the French tradition, including Olivier Messiaen (1908–1992), whose unique musical language, built by arranging the tones of the scale in special symmetrical patterns, and also incorporating bird calls, gave rise to what he termed "a glistening music . . . giving to the aural sense voluptuously refined pleasures." The sheer splendor of his conceptions could convey a sense of timelessness. Messiaen relished what he termed "the charm of impossibilities," creating exotic scales that could be transposed—shifted to another key—only a limited number of times before they repeated themselves. The great composer and conductor Pierre Boulez (1925–2016), a student of Messiaen's, wrote virtuosic and dazzling works of "organized delirium," luminous and explosive, where improvisatory-sounding flurries of fast notes moved into resonant clouds of frozen harmonies, and always with an intoxicating beauty.

As the features that comprised the fair coalesced, they formed the nexus out of which radical new directions arose. The electric current that energized the spectacle's lights, for example, became yet another impressionist tributary. At the 1881 Exposition Internationale de l'Électricité in Paris, telephones had been used to transmit performances over a distance. This time around, 120 listening stations were set up to give participants the opportunity to hear performances transmitted to them directly from the opera stage, and patrons marveled at the quality of the sound. The impact of electricity, harnessed for artistic experimentation, was now about to be fully recognized.

In 1893 composer and pianist Ferruccio Busoni (1866–1924) suggested that science had the potential to expand music's expressive range—especially, as mentioned earlier, through the exploitation of microtones, those pitches hidden in the cracks between the keys of the piano. Even before that, in 1867, scientist Matthias Hipp—whose inventions included railway signaling equipment, clock mechanisms, telexes, fire alarms, microphones, and seismographs—created an "Electromechanical Piano," with a keyboard that activated electromagnets, which in turn affected small generators. By 1893, Busoni's vision was truly being realized, as American Thaddeus Cahill revealed the Telharmonium, an artificial orchestra of sorts, with tones broadcast telephonically. Though it had a mixed reception, Mark Twain weighed in positively with his usual wit: "The trouble about these beautiful, novel things is that they interfere so with one's arrangements," he complained. "Every time I see or hear a new wonder like this I have to postpone my death right off. I couldn't possibly leave the world until I have heard this again and again."

And the evolution continued. By 1928 new electronic instruments were being launched, like the ethereal-sounding ondes martenot, invented by French cellist Maurice Martenot, and the theremin, invented by Russian Leon Theremin and operated by means of waving one's hands near antennas, without any physical contact between the player and the instrument. Both eventually enjoyed a vogue on Hollywood sci-fi soundtracks. American violinist Clara Rockmore (1911–1998) championed the theremin, tapping its magical properties and performing Schubert's "Ave Maria" on her knees while waving her arms in space. The theremin has found a present-day champion in keyboardist Rob Schwimmer.

Envisioning radically new sounds had once been the province of philosophers like Francis Bacon, who set out a future of music in his *New Atlantis,* published posthumously in 1626. The new art, he wrote, would accommodate quarter tones, what we would later call microtones, and "lesser slides of sounds," to be performed on unknown instruments "with bells and rings that are dainty and sweet," conveyed through "trunks and pipes, in strange lines and distances." Allowing for a broad interpretation, his description was not far off from the state of music that would materialize three hundred years later.

Many joined in the new wave: French-American composer

Edgard Victor Achille Charles Varèse (1883–1965), a student of Busoni's who began his career as an impressionist—his "Un grand sommeil noir" (1906), based on a poem by Paul Verlaine, included a quotation from Debussy's opera *Pelléas et Mélisande*—gravitated to the atmospheric potential of electronics and magnetic tape, media in which he would become a leading light. And American composer Harry Partch (1901–1974) would become one of the first modernists to use microtonal scales in earnest, building custom-made instruments to execute them—contraptions with names like the Chromelodeon, the Quadrangularis Reversum, and the Zymo-Xyl.

Yet another opportunity to integrate technology and enchantment had arisen when recordings made their appearance in 1877 with Edison's phonograph. The inventor, who first used wax paper, graduated to tinfoil, and then moved on to a hollow wax cylinder as the raw material for his soundtracks, paved the way for the emergence of an entire industry based on audio discs that could be spun on turntables—marketed in 1889 by Emile Berliner, shortly before Leon F. Douglass and Eldridge R. Johnson formed the Victor Talking Machine Company in Camden, New Jersey, in 1901. The first Victor classical recording was of Alfred Cortot performing Chopin and Schubert.

Audio reproduction provided new opportunities for inveterate avant-garde musicians, who began to play the discs in reverse, pursuing the impressionist goal of freeing musical sounds from their conventional contexts. John Cage further expanded the expressive potential of turntables by varying their speeds in his *Imaginary Landscape* no. 1 for piano and percussion (1939). His *Imaginary Landscape* no. 5 (1952), choreographed by dancer Jean Erdman, recorded fragments from forty-two phonograph records transferred to magnetic tape—"so far as I can ascertain," he said, "the first piece of music for magnetic tape made in this country [the United States]."

Other countries were also becoming hotbeds of electronic music production, with haunting sounds emanating from laboratories throughout Europe. In Germany, Karlheinz Stockhausen created *Gesang der Jünglinge* (1955–1956), a work routinely called the first masterpiece of electronic music, using recorded vocals by twelve-year-old Josef Protschka, seamlessly integrated with electronic sounds. Italian composer Luciano Berio worked with his wife, Cathy Berberian, to produce a piece in 1958 in which a text by James Joyce was altered and elaborated upon by electronic means. Building on these landmark pieces, American Milton Babbitt, one of the founders of the Columbia-Princeton Electronic Music Center, issued *Philomel* in 1964, combining synthesizer with live and recorded soprano voice.

The development of the synthesizer took a large leap forward through the ingenuity of American inventor Robert Moog, who had been contacted by Cage in 1965 when Moog was a recent PhD graduate in engineering physics at Cornell University. He helped Cage and choreographer Merce Cunningham create *Variations V*, fashioning twelve five-foot-high antennas to sense the movements of the dancers on stage. After composing *Imaginary Landscape* no. 5, Cage set about exploring the possibilities of "synthetic music," using sound generators and having volunteers toss coins to determine the order of things. Moog later became world-famous for creating an instantly popular simple, compact synthesizer.

The shock of the new provided the spark of awe—the moment of alchemy—that these composers were hoping to ignite. Just as in the case of audio discs, sometimes this entailed repurposing old devices, like the mechanical player piano, which had been in popular use since Muzio Clementi (in his role as piano maker) offered a "self-acting pianoforte" in London around 1825. The Pianola, a version created by American Edwin Scott Votey in 1895, became all the rage in his day. Igor Stravinsky composed an Étude for Pianola in 1917, and Paul Hindemith offered up a Toccata for Mechanical Piano in 1926. But earlier composers never suspected the instrument's radical potential.

American composer Conlon Nancarrow (1912–1997) pushed the device further to produce jaw-dropping outcomes beginning in the 1940s, with his Studies for Player Piano. These pieces transformed the quaint parlor instrument, whose rolls filled with punched holes allowed families to hear great piano performances in their own homes, into a medium for music technically beyond the ability of mere mortals to execute. In Nancarrow's works, musical lines shoot by like lightning; phrases run, skip, dance, and collide at different speeds; bursts of energy seem to threaten to tear the instrument apart.

Nancarrow's focus on super-performance continued in the music of composer Noah Creshevsky (1945–2020), who called his approach "hyperrealism." Creshevsky, whose background included studies with Berio and with famed French teacher Nadia Boulanger and a close association with composer Virgil Thomson, had always been fascinated by the idea of transcending human limitations. He remembered an uncle who did magic tricks, and begged him for explanations of how they were done. "When I finally learned the answers, I was disappointed," he remembered, "because the tricks became commonplace. Boulanger talked about this: How we lose the wonder of childhood and, as artists, have to recapture it somehow in a new, 'informed' second childhood. Music ought to be magic, and I'm always aiming for something that goes beyond the ordinary—I don't even want to be able to put my finger on it."

It spurred Creshevsky to take materials that are recognizably of this world—real instrumental and vocal performances—and exaggerate them electronically, creating performances that normal human beings are incapable of producing. As a student he was aware that Liszt was frequently criticized for empty virtuosity. "But I was always intrigued by that supreme degree of technical accomplishment. My music pushes virtuosity to new levels, resulting in sounds that are lifelike and yet not real. I like that point which hovers between reality and the magical." It's a state to which all the alchemists aspired, where music and enchantment find common ground.

Creshevsky offered insights into the special place that electronic music holds in the artform, and the unique possibilities it offers. "What is it that induces musicians to endlessly compose string quartet after string quartet, or an infinite number of pieces for solo piano?" he asked. "These prefabricated musical formats are generally chosen because composers imagine their music being played by live players in concert halls. In fact, most music is heard through speakers or headphones, at home. The home theater has nearly replaced the concert hall, especially in the area of contemporary non-pop music.

"Composing for recordings instead of for live concerts closes some doors, but opens others. What of the composer who had dreamed of having a flutist imitate some bird sounds at the end of the last movement of a quartet that has been limited to four strings? Can we hire a flutist to play for only one minute of a thirty-minute piece?"

Curated concerts of electronically produced and recorded works offer new possibilities. "If this were a recording instead of a live concert, no one would care about the dramatic or economic comings and goings of the cello and flute. If this were a recording, and if the composer wanted birdcalls, he or she could make a recording of some real birds and dispense with the flutist altogether. If music—including music for standard ensembles—was conceived for recordings instead of live concerts, the music composed could be very different." Creshevsky's music fulfills that vision.

Like other revolutionary approaches, this one was tied to a singular place and time. On the other hand, jazz emerged from a vast array of sources, some of them mysterious, encompassing generations of contributors. Perhaps the most important development in the modern era—America's musical gift to the world—jazz was a revolution that could have grown only in the fertile ground and extraordinarily open milieu of a country that welcomed myriad ethnicities to live, work, and interact as neighbors. Its elements can be traced, among other influences, to African drumming; the fiddling traditions of the British Isles; some claim the exotic music of the Middle East; and the rhythmic inventiveness of Latin America; with pockets of local influence arising in such American regions as the blues-infused Mississippi Delta, New Orleans's historically rich Congo Square, and the Five Points section of New York, where the culture of Irish immigrants collided with that of freed slaves as dance contests gave rise to tap dance as an art form. Added to that mix was the cultivated musical art of the European royal courts, as it proliferated in the West. All of these strands were mined, milled, and mashed together in the capacious melting pot of the New World, where traditional forms, familiar melodies, and intoxicating rhythms melded together into a new improvised art, nurtured mostly by the descendants of slaves.

# CHAPTER 7

# Jazz Goes to Paris

Everybody has the Blues. Everybody longs for
meaning. Everybody needs to clap hands and be happy.
Everybody longs for faith. In music, especially this
broad category called Jazz, there is a stepping stone
towards all these.

——MARTIN LUTHER KING JR.,
in the 1964 Berlin Jazz Festival program

THOUGH MUSICIANS from vastly different backgrounds
and ethnicities contributed to its evolution, jazz came to
embody "the eternal tom-tom beating in the Negro soul," as
Langston Hughes, esteemed poet of the Harlem Renaissance,
put it. "Their joy runs, bang! into ecstasy," Hughes explained,
linking this music to the uplifted spirits of Black folk. "Their
religion soars to a shout," he wrote. Their credo: "Play awhile.
Sing awhile. O, let's dance!" Of course, jazz also encompassed
darker aspects of life. As Harlem bandleader James Reese
Europe (1880–1919) explained, "We colored people have our
own music . . . created by the sufferings and miseries of our
race."

Though the impulse behind it was deeply personal, jazz's
appeal was instantaneous and widespread. There were some

*An American military band led by Lt. James Reese Europe,
in the courtyard of a Paris hospital for the American wounded,
entertaining patients with "real American jazz"*

naysayers, like "March King" John Philip Sousa, who charged that jazz's earliest incarnation, ragtime, featuring relentless syncopations—metrical disruptions that create a feeling of giddy disorientation—made you "want to bite your grandmother." In classical music such moments of rhythmic disruption are temporary, quickly dispelled through a reassertion of the regular accents of meter. In ragtime, and later in the less rigid sounds of jazz (the two similarly fell along a gradual spectrum of rhythmically unsettling styles, with ragtime the more formulaic and predictable), things were left more permanently off-kilter. But songwriters Chris Smith, Tom Lemonier, and Will Dixon proffered a more popular opinion of the approach that had set Sousa back on his heels: "Ragtime music," they asserted, "is the only real melody that thrills the heart and moves the feet."

It moved feet all over the country. In Chicago, ragtime and early jazz stars like W. C. Handy and Scott Joplin made toes tap at the local World's Fair in 1893, as well as at venues like the Pekin Theatres on South State Street, where Black and white patrons soaked in the sounds together. By 1917, William Bottoms's immense Dreamland Café—which advertised eighteen electric blow fans, five exhaust fans, 125 electric lights, and an eight-hundred-person dance floor—was presenting the "Original Jazz Band" (initially spelled "Jass"). Two years later it hired legendary cornetist Joseph "King" Oliver, the musical leader whose ensemble served as a training ground for Louis Armstrong, who brought a new level of rhythmic flexibility to the art. As time went on, ragtime's stiff formulations loosened and modern jazz's more elastic approach took hold.

Other jazz hot spots included Jelly Roll Morton's New Orleans, with its Storyville section, boasting bawdy houses with the best piano "ticklers" of the day—that is, until the sector was shut down by the United States Navy on November 12, 1917. The sounds migrated elsewhere, including New York. The Tenderloin district, which encompassed Tin Pan Alley on West Twenty-Eighth Street, became dotted with jazz clubs early in the century. Black musicians learned to hone their trade in the growing cluster of music venues, reaching wealthy clientele at spots like Barron Wilkins's Little Savoy on West Thirty-Fifth Street, and networking at the Marshall Hotel on West Fifty-Third Street, which became an unofficial base of operations for jazz professionals. The musicians and crowds gravitated uptown to Harlem, the section of Manhattan that became a national symbol of America's Black culture.

Remarkably, by the 1920s, the music had traveled clear across the Atlantic, setting Paris ablaze with its unconstrained energy, opening the doors of opportunity to itinerant American musicians overwhelmed by racial prejudice at home, and spreading the new musical gospel to European audiences eager in the wild pre-Depression era to succumb to its charms. Black theatrical entertainers—comedians, exotic dancers, husky blues singers—joined the exodus as the City of Light took on a distinctly American cast, and Harlem migrated, step by step, to Montmartre. The world had conspired to make it happen—by going to war.

Musical history is filled with instances when armed conflict spawned artistic change: the fifteenth-century English musician John Dunstable, accompanying the Duke of Bedford on his military adventures, influenced generations of European composers with his modern harmonic ideas. The Turks, as they attacked Austria in the eighteenth century, introduced cymbals and percussion instruments to Viennese musicians through their military janissary bands, sounds that were quickly absorbed by composers like Haydn, Mozart, and Beethoven as essential elements into the European symphony. Thus it was with America's Black soldiers who fought German aggression in World War I, troops that included many professional musicians. Under the leadership of Harlem conductor James Reese Europe, they performed in French towns during and after the conflict, and became an enduring presence.

There had been few opportunities for African Americans in the United States military, though at the outbreak of the Spanish-American War in April 1898 a scattering of Black National Guard units joined the effort. Once the Great War began, African Americans had little incentive to enroll in the war effort. Indeed, their help was initially discouraged. Nevertheless, the 15th Infantry Regiment (Colored) of the New York National Guard—consisting of Black men recruited from the Williamsburg section of Brooklyn, the San Juan Hill section of Manhattan, and Harlem—was established in mid-June 1916 with one white officer, and no rifles, ammunition, uniforms, or even a headquarters. However, once the Black soldiers were equipped and sent into battle, they more than made up for the meager early support with grit and valor: terrified Germans came to call them *blutlustige Schwarzemänner*, bloodthirsty Black men, and the French dubbed them "the Harlem Hellfighters."

Early recruitment of Black soldiers was accomplished through announcements in a Black publication, *The New York Age*, and bolstered by endorsements from celebrities like Bert Williams, the Ziegfeld Follies comedian. The campaign was only minimally successful beyond the 15th Infantry Regiment, but that changed on September 18, 1916, when James Europe signed on, seeing it as a civic responsibility to his African American brethren. As he explained to musician Noble Sissle, a member of his band and an artistic partner with ragtime composer Eubie Blake in producing such hit shows as *Shuffle Along:* "Our race will never amount to anything, politically or economically, in New York or anywhere else unless there are strong organizations of men who stand for something in the community."

The moral example had been set by Frederick Douglass, who in 1863 urged fellow "men of color," despite their consistently dismal treatment, to join in the fight against the Confederacy. "By every consideration which binds you to your enslaved fellow countrymen and the peace and welfare of your country . . . ," he proclaimed, "I urge you to fly to arms, and smite with death the power that would bury the government and your liberty in the same hopeless grave."

It helped that James Europe's reputation in the music community was unimpeachable. He had established the Music School Settlement for Colored People in Harlem, with help from David Mannes, concertmaster of the New York Symphony Orchestra and son-in-law of celebrated conductor Walter Damrosch. Mannes, in turn, enlisted the support of philanthropists, proclaiming that music was "a universal language [through which] the Negro and the white man can be brought to have a mutual understanding."

In 1910, when a number of Marshall Hotel regulars formed a new organization, the Clef Club of the City of New York, they chose Europe as its first president. His dream of bringing a symphony-sized orchestra of African American musicians before the public could now be realized, though the Clef Club ensemble was in truth no more than a ragtag amalgam of talent. Some of the musicians involved played standard instruments, like pianos, but others used folk instruments like the bandoris (a cross between a banjo and mandolin) and the harp guitar. Their initial public offerings included a "Musical Melange and Dance-fest," featuring one hundred musicians and dancers, held at the Manhattan Casino on 155th Street and Eighth Avenue. Yet by the opening of the Clef Club's official headquarters in 1910, at 134 West Fifty-Third Street, across the street from the Marshall Hotel, a plan had been formalized to hold a concert in New York's famed Carnegie Hall.

Not everyone thought that using that upscale venue was a good idea. Black composer Will Marion Cook, a student of Antonín Dvořák's and the Clef Club's assistant conductor, predicted to Noble Sissle "that Jim [Europe] would set the Negro race back fifty years." But Cook, whose conduct was notoriously erratic, had attempted to organize a similar event in 1890, and failed, despite the backing of Frederick Douglass. (Cook's Black musical revue *Clorindy, or The Origin of the Cake Walk*, had opened on Broadway in 1898. In 1918, he would establish the New York Syncopated Orchestra [later, the Southern Syncopated Orchestra] out of the remnants of the Clef Club, and take it on tour. The ensemble's high artistic level impressed even the revered Swiss conductor Ernest Ansermet, who wrote, "The first thing that strikes one about the Southern Syncopated Orchestra is the astonishing perfection, the superb taste, and the fervor of its playing.")

Commenting on his group's strange instrumentation, James Europe explained how it enhanced the ensemble's unique charms. The "steady strumming accompaniment" from all the mandolins and banjos gave them a sound similar to a Russian balalaika orchestra, he noted. And the multiple pianos were, he said, "sufficient to amuse the average white musician who attends one of our concerts for the first time. The result, of course, is that we have developed a kind of symphony music that, no matter what else you may think, is different and distinctive, and that lends itself to the playing of the peculiar compositions of our race."

On May 1, 1912, the day before the Clef Club's Carnegie Hall concert, two thousand seats remained unsold. Then an editorial in the *New York Evening Journal* appeared, asking the public for support: "The Negroes have given us the only music of our own that is American—national, original, and real. . . . The proceeds of the concert will be devoted to the Music School Settlement for Colored People." It made all the difference. People had to be turned away at the door.

Musicologist Natalie Curtis Burlin described the group's instrumental assemblage, with its sections of banjos, mandolins, guitars, strings, percussion, and a contingent of fourteen upright pianos played by the best ragtimers in town, as having an "absolutely distinctive sound, [with] a 'tang' like the flavor of pineapple amid other fruits." When the concert opened with a syncopated march, played "with a biting attack and an infectious rhythm," reported writer James Weldon Johnson, author of *Black Manhattan*, "the applause became a tumult."

That success fostered ever more triumphs, both for Europe and for his musicians. Before long the Clef Club players held a near-monopoly on providing music for private parties in town. And though it was common practice at the time for hotels and restaurants to pay Black musicians to perform menial tasks, like housekeeping, and to expect them to provide their music for mere tips, Europe changed that pattern, insisting that employers pay his band members a fixed salary, plus transportation and room and board. And he instilled in the musicians a new sense of pride by instituting a dress code, requiring tuxedos and dark suits on the job.

A new era for Harlem's talent dawned as a dance craze began to grip the nation, creating an even greater demand for their musical services. "People who have not danced before in twenty years have been dancing," noted the October 1913 issue of *Current Opinion*. "Cabaret artists are disappearing except as interludes while people recover their breaths for the following number. One wishes either to dance or to watch and to criticize those who dance."

James Europe and the English ballroom-dancing star Vernon Castle and his American wife, Irene, had met in the summer of 1913, at Mrs. Stuyvesant Fish's dinner and dance in Newport, Rhode Island (where the society crowd was, like the rest of the country, caught up in a Turkey Trot craze). The husband-and-wife dance team were a popular item with the highbrows despite the ragtime aspect of their act, explained Irene, because "we were clean-cut, we were married and when we danced there was nothing suggestive about it. We made dancing look like the fun it was and so gradually we became a middle ground both sides could accept." With Europe's Society Orchestra playing, they improvised a new step called the Castle Walk. "Instead of coming down on the beat as everybody else did, we went up" was the way Irene described it.

"Vernon was astonished," remembered historian Douglas Gilbert, "first at Europe's rhythms, then at the instrumental color of his band." The Castles decided on the spot to include in their contracts a demand that Europe provide the music for their act, supporting such entertaining dance moves as the Texas Tommy—which required a male dancer to whirl or toss his partner and then catch her at the last moment—and the off-kilter Castle Half and Half, which rapidly alternated between meters of 3/4 and 2/4.

The artistic partnership fostered genuine friendship. When the Castles accepted an offer of two thousand dollars a week to perform at two Times Square theaters, the Palace and Hammerstein's Victoria, they insisted, as usual, on using Europe's musicians. The powerful, segregated musicians' union, though, refused to allow Blacks to enter the pit of any Broadway house, voicing concerns that Black orchestras would soon dominate the theaters just as they already had taken over the cabarets. Neither Europe nor the Castles were prepared to cave in to that ban, however; so they simply placed chairs for the musicians on the stage.

Overcoming pervasive racism in the greater world was less easy, however. Even heeding the patriotic call in the fight against Germany was no guarantee of just treatment or safety for the Black recruits. In the armed forces, conflicts between Black and white soldiers were a constant. By August 1917 ongoing tensions had erupted into a gun battle in Houston that left seventeen white citizens dead, with thirteen Black soldiers tried and hanged, and forty-one others jailed. Houston's mayor, J. F. Floyd, had carped: "With their northern ideas about race equality, they will probably expect to be treated like white men." When James Europe's troops finally shipped off to France aboard the *Pocahontas* at the end of 1917, they were entering a fraught world, but it was one prepared to offer them a measure of respect they couldn't get at home.

As Europe wrote to Fred Moore, editor of *The New York Age:* "The French simply cannot be taught to comprehend that despicable thing called prejudice. . . . 'Viva [*sic*] la France' should be the song of every Black American over here and over there." (The same could not be said of the United Kingdom, where drummer Louis Mitchell and his Southern Symphonists' Quintet opened at the Piccadilly Restaurant in 1914, but found that racism continued there unabated. Later, Duke Ellington and Cab Calloway were both refused first-class accommodations in London.) But the French were aware that the color line was a delicate matter: a memo entitled "Secret Information Concerning Black American Troops" warned French officers that "we may be courteous and amiable with these [Black troops], but we cannot deal with them on the same plane as with the white American officers without deeply wounding the latter."

Fronting the best band in the United States Army eased the way for James Europe, but assembling the group had required special efforts. Funds were hard to find, and regulations limited the number of band members to twenty-eight, while Europe said he needed at least forty-four. His superior officer Col. William Hayward solicited help from Daniel G. Reid of the U.S. Steel Corporation and the American Can Company, who wrote a check for ten thousand dollars. Then, when Europe needed skilled woodwind players, he was allowed to recruit them from Puerto Rico, placing Noble Sissle in charge of the group.

Overseas, the Harlem musicians fought in the trenches, passing through a dozen towns, including Angers, Tours, Moulins, Lyon, and Culoz, and played their early jazz music in hospitals and public squares. In Paris, they were ordered to play at the

Théâtre des Champs-Élysées, where the audience went wild. "The leader of the band of the Garde Republican came over and asked me for the score of one of the jazz compositions we had played," recalled Europe. "He said he wanted his band to play it. I gave it to him, and the next day he again came to see me. He explained that he couldn't seem to get the effects I got, and asked me to go to a rehearsal. I went with him. The great band played the composition superbly—but he was right: the jazz effects were missing. I took an instrument and showed him how it could be done, and he told me that his own musicians felt sure that my band had used special instruments." In fact, the French musicians examined one of the Americans' horns, searching for a hidden valve that might be used to create the wails and wah-wahs of the band's "talking trumpets," and falsely concluded that the effect was simply a Black anomaly, beyond their abilities.

It was true that the Americans had demonstrated skills beyond conservatory training, with finely honed ears and a responsiveness to the demands of the moment. "I always put a man that can read notes in the middle where the others can pick him up," Europe told Natalie Curtis Burlin. They "can catch anything if they hear it once or twice, and if it's too hard for 'em the way it's written, why they just make up something else that'll go with it." But the idea that this music could only be played by Blacks was of course a fiction—an example of the nature-versus-nurture debate, with the French coming down on the wrong side of the issue.

Journalist Charles Welton of the *New York World* conducted a series of interviews with James Europe in 1918, and tried to explain the technically intricate nature of jazz to his public. This music, he wrote, "isn't merely a series of uncontrollable spasms or outbursts of enthusiasm scattered through a composition and discharged on the four winds, first by one wing and then by another of the band. Of course, if a player feels an attack of something which he believes to be a jazz novelty rumbling in his system it is not the Europe rule to make him choke it back and thus run the risk of cheating the world out of a good thing. Any player can try anything once. . . ."

The result was at times a kind of wild abandon, like that of a New Orleans marching band. The ensemble was helped along by the rhythmic impetus of legendary tap dancer Bill "Bojangles" Robinson, who served as the unit's drum major. Special effects were merely a natural part of the process. "When a leather cone is wrung out and fitted into the vestibule of a horn, and the man back of the works contributes the best that is in him," Welton wrote, "it is somewhat difficult to explain what happens in mere words. You get it in both ears and almost see it. The cone being wet, the sound might be called liquified harmony. It runs and ripples, then has a sort of choking sensation; next it takes on the musical color of Niagara Falls at a distance, and subsides to a trout brook nearby. The brassiness of the horn is changed, and there is a sort of throbbing nasal effect, half moan, half hallelujah. Get me?"

But James Europe was not the only American stoking the jazz fires across the Atlantic. Louis Mitchell's Jazz Kings, who in 1917 had taken up residence at Le Perroquet, a cabaret in the basement of the Casino de Paris, introduced the French public to the assorted drums and cymbals known collectively to jazz musicians as "traps" (including snare drums, tom-toms, and more), and labeled them *un jazz*. Influential French musician Léo Vauchant listened to Mitchell's group in wonder, amazed that they were totally uninhibited by "the sacredness of the written notes." His fellow musicians played the scores as they were written, he noted, while the Americans "added something, syncopations, notes. . . . And I couldn't understand where that came from!"

Europe even had a rival within the United States fighting forces, another Black American who led his own jazz-inflected military band throughout the conflict. Lieutenant James Tim Brymn (1881–1946) conducted the African American 350th Field Artillery Regiment Band, known as the Black Devil Orchestra. Like Europe, he signed up to fight in World War I. Afterward, in 1919, Brymn's Black Devil Orchestra performed before President Woodrow Wilson and General John Pershing during the Paris Peace Conference. Jazz pianist Willie Smith, who also served in the 350th Field Artillery Regiment, received the nickname "the Lion" for his bravery.

After their return to the United States Brymn and his Black Devil Orchestra would release twelve records over the next decade; he also led orchestras at Ziegfeld's Roof Garden and Reisenweber restaurant's Jardin de Dance, two prominent nightclubs in New York City. In the 1920s he served as the musical director of Europe's Clef Club, despite the competition that had brewed between them.

The French were already predisposed to regard Blacks as a people secretly "teeming with a disquieting and robust life, the generator of a power that will one day revolutionize any exhausted societies through contact alone," as Parisian critic François de Nion wrote of the visiting Africans who exhibited at the 1889 fair. The idea inflamed the libidinous fantasies of many a repressed white socialite, insinuating itself into the art world in paintings like Picasso's highly charged *Les Demoiselles d'Avignon* (1907). Cubist Georges Braque (1882–1963) confessed that the popular displays of African masks that had sprung up throughout Europe had helped him "to make contact with instinctive things, with inhibited feeling that went against the false [Western] tradition which I hated." It paralleled the contrast between Western musical traditions and the free-and-easy spontaneity of jazz musicians.

But French classical musicians had actually shown a jazz sensibility even before the arrival of the Americans. Claude Debussy created raggy piano pieces like "Golliwog's Cakewalk" (1908) and "Le Petit Nègre" (1909), likely after having heard some cakewalks in London around that time. Print music was available as another early source of ragtime style in French composition: Tom Turpin's "Harlem Rag" was published in 1897, and Scott Joplin's instructional *School of Ragtime* appeared in 1908.

Still, viewing this music in print was a far cry from experiencing it live. After hearing a jazz performance in 1918 at the Casino de Paris, Jean Cocteau described the art, in *Cock and Harlequin: Notes Concerning Music,* as a "cataclysm in sound." Adding to Cocteau's portrayal, French composer Darius Milhaud drew a larger picture: "The saxophone breaking in, squeezing out the juice of dreams, or the trumpet, dramatic or languorous by turns, the clarinet, frequently played in its upper register, the lyrical use of the trombone, glancing with its slide over quarter-tones in crescendos of volume and pitch, thus intensifying the feeling; and the whole, so various yet not disparate, held together by the piano and subtly punctuated by the complex rhythms of the percussion, a kind of inner beat, the vital pulse of the rhythmic life of the music. The constant use of syncopation . . . gave the impression of unregulated improvisation. . . ."

Milhaud's own jazz ballet, *La Création du monde*, premiered in 1923. Other classical composers were similarly smitten by the new sounds, with syncopated stylings permeating Satie's "Rag-Time du paquebot" in his ballet *Parade* (1917); Georges Auric's foxtrot "Adieu, New York!" (1919); and Igor Stravinsky's cubist depiction of the musical fad, *Ragtime for Eleven Instruments* (1918). Soon after, Maurice Ravel composed his Violin Sonata no. 2 (1923–1927), whose second movement is an homage to the blues; in the years that followed, he would be strongly influenced by George Gershwin. By 1927, Ernst Krenek's jazz opera, *Jonny spielt auf* (Jonny Strikes Up), was touching off violent protests among conservative critics, as an archetype of Weimar decadence.

Once the troops returned home, Paris would open its arms wide to America's other musical expeditioners. Louis Mitchell opened his venue, Mitchell's, in 1924, which he renamed Chez Florence for singer and hostess Florence Embry Jones. Other exciting venues soon followed. The Black boxer, fighter pilot, soldier, and spy Eugene Bullard made friends with Mitchell, took drum lessons, and opened his own club, Le Grand Duc, in 1924; in short order it was run by Harlem singer Ada Beatrice Queen Victoria Louise Virginia "Bricktop" Smith, a celebrated presence in Montmartre. Bricktop, who acquired her nickname because of her red hair and freckles, found the small size of Le Grand Duc to be disheartening, but was comforted by a penniless Langston Hughes, who worked there as a dishwasher, backup cook, and waiter. In fact, the club featured only twelve tables, but the place made a huge impact on Parisian society: patrons included Elsa Maxwell, Fatty Arbuckle, the Prince of Wales (who sat in on drums), Gloria Swanson, Sophie Tucker, F. Scott Fitzgerald, Ernest Hemingway, Picasso, and Man Ray. In 1926, Bricktop opened her own place, which she described as "a combination nightclub, mail drop, bank and neighborhood bar for the most elegant people." Cole Porter auditioned many of his songs at Bricktop's, with Mabel Mercer singing them.

In 1925, orchestra leader Claude Hopkins brought *La Revue Nègre* to Paris, along with the iconic sex symbol Josephine Baker, who had danced in Sissle and Blake's *Shuffle Along*. Baker's antics scandalized and enthralled the town. As writer Djuna Barnes reported, "She made her entry entirely nude except for a pink flamingo feather between her limbs; she was being carried upside down and doing the split on the shoulder of a Black giant. Midstage he paused, and with his long fingers holding her basket-wise around the waist, swung her in a slow cartwheel to the stage in an instant of complete silence. She was an unforgettable female ebony statue. A scream of salutation spread through the theater." Baker's adopted son, Jean-Claude Baker, placed her act in historical context: "In 1905, Mata Hari had danced at the Museum Guimet, bare-breasted except for two metallic shells, and shocked Parisians," he wrote. "Four years later Colette, that most sensual of writers, proved she was an equally uninhibited actress. In a melodrama called *The Flesh*, she played an unfaithful wife whose husband rips off her clothes. Audiences gasped as her breasts were exposed." Yet, claimed Jean-Claude, Josephine outdid them all. When jazzman Sidney Bechet blew his horn on the opening night of *La Revue Nègre*, socialite Caroline Reagan, who had enticed Baker into joining the show, compared the theater to the walls of Jericho, and announced, "The house came tumbling down."

Josephine's gold fingernails led artist Marie-Laure de Noailles to dub her "the pantheress with golden claws." It was especially fitting for a celebrity with an ever-changing menagerie. One day, remembered Sissle, she would promenade down the

*Josephine Baker performing in Paris*

Champs-Élysées with two cheetahs; on another day, with two swans. Her pet leopard, Chiquita, wore a different collar for each of Josephine's dresses, and her apartment was filled with boa constrictors, monkeys, and a pet pig named Albert.

Poster artist Paul Colin left an eyewitness account of *La Revue Nègre:* "At ten o'clock one morning I watched a colorful raucous group swarming toward the theatre, devouring their latest find, croissants from a bistro on the avenue Montaigne," he recalled. "Harlem was invading the Champs-Élysées Theatre. Leaping onto the stage like children at play, the troupe broke out into a frenzied tap-dance. With bright-colored neck ties, dotted pants, suspenders, cameras, binoculars and green- and red-laced boots, who needed costumes? What style. The stage-hands stopped open-mouthed in the wings, and from our seats in the hall, Rolf de Maré, the theatre manager, André Daven, the director, and I sat gaping at the stage. The contortions and cries, their sporty, perky breasts and buttocks, the brilliant colored cottons, the Charleston, were all brand new to Europe."

In the years following her *Revue Nègre* performances, Josephine Baker acted in films, launched her own hair product, and opened her own nightclub. Paris was hers for the moment; but American jazz musicians, singers, dancers, and entertainers continued to arrive and make their own marks. Soon, European musicians like violinist Stéphane Grappelli and guitarist Django Reinhardt began to join the jazz pantheon.

In the United States, the Original Dixieland Jass Band migrated in 1917 from Chicago's Schiller Café to New York's Reisenweber's. In both cities and elsewhere, though the music was causing excitement, it continued to come under attack. In Pittsburgh in 1921, the head of the musicians' union sent a letter to its membership, reprinted in *Variety* under the heading "Death to Jazz." It condemned the music as "socially demeaning" and "immoral." The jazz musicians were accused of "acting like a bunch of intoxicated clowns." Some distinguished classical musicians, on the other hand, found the music praiseworthy, conductor Leopold Stokowski among them.

Despite the resistance the new style blossomed as the twenties got under way. In Chicago in 1923, songwriter Hoagy Carmichael waxed poetic over King Oliver's Band, featuring trumpeter Louis Armstrong and his future wife, pianist Lil Hardin. "The joint stank of body music, bootleg booze, excited people, platform sweat," he wrote. "I couldn't see well but I was feeling all over, 'Why isn't everyone in the world here to hear this?'

"The muggles [marijuana] took effect, making my body feel as light as my Ma's biscuits. I ran over to the piano and played 'Royal Garden Blues' with the band.

"Music meant more than flesh, just then. I had never heard the tune before, but full of smoke, I somehow couldn't miss a note of it. . . . I was floating high around the room in a whirlpool of jazz."

Legal and economic conditions underlying the spread of the new music were rapidly shifting. In 1919 the Eighteenth Amendment to the United States Constitution had been ratified, outlawing alcoholic beverages. The sense of rebellion it engendered soon permeated the culture, setting the stage for a moral free-for-all for gangsters, "flappers," and underground entrepreneurs operating illegal "speakeasies." As bandleader Vincent Lopez remembered, "Crime and gangsterism, once a smalltime operation, was handed a billion-dollar tax-free business to organize with blood and bullets. No binge in history equaled the one in the Prohibition Era." Then along came the Nineteenth Amendment, giving women the right to vote, spurring even more changes: the victors began to smoke in public, raised the hems of their skirts, and bared their knees. Hot, syncopated music fit the times.

On the cusp of these changes, James Europe's troops returned triumphantly in February 1919. In celebration of their victories, they marched up Fifth Avenue from Twenty-Third Street to Harlem, where the band played the popular song "Here Comes My Daddy Now" as onlookers rushed forward to hug their sons, husbands, and friends. It should have been a perfect setup for the bandleader's continuing success, but in a tragic turn, he performed for the last time just three months later, on May 9, in Boston. During an intermission, Europe criticized two of his drummers, Steve and Herbert Wright, for their feuding behavior with each other. Herbert became agitated and stabbed the bandleader in the neck with a penknife. Thinking the wound superficial, Europe ignored it, and bled to death.

W. C. Handy reflected on the sadness of that moment. "The man who had just come through the baptism of war's fire and steel without a mark had been stabbed by one of his own musicians. . . . The sun was in the sky. The new day promised peace. But all the suns had gone down for Jim Europe, and Harlem didn't seem the same." The bandleader was given the first-ever public funeral for a Black American in the city of New York.

A young George Gershwin had once sat outside the clubs where James Europe played, soaking up the music and learning to put his own spin on it, combining the Harlem sounds with Broadway tunefulness and the cultivated harmonies of French impressionism. With Europe's passing, he would assume a large role, unveiling his *Rhapsody in Blue* at Paul Whiteman's "Experiment in Modern Music" concert in New York in 1924. That work rapidly spread throughout the world, making its European debut in Berlin in 1924 as part of *An Alle*—the first revue of director Erik Charell ("the Ziegfeld of the German musical comedy stage"), described by one critic as a mix of German operetta, "Negro music," and "the most enchanting Dancing-Girls, with divine legs."

*The New Republic* carped that Gershwin and Whiteman were ushering in the "vanilla epoch of jazz." Nevertheless, sales of the *Rhapsody in Blue* recording with Gershwin at the piano totaled a million copies. And the advent of such "symphonic jazz" owed much to the pioneering efforts of James Reese Europe.

"Vanilla epoch" or not, those white musicians were capable of true art, though, sadly, they received royal treatment in comparison with that of their Black colleagues. While touring with the Clef Club in Marion, Ohio, Will Marion Cook felt compelled to castigate the enthusiastic audience. "We don't want your applause," he scolded. "We just want to fulfill our obligation here and leave. Early this morning this group of great musicians and myself arrived here. All day long we've sought places to sleep, to eat. Everywhere we went we were turned down because we're Negroes.

"The only rest we've had was the little we could get on trunks and boxes backstage. Our only food has been sandwiches made from cold meat we bought in shops along the avenue.

"Then you come here tonight and have the audacity to applaud our singing. It's hypocrisy and we don't appreciate it."

In the audience was newspaper editor, state senator, and future United States president Warren G. Harding, who promptly organized a committee to place orchestra members in

the homes of the city's "best." Cook was not on their list, purportedly because everyone assumed he had been taken care of.


Across the Pond, where jazz was now a permanent fixture,
people continued to ruminate appreciatively about "Lieutenant Europe's band" following its departure. In a letter to *The
New York Age*, Mrs. Addie Hunton, a YMCA worker in France,
reported that talk about the American troops continued among
French and Americans alike after they returned home. "At Aix-
les-Bains, Chambéry, and Challes Eaux we were being told how
wonderful [the American band] was," she wrote.

   With the advent of jazz, beloved by some yet scorned by
others, the issue about what distinguishes music from noise was
still relevant. The innovations of Cowell, Cage, and others certainly made the matter challenging, but it became even more so
as musical composition continued to encompass a greater range
of sound possibilities, especially with mechanical contrivances
ushering in yet another revolutionary wave. A 1926 event in
Paris, where acoustic instruments and automated contraptions
formed an unorthodox marriage, illustrates why the question
continued to loom.

# CHAPTER 8

# A Great Noise

In your silence
Every tone I seek
Is heard.

—LANGSTON HUGHES, "Silence"

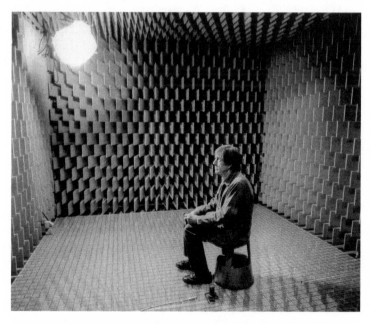

*John Cage in an anechoic chamber (designed to suppress reflected sound),
1990, Festival des Hörens, Erlangen, Germany*

At the 1926 house concert, with seats in short supply, the elegant guests were forced to huddle together, filling in small spaces around and under a bevy of grand pianos, with their arms and legs emerging through the interstices between the instruments. One imagines that the air was thick with the stale mixture of smoked Gauloises and Chanel No. 5, engendering a stifling sense of claustrophobia. Even a cadre of white-gloved butlers dispensing champagne brought little comfort. Still, no one complained. The occasion promised to be *the* musical performance of the year—an alluring draw even in a city filled with artistic exotica.

This evening's affair was the brainchild of George Antheil, who recounted the event in his memoir, and Virgil Thomson, two vagabond American composers who floated through the cultural eddies of 1920s Paris like rudderless ships, scouting for opportunities to advance their fledgling musical careers. They finally found what they were looking for in a wealthy young American housewife and her polo-playing husband, both desperate to gain a higher social standing. The couple was easily seduced into offering the use of their residence for a series of Friday-afternoon musicales, in the hope of being welcomed into the arms of the avant-garde-loving cream of Parisian society.

Antheil had placed his own massive new piece, *Ballet mécanique*, on the program. Its required eight grand pianos filled the small living room to the brink, while additional instruments—xylophones, percussion, and sirens—were set out in a side room and along the giant staircase. Large fans stood in place of the airplane propellers that were called for in the score. The instrumental assemblage left almost no space for the two hundred guests who, reported Antheil, seemed to have been poured through the chimney into the house, where they sweltered while waiting for conductor Vladimir Golschmann, standing atop the center piano, to give the signal for the musicians to begin. At his gesture, wrote Antheil, "the roof nearly lifted from the ceiling! A number of persons instantly fell over from the gigantic concussion! The remainder of our guests squirmed like live sardines in a can; the pianos underneath or above or next to their ears boomed mightily and in a strange synchronization."

The fans blew the wigs off the heads of some of the men. The invitees more resembled prisoners under duress than concertgoers. In the din, several patrons began to brawl. As the music unfolded, their heads spun, their bodies spasmed, and the uproar went on without a break for nearly a half hour. When the performance was finally over, the audience, dripping with perspiration and relieved to find the room finally quiet, crawled out from their spaces, reached for the refreshments, and began celebrating. Antheil and Thomson, the two impresarios, surveyed the spent battleground and spotted their young hostess being tossed up and down in a blanket "by two princesses, a duchess, and three Italian marchesas." Clearly, she had succeeded in her pursuit. And for a brief period, her American co-conspirators had gained a new status as power brokers in the salons of Paris, founts of musical authority and prestige.

Of course, both men had other compelling interests. Antheil had left the factory town of Trenton, New Jersey, for Europe at the age of twenty-one, determined to gain a reputation, he reported in his autobiography, as a "new ultra-modern pianist composer" and "futurist terrible," and by 1921 he was well on his way, with works like his Second Piano Sonata, *The Airplane*—a percussive insurrection of a piece that predated his eventual use of actual airplane propellers as a musical element. Halfway through that early performance, people were fighting in the aisles, yelling, clapping, and hooting. As the composer remembered it, "Any number of surrealists, society personages, and people of all descriptions were arrested." Antheil was often accused of hitting the piano rather than playing it, and he had developed the habit of pulling a revolver from his jacket and laying it on the piano before beginning a performance, as if to warn detractors.

In the audience sat many leading lights of contemporary French art: composer Erik Satie; writer Jean Cocteau; prankster-artist Man Ray, known for his absurdist films and photographs; and painters Pablo Picasso and Francis Picabia, whose catalog included a work titled *St. Vitus's Dance (Rat Tobacco)*, an empty frame strung with yarn. Picabia was a chameleon, adopting and then violating one artistic style after another, proving himself brilliant at them all.

The group comprised a new French wave in the art world, a brotherhood of provocateurs out of which important collaborations had already emerged, such as the strange aforementioned 1917 ballet *Parade*, based on a scenario by Cocteau with music by Satie and designs by Picasso. (The poet Guillaume Apollinaire described *Parade* as "a kind of surrealism," thus coining the term.) Picabia and Satie together later devised yet another ballet with Rolf de Maré, impresario of the Théâtre des Champs-Élysées, the site of the violent 1913 premiere of Stravinsky's ballet *The Rite of Spring*. That notorious event remains a seminal point in modernist history. The ballet was choreographed by Vaslav Nijinsky, who had caused a minor scandal a year earlier with an erotic portrayal of the lovesick faun in his ballet set to Debussy's *Prelude to the Afternoon of a Faun* and performed, like *The Rite*, by Serge Diaghilev's Ballets Russes.

*The Rite of Spring* set off tremors in the music world. In the hall, patrons protested from the beginning as "the curtain opened on the group of knock-kneed and long-braided Lolitas jumping up and down," remembered Stravinsky, while a solo bassoon strained to perform in its highest range. The "smart audience," noted Cocteau, "in tails and tulle, diamonds and ospreys, was interspersed with the suits and bandeaux of the aesthetic crowd. The latter would applaud novelty simply to show their contempt for the people in the boxes." Stravinsky himself was above such superficial games. But there was no denying that the work represented at times a celebration of something close to noise.

The music's emotional message from the start was savage—thunderous collisions inducing a kind of sonic whiplash. Nevertheless, the raw and rhythmically complex onslaught was barely able to cut through the uproar of the audience. In the commotion, Stravinsky ran backstage to help the dancers keep time, and ended up holding on to Nijinsky's tails as the dancer stood on a chair while shouting out the music's count. Poet T. S. Eliot wrote that Stravinsky had seemed to transform "the rhythm of the steppes into the scream of the motor horn, the rattle of machinery, the grind of wheels, the beating of iron and steel, the roar of the underground railway, and the other barbaric cries of modern life; and to transform these despairing noises into music." After the riot, remembered the composer, Diaghilev's only comment was, "Exactly what I wanted."

The trio of Cocteau, Satie, and Picabia also collaborated on the notorious film *Entr'acte*, a bellwether of the age, which featured slow-motion action; scenes that ran in reverse; people appearing and disappearing willy-nilly; the transmutation of an egg into a bird; and a hilarious scene of a runaway hearse at a funeral. Satie seemed generally incapable of repressing his most outrageous inclinations; even his performance instructions in his various musical pieces were designed to provoke: "With inane but appropriate naiveté." "Hypocritically." "Like a nightingale with a toothache." "Courageously easy and obligingly alone." "Be unaware of your own presence." Nevertheless, Satie's works themselves are often unpretentious and exquisitely direct. John Cage found his music spellbinding because he couldn't explain "why something that absurdly simple should be so fascinatingly beautiful."

These men were linked in a common pursuit: questioning the very meaning of art. Of course, in the age of the individual, working together wasn't always smooth sailing. Cocteau annoyed Satie by adding noisemaking instruments to the score of *Parade*—a typewriter, a foghorn, milk bottles, and a pistol—though the composer saved most of his fury for a critic who attacked the work, sending the man a postcard describing the reviewer as an ass. Satie was sued for offending the critic, and given a short jail sentence, and Cocteau was arrested and beaten by police for repeatedly yelling "Ass!" in the courtroom.

The idea of using sirens, foghorns, pistols, and typewriters in musical works was unusual, but not entirely baffling. Percussive, nontonal sounds already had a long-established history in the Western tradition, such as through the influence of the aforementioned Turkish janissary bands. But in incorporating nonmusical, everyday sound sources into the instrumental mix, Cocteau became a leader of a new conceptual direction—a revolution of sorts—that would shape the arts in various ways for a century to come. American composer Leroy Anderson (1908–1975), for example, would create a huge novelty hit in 1953 with "The Typewriter," for orchestra and solo typist. In 2021, flutist Claire Chase recorded *Magic Flu-idity* by Olga Neuwirth

(b. 1968), revisiting the concept by adding the sound of carriage returns and pings, executed by percussionist Lukas Schiske, to scurrying flute lines.

The genesis of such odd couplings of music and machine could be found in the social turmoil that gave rise to an artistic movement called Dada around the time of World War I, in which musicians, filmmakers, and painters elevated the nonsensical to high art. Life is absurd, they reasoned, so why not have the last laugh? And they did—especially in Paris, New York, and Zurich, with works that were both strange and socially transgressive.

Henri-Robert-Marcel Duchamp (1887–1968), a leader of the movement, became famous for his "readymades"—mundane items (a bicycle wheel, a bottle-drying rack) that, when formally displayed, were elevated to the status of art. His *Fountain*, a urinal signed with the pseudonym "R. Mutt," jolted the art world at an exhibit in 1917; in 2004 it was selected as the most influential artwork of the twentieth century by five hundred renowned artists and art historians. Duchamp's readymades were the visual equivalent of commonplace objects put to musical use, such as Antheil's airplane propellers and sirens and Cocteau's foghorn.

The philosophical justification for this aesthetic was laid out by Italian futurist Luigi Russolo in his 1913 manifesto, *The Art of Noises*. He catalogued six types: (1) bangs, thunderclaps, explosions; (2) whistles, hisses, snorts; (3) whispers, murmurs, rustling, gurgling; (4) screams, shrieks, buzzing, crackling, friction sounds; (5) striking metal, wood, stone, china; (6) animal and human cries, roars, howls, laughter, sobs, and sighs. In part, the idea stemmed from the futurist embrace of industrialization. Since the human ear has become accustomed to the industrial landscape, Russolo argued, it is time for new approaches to musical instrumentation and composition. Technology, he mused, will allow musicians to "substitute for the limited variety of timbres that the orchestra possesses today the infinite variety of timbres in noises."

Others had contributed early on to the mounting desire for a music that expanded the usual range of musical sounds. By 1912, American composer Henry Cowell, who would later come up with the idea of playing inside the piano on its strings, had invented the "tone cluster"—a chord using at least three adjacent tones, usually played by a pianist's fist or forearm. (For once, the stream of influence in the classical realm flowed from America to Europe: Hungarian Béla Bartók [1881–1945] heard the American composer perform his unusual harmonies and asked his permission to use clusters in his own music, a device for which Bartók became famous.) Cowell had early on studied with modernist composer Leo Ornstein (1895–2002), whose radical piano piece "Suicide in an Airplane" (1916) employs the cluster effect, along with dissonant tremolos, though it's not clear whether the cluster idea originated with the student or teacher. Cowell also cited French composer Edgard Varèse as an inspiration. This iconoclastic musician wrote *Amériques* between 1918 and 1921, his first piece after emigrating to the United States (the work premiered in 1926), with parts for every conceivable imprecisely pitched percussion instrument, including sleigh bells, rattles, lion's roar (a drum with strings attached), whip, gong, cymbal, and loud siren—"deep and powerful," says the score, "with a brake for instant stopping [of the mechanism to silence it]."

Such sounds were sometimes incorporated with a sense of humor. In 1923, composer Arthur Honegger (1892–1955) introduced his orchestral work *Pacific 231*, a depiction in music of a train traveling from station to station—a journey that begins with metaphorical steam whistles and groaning gears, a locomotive slowly chugging against inertia, before picking up the pace to suggest an engine at full throttle. In 1928, George Gershwin placed French taxi horns in his orchestral tone poem *An American in Paris*, offering audiences the shock of the new with a wink and a smile Noise in the service of musical farce continued on with English composer Malcolm Arnold (1921–2006), whose *A Grand, Grand Overture* featured four gunners, three vacuum cleaners, and a floor polisher.

There were even earlier explorations of strange musical sonorities, like the dense, eerie harmonies of baroque composer Jean-Féry Rebel's (1666–1747) *The Elements,* which begins with a representation of the chaos that preceded the creation of the world—"that confusion," explained Rebel, "which reigned among the Elements before the moment when, subject to immutable laws, they assumed their prescribed places within the natural order." To accomplish this, he had all the notes of a minor scale "played as a single sound. . . . The bass expresses Earth by tied notes which are played jerkily. The flutes, with their rising and falling line, imitate the flow and murmur of Water. Air is depicted by pauses followed by cadenzas on the small flutes, and finally the violins, with their liveliness and brilliance representing the activity of Fire." Rebel's contemporary, composer Georg Philipp Telemann, wrote an equally jarring Overture in F in which he conceived of frogs and crows joining together in raucous cacophony. The result was fairly outrageous, every bit as modern as Stravinsky.

Pieces depicting scenes from war formed yet another musical tradition that teetered on the edge of unruly commotion. *The Battle of Manassas*, by former slave Thomas "Blind Tom" Wiggins (1849–1908), an autistic savant who demonstrated uncanny piano skills, used the piano to convey the noise of cannon fire and the turmoil of civil war. Mark Twain witnessed Blind Tom in action and described his effect on the audience: "He swept them like a storm, with his battle-pieces; he lulled them to rest again with melodies as tender as those we hear in dreams; he gladdened them all with others that rippled through the charmed air as happily and cheerily as the riot the linnets make in California woods; and now and then he threw in queer imitations of the tuning discordant harps and fiddles, and the groaning and wheezing of bag-pipes, that sent the rapt silence into tempests of laughter. And every time the audience applauded when a piece was finished, this happy innocent joined in and clapped his hands, too, with vigorous emphasis."

But these explorations paled in comparison to what was to come. John Cage, as we've seen, elevated the everyday sounds of a noisy contemporary world to the stature of musical splendor, simply by force of his personality, turning the normal order on its head. Cage became a revered leader of his own musical revolution, a celebration of the unexpected, that continues to this day. He rejected the scientific distinction between "noise" and "signal," the former usually regarded as a degradation of the latter. Traditionally, music derives its potency from its tonal stability and organization. Yet, even under the most ideal conditions, chaos threatens that solidity at every moment: human touch wavers, rhythms falter, the shapes of vibrating strings become distorted as a result of material impurities.

And in many quarters such chaos is traditionally welcomed.

Around the world, societies manage to reshape the messy sounds of everyday toil into artful experience. In Africa, as writer Kofi Agawu has pointed out, whole symphonies emerge from the commonplace rhythms of life—the sounds of chopping, grinding, and pounding food, for example, or the fetching of water. Through these daily communal efforts, villages collectively sing music into existence, investing effort to convert sounds into music.

Of course, noise can also be vexing. As philosopher Arthur Schopenhauer wrote, "The most eminent intellects have always been strongly averse to any kind of disturbance, interruption and distraction, and above everything to that violent interruption which is caused by noise . . . [the] infernal cracking of whips . . . which paralyzes the brain." Yet even contemporary science has at times found noise a useful property. Albert Einstein, for example, traced the jitter of pollen grains in fluid to their random encounters with molecules, and this enabled him to better describe the nature of the world. "I often think in music," the physicist once said.

But the work of John Cage represents an extreme case. The four-thousand-year-old Sumerian/Babylonian poem *Epic of Gilgamesh* described how one of the gods, annoyed by mankind's clamor, decided to quash the din by exterminating the human race altogether through a great flood. Cage's radical conceit was to embrace and magnify the very haphazardness that is normally avoided by composers, and to present it as music. For Cage, life's unceasing flood of vibrations—some manmade, others simply arising from nature—was not a portent of calamity, but rather the stuff of beauty. "When I was setting out to devote my life to music, there still were battles to win . . . ," he remembered. "People distinguished between musical sounds and noises. I followed Varèse and fought for noises." His point of view grew from a life devoted both to mystical pursuits and musical explorations, along with an honest assessment of his own limitations.

In 1936, Oskar Fischinger, a renowned abstract music animator, spoke to Cage about the idea of liberating the essence of an object by brushing past it, to "draw forth its sound." The concept, said Cage, "set me on fire," and he began directing his attention to percussion music, which, he declared, "really is the art of noise." As this philosophical underpinning took hold, he began translating Russolo's *The Art of Noises*. At the same time, spiritual transcendence, with an Eastern slant, became an ongoing obsession. He turned to the Chinese *I Ching* (Book of Changes)—a compilation of hexagrams often used in conjunction with chance operations, for the purpose of divination—to explore composing through random procedures, "making my responsibility that of asking questions instead of making choices." Eliminating choice meant disengaging the human ego, the commanding force that fueled Western society, and this became a serious goal in both Cage's life and his music; he found Beethoven's music repulsive, for example, because of the sheer will that drove it.

He began attending classes in Zen Buddhism taught by D. T. Suzuki at Columbia University in the late 1940s. Zen is a discipline that aims to instill in its practitioners what Suzuki had termed "beginner's mind"—a cultivated, wide-eyed, unfiltered sense of openness toward the world. "Zen had the right flavor for me," Cage noted, "humor, intransigence, and a certain feet-on-the-ground character." At the Suzuki lectures, he experienced "a beautiful quietness that you wouldn't even encounter in a Quaker meeting."

For Cage, embracing the Zen of music required cultivating an acceptance of every sound, even noise, rejecting nothing. His *Second Construction* of 1940 had included a rattle, thunder sheet, maracas, temple gongs, sleigh bells, and a "prepared piano," in which objects inserted among the piano's strings produce an altered instrument yielding an array of sonorities.

He also came to pay more attention to silence. He had been working as a WPA recreation leader during the New Deal, entertaining the children of visitors at a San Francisco hospital, where he was instructed not to make any noise, so as not to disturb the patients. This experience, he believed, may have led to his most radical conception: what he later called "the silent piece." At a 1948 lecture at Vassar he spoke of selling "a piece of uninterrupted silence" to the ambient music company Muzak. "It will be 3 or 4½ minutes long—those being the standard lengths of 'canned' music." Apparently, they didn't buy the idea.

But that notion took on new dimensions in 1950, when Cage visited the anechoic chamber at Harvard University, a room specially insulated to suppress any external noise. Despite those auditory blockades, he still heard two sounds, one high and one low. He asked an engineer why: "The high one was your nervous system in operation" was the reply. "The low one was your blood in circulation." So, he concluded, there really is no absolute silence. Still, in 1952, Cage wrote *Waiting*, a three-and-a-half-minute piano solo that begins with a minute and a half of stillness and ends with another twenty seconds of quietude. Later that year, seeing the all-white paintings of Robert Rauschenberg, he felt a compatibility with the artist: these paintings expressed, he said, "the plastic fullness of nothing."

It all led to his most famous work of all: *4'33"*. The premiere was given by pianist David Tudor on August 29, 1952, in Woodstock, New York. Philosophically, it was a piece purportedly focused on nothingness. Using chance methods, Cage found and noted various durations on standard music paper, shuffling the sheets of numbers to set the time lengths of the three movements, which added up to a total of 4'33''. In the performance, Tudor sat at the keyboard and consulted a stopwatch while following the score—on which there were no written tones—announcing the beginnings of movements by closing the keyboard lid, pausing for the required duration, and then signaling their endings by opening it up again. All else was stillness.

But by now the composer's view of the sonic world had undergone a transformation: *4'33''* is actually not about silence at all, but about ambient sound. In fact, the composer explained, it is about attention. Tudor called it "one of the most intense listening experiences you can have. You really listen. You're hearing everything there is." And though perhaps most members of the audience experienced silence, Cage said, there were ambient sounds they ignored: wind stirring outside, raindrops pattering the tin roof—and toward the end, the listeners themselves making "all kind of interesting sounds as they talked or walked out. Music is continuous," he explained. "It is only we who turn away." Any disturbance that arose in the hall or outside it, from sniffles and coughs to rumbling car engines or the wet smacks of gum being chewed, was, in his view, legitimate music.

Not everyone understood. Composer Christian Wolff's mother was so embarrassed at having invited friends to the performance, she complained to Cage that it was merely "a schoolboy's prank, and can give pleasure only to an immature portion of yourself." She asserted that she had consulted the *I Ching* about the piece and that it gave her the hexagram for "Youthful Folly." Cage's music had drifted as far as possible from the ideals of his onetime teacher Arnold Schoenberg, with whom he had studied privately and then at UCLA. Although Cage had idolized Schoenberg, the teacher felt compelled to inform his student that he had no feeling for harmony. Given that situation, Cage ultimately embarked on a course of composition for which the rules of harmony were simply irrelevant.

Ironically, Schoenberg upended musical tradition in his own ways, early on through his 1909 Five Pieces for Orchestra, which contained a movement in which shifting instrumental "colors"—the distinguishing characteristics that made a trumpet sound different from a flute—replaced standard notions of melody; in his 1912 *Pierrot lunaire,* which instructed the singer to half-sing, half-speak the musical lines; and in the revolutionary method he invented for composing "atonally"—using mathematical permutations for determining which tone to use, completely abandoning the traditional notions of consonance (repose) and dissonance (tension) on which musical harmony and structure had rested for hundreds of years. Yet there was no way to reconcile the two worlds in which these composers lived. When Cage invited his former teacher to a performance of his compositions, Schoenberg declined, saying he wasn't free. Cage invited him to another performance, so Schoenberg clarified his position: "I am not free at any time," he explained.

Cage's continuing musical adventures began to incorporate the ballooning technical advances taking shape at places like the RAI Musical Phonology Studio in Milan, which had been set up by composer Luciano Berio and conductor Bruno Maderna, where Cage experimented with magnetic tape. And as the American investigated the expressive links between noise and silence, French composer Pierre Schaeffer was also pursuing a Cagean aesthetic, using technological tools, like recording noises on a gramophone record, and calling the result *musique concrète*. The name stuck. In 1948 his experiments included playing a 78 rpm record at 33 rpm, and he broadcast on French radio a compilation of the sounds of a train, a cough, an accordion, and a priest's song from Bali. In 1950, he and Pierre Henry produced *Symphonie pour un homme seul* (Symphony for a Solo Man), which later was turned into a ballet by Maurice Béjart. It consisted of human sounds (breathing, vocal fragments, shouting, humming, whistling) and nonhuman sounds (a footstep, knocking on doors, percussion, prepared piano, and orchestral instruments).

American composer Kirk Nurock was barely two years old when Schaeffer and Henry's *Symphonie* was first performed, yet he picked up its philosophical threads in the 1970s, forming the Natural Sound Workshop, a touring chorus of twenty-five that based its music on bodily sounds, including cackles, moans, slaps, claps, and vocalized gibberish. In the 1980s Nurock began exploring "cross-species" communication, producing works with a variety of animals: sea lions, wolves, a screech owl, and a Siberian tiger.

There were other adherents to the sensibility. Award-winning film composer Ennio Morricone (1928–2020), whose famed soundtracks for Italian "spaghetti westerns" included unusual instrumentation (ocarina, slapstick, whistling, grunts, electric-guitar noises, howls, and more), brought *musique concrète* to even greater numbers of listeners. His unusual, playful use of all sorts of sounds made noise acceptable as a dramatic enhancement to movie scores.

And the increasing acceptance of noise as an artistic element opened new windows on the great cosmic puzzle in which music and science connect. Computer music composer

Charles Dodge (b. 1942) mapped *Earth's Magnetic Field* (1970), converting the shifting data into musical tones. Collaborating with physicists Bruce R. Boller, Carl Frederick, and Stephen G. Ungar at the Columbia-Princeton Electronic Music Center, Dodge traced the magnetic fluctuations that influence the solar winds. The resulting vortex, not normally heard, was thus translated into audio waves, finally turning the theoretical "music of the spheres"—the ancient idea that celestial bodies, as they travel in their orbits, emanate a heavenly harmony—into something truly tangible.

If adherents of that theory pictured the resulting music to be beauteous, they would be in for a surprise upon listening to Dodge's rendering, because such early thinkers subscribed to the traditional idea that particular combinations of tones create a heightened state of tension, while others bring about repose, an endless cycle fulfilling to the ear and the soul. Then the "atonal" revolution established by Arnold Schoenberg sabotaged the entire scheme.

# CHAPTER 9

# Emancipating the Dissonance

Art is the cry of distress uttered by those who
experience firsthand the fate of mankind.

—ARNOLD SCHOENBERG, *Aphorisms*

F OR CENTURIES, the held breath of dissonance, followed
by the exhalation of consonance, imbued classical music—
the works of Bach, Haydn, Mozart, and others—with a sense
of respiration, propelling whole works forward like a ship carried on undulating waves. The cycles of tension and release
settled into fixed structures, varieties of musical architecture, as
composers imagined borders around the individual harmonic
sequences, treating them as separate building blocks in a well-
ordered narrative.

But in the Romantic age, as art increasingly embraced an
aesthetic of unrequited yearning, and music joined literature
and painting in reflecting the era's existential restlessness, the
long-established classical demarcations became blurry, the once
steadfast anchors now untethered buoys. Melody lines length-

ened, as if reaching toward an invisible, unattainable target. Harmonic resolutions grew increasingly elusive (as in the prelude to Richard Wagner's *Tristan und Isolde*, where the pursuit of a conclusive ending is frustrated at every turn), and music's very foundation seemed to be shifting beneath everyone's feet. Finally, it completely crumbled.

Composer Arnold Schoenberg was a chief saboteur of the system, even in his early works, like the melodramatic string sextet *Verklärte Nacht* (Transfigured Night, 1899), written when he was just twenty-five. Based on a poem by Richard Dehmel about a man walking through a "bare, cold wood" along with a woman holding a dark secret, this composition pushed typical Romantic writing to extremes. "It sounds as if someone had smeared the score of *Tristan* while it was still wet," remarked a contemporary. A musical society in Vienna refused to allow the work to be performed because it contained one dissonant chord as yet unclassified by any textbook (today considered tame). Yet this was merely a prelude to even greater provocations.

For Schoenberg, it would never be an easy road. In 1913, when he was hoping to receive a grant from the Mahler Memorial Foundation, committee member Richard Strauss wrote to Mahler's widow, Alma: "Only a psychiatrist can help poor Schoenberg now. . . . He would do better to shovel snow instead of scribbling on music paper." But Strauss lacked the courage of his convictions. "Better give him the grant anyway," he wrote. "You can never tell what posterity will say." Alma reported the remarks to Schoenberg, who was still bitter when asked the following year to write something for Strauss's fiftieth birthday. "He is no longer of the slightest artistic interest to me," replied Schoenberg, "and whatever I may once have learned from him, I am thankful to say I misunderstood."

From the evidence, Schoenberg derived little personal happiness from his pioneering efforts. Photographs of the composer consistently reveal a dour, intense persona with a ravaged stare, like someone burdened by a great weight. He had a "pained, too sensitive face, difficult to look into and impossible not to look into," recalled conductor Robert Craft. Max Deutsch, an early student, claimed "his face was [all] eyes," and when they looked at you, "you disappeared." Perhaps the weight he felt was the yoke of providence: to be true to himself, Schoenberg believed, he had no choice but to follow the path that ultimately led to the demise of an art to which he had devoted his life. Once, when asked if he was "the notorious Schoenberg," his response was cheerless resignation: "Nobody wanted to be, someone had to be, so I let it be me."

What had driven him? He was born into a Jewish family in Vienna at a time of pervasive anti-Semitism, and circumstances helped forge in him a high degree of seriousness along with a fervent desire to find answers for life's philosophical riddles. To fit in, he gave up his affiliation with Judaism, converting to Christianity, as so many European composers had before him, but then discovered he was still unable to escape the onus of being the "other." Perhaps subconsciously, Schoenberg continued to cling to aspects of Jewish thought—for example, the spiritual longing for a singular solitary principle at the root of everything: a perspective that also influenced Marx's quest for the historical imperative and Einstein's pursuit in physics of a unified field theory. (The highly influential Austrian Jewish musicologist Heinrich Schenker similarly cited the "one origin in God" when describing his groundbreaking analysis of musical structure, tracing the fundamental idea behind his theories to "monotheistic thinking.") In time, Schoenberg would follow that impulse to erase the distinction between "consonance" and "dissonance" entirely, creating a compositional approach in which the two terms no longer had any meaning. Afterward, he felt compelled to boast that his new post-tonal method, "emancipating" the dissonance that had been held prisoner to the rules of tonality, would ensure the hegemony of German music for a hundred years. Painful life lessons gave him cause to regret that avowal.

Painter Wassily Kandinsky was a kindred spirit, describing his own works in terms like "tangled lines," "blurred dissolution with gloomy little disintegrations," and "inner seething in unclear form." He wrote to Schoenberg: "You have realized what I, albeit in uncertain form, have so longed for in music. The independent life of the individual voices in your compositions is exactly what I am trying to find in my paintings." The idea was to exult in pure abstract expressionism. Schoenberg, for his part, told Kandinsky, "You are such a full man that the least vibration causes you to overflow." Yet when Kandinsky invited him in 1923 to join the staff of the Weimar Hochschule and the prestigious Bauhaus school of design, he felt compelled to warn Schoenberg that Jews were not normally welcome. The composer balked: "I have at last learned the lesson that . . . I am not a German, not a European, indeed perhaps scarcely a human being (at least the Europeans prefer the worst of their race to me), but I am a Jew."

That uncomfortable situation represented a way of life, especially in the heavily conservative atmosphere of Vienna, where Schoenberg's anarchic stance toward the rules of tonality was seen as an affront. (Viennese society was so closed to new ideas that Adolf Loos, one of the greatest architects of the early twentieth century, founded a review dismissively entitled *The Other:*

*A Paper for the Introduction of Western Culture into Austria.*) At a 1913 concert conducted by Schoenberg in the Great Hall of Vienna's Musikverein, the reaction was violent, set off in large part by the music of Schoenberg's most famous students, Anton Webern (1883–1945) and especially Alban Berg (1885–1935), who had composed songs for voice and orchestra set to words sent on a picture postcard by Viennese writer Peter Altenberg. The audience, stunned by Berg's expressionist, experimental sounds, clamored for both him and Altenberg to be committed to an asylum, not realizing that the writer was in fact already a confined mental patient.

Amid the audience's reflexive shouting, scornful laughter, hissing, and whistling, Schoenberg stopped mid-performance and scolded the crowd. Despite pleas for calm, the rioting continued, and the musicians onstage were even physically attacked. Finally, the police were called and the program halted. During the melee, the concert's organizer, Erhard Buschbeck, slapped a concertgoer in the face, leading to a lawsuit. Operetta composer Oscar Straus, who witnessed the event, swore that the slap had been the most harmonious sound of the evening. A doctor testified in court that the music had been "injurious to the nervous system." And this was long before Schoenberg's compositional procedure had been formalized into the mathematically precise but subversive atonal method, setting in motion a powerful movement that continues to this day.

The year 1913 was, of course, a marker for revolutionary change on many fronts, including Stravinsky's notorious ballet *The Rite of Spring*, music that was loud and cacophonous and rhythmically intense. T. S. Eliot noted that what made the music of *The Rite* original was its combination of the primitive and the modern. Schoenberg's contribution was less quantifiable.

.   .   .

Once he embarked on his quest to revoke the principles of tonality, it took Schoenberg twelve years to come up with his famous fixed formulas. Why did he bother? "The method of composing with twelve tones [related to each other only through the prescription of a predetermined formula] grew out of a necessity," he explained—a need to replace the prevailing system, because it had played itself out. Advancing a remedy for this new circumstance was, in his view, an artist's responsibility: "An idea is born," he wrote; "it must be molded, formulated, developed, elaborated, carried through and pursued to its very end."

Previously, in tonal music, the structure was determined by the gravitational pull exerted by a key center—known as the tonic—in relation to other tones. In sonata form, for example, the music would begin in a principal key—say, C major (which utilized the white notes of the piano)—then migrate (modulate) to a key a fifth or fourth away, before finally returning to the home key once again. The result was a kind of voyage in sound. "Form in the arts, and especially in music, aims primarily at comprehensibility," wrote Schoenberg. "The relaxation that a satisfied listener experiences when he can follow an idea, its development, and the reasons for such development is closely related, psychologically speaking, to a feeling of beauty."

But as modern composers pursued increasingly expressive techniques, they pushed the parameters of form to the breaking point. This was especially true, said Schoenberg, of Richard Wagner, who had promoted "a change in the logic and constructive power of harmony." Another such effort was the impressionistic approach, explained Schoenberg, "especially practiced by Debussy . . . [which] often served the coloristic purpose of expressing moods or pictures."

At this juncture in history, explained the composer, "the idea that one basic tone [the fundamental root] . . . dominated the construction of chords and regulated their succession" had been seriously weakened. The old dramatic structures were no longer clear. In regard to sounds built above a fundamental tone, "it became doubtful whether such a root still contained the center to which every harmony and harmonic succession must be referred," said the composer. Schoenberg's approach renounced the necessity of a tonal center altogether.

While thinking long and hard about the issue, Schoenberg had already written pieces free of tonality's sense of push and pull, with his compositional choices based solely on intuition. But his 1923 "method of composing with [all] twelve tones related only to each other"—that is, without a pervasive sense of tonal gravity, first employed in the last of the composer's Five Piano Pieces, op. 23 (the Waltz) opened the door to an entirely new world. With this system, musical composition again had a tangible and well-defined prime mover: a predetermined arrangement of all twelve possible pitches, called a "tone row," which would serve as a work's DNA, threading its way through the music while undergoing a set of strictly controlled permutations. Schoenberg's idea completed a revolution: the old order had given way to chaos, which in turn yielded a new order.

Maintaining the integrity of the row became the essential law of a new landscape. Variations were created in four distinct ways: the row could be used as initially stated (prime); it could run backward, from last note to first, in retrograde motion; it could be played in mirror form (inversion), so that a melodic leap that went down a fifth, say, would now go up a fifth; or it could be played in retrograde inversion, both backward and in mirror form. The formula that governed consecutive intervals could be transposed (begun again on any new note) after being completely played through. And members of the row could be conjoined to form harmonies. But no tone would be allowed to repeat until the entire row unfolded, lessening the chance that, thus emphasized, the ear would construe it as a tonal center. (Composer Josef Matthias Hauer [1883–1959] issued a competing system of working with twelve tones; the two argued over who was first, and remained bitter rivals.)

These rules were created to free the music from any sense of a tonal hierarchy, of the sense that the tones should lead from one to another in any particular way, thus producing a musical universe in which all pitches have equal status to move in any direction whatsoever. "The playing of even one tonal triad will bring its own consequences and demand a certain space, which cannot be allowed inside my form," Schoenberg warned. "A tonal chord arouses expectations of what is to follow. . . ." Philosophically, the new method perfectly suited Schoenberg's interest in composition as "developing variation," the spinning-out of a work through constant elaborations of basic thematic material, a process that he found especially admirable in Brahms. He was less enamored of Stravinsky, who, he claimed, favored style over idea. Stravinsky, regarded by many as the alternative to Schoenberg as the de facto leader of the modernist movement in music, for his part considered his rival overly complex, though late in his career he actually adopted Schoenberg's method.

Citing numerous examples of variation formulas in the works of the great composers, Schoenberg felt his approach to be a continuation of tradition, not a break with it. (He even made a point of using the theme B-A-C-H—rendered as B-flat, A, C, and B natural—in his Variations for Orchestra, which premiered in 1928, to tumultuous disdain.) And he believed his efforts would provide listeners with the much-desired clarity he associated with beauty, even when the initial theme (row) was disguised by, say, being played backwards. "Just as our mind always recognizes, for instance, a knife, a bottle or a watch, regardless of its position, and can reproduce it in the imagination in every possible position," he explained, "even so a musical creator's mind [and, presumably, an educated listener's] can operate subconsciously with a row of tones, regardless of their direction." That was, perhaps, too optimistic a view.

Some of his most inventive and striking compositions were created before he set out his method. His earliest works, like the mammoth, gorgeous *Gurrelieder* (completed in 1910) or the intense monodrama *Erwartung* of 1909 (which aimed at representing "in slow motion," according to the composer, "everything that occurs during a single second of maximum spiritual excitement, stretching it out to half an hour"), are firmly rooted in the Romantic tradition. But free atonality saturated the atmosphere of many of his works, including *Pierrot lunaire*, the madcap, kaleidoscopic piece that Stravinsky, though initially disdainful, eventually called the "solar plexus" of early-twentieth-century music. One critic called it "verbal insanity," matched by "musical madness." (In a preview of indignities to come, *Pierrot* prompted an audience member to point at the composer and yell, "Shoot him! Shoot him!") The work, Stravinsky admitted fifty years after its premiere, had simply been "beyond me, as it was beyond all of us at that time." Today, *Pierrot* remains a masterpiece, fascinating, enchanting in its range of instrumental colors, and deeply influential to many who came after. Even the specific instrumentation of its ensemble—flute, clarinet, violin, cello, and piano—became a model for latter-day chamber groups like the Fires of London (originally known as the Pierrot Players) and Eighth Blackbird, and embraced by numerous contemporary composers, including Milton Babbitt, David Lang, and Steve Reich.

*Pierrot's* score uses three groups of seven poems by Belgian writer Albert Giraud, translated into German by Otto Erich Hartleben. The text runs over with surreal, provocative images, as in the first entry, "Drunk with Moonlight"—"Lusts, thrilling and sweet / Float numberless through the waters! / The wine that one drinks with one's eyes / Is poured down in waves by the moon at night." The singer is required to employ *Sprechstimme*—a kind of speech-song used by cabaret performers (think of Marlene Dietrich singing "Falling in Love Again," with her imprecise pitch exaggerated). According to the composer, the job of the singer in this style is to hit the pitch and then immediately abandon it by falling or rising—an effect perfectly suited to *Pierrot's* dream world. (From 1901 Schoenberg was composer, orchestrator, and music director for a Berlin cabaret called Überbrettl, inspired by Parisian models like Le Chat Noir.)

Schoenberg's method was rigorous, but not a straitjacket. Its inventor was an artist first and a theorist second. When Webern questioned why his teacher had made a particular decision in one piece, Schoenberg replied, "I don't know." Webern was pleased by this, because it meant that despite all the rules, the ear was still vital. Rules are necessary, but "the laws of art," wrote Schoenberg in his *Theory of Harmony,* "consist mainly of exceptions."

In fact, Webern's famous Piano Variations, op. 27, in which the tone row and its permutations are laid bare like the scaffolding of a building under construction—its composer, the most stringent twelve-tone practitioner of all, gaining a reputation for works that seemed like a skeletal structure, mere outlines without muscles or sinews—contains one pitch that actually doesn't fit the tone row, placed in the texture for strictly thematic reasons.

Like mighty Zeus casting a shadow over his sons Apollo and Dionysus, Schoenberg the teacher exerted a huge influence in the lives of his students Anton Friedrich Wilhelm von Webern and Alban Maria Johannes Berg. Webern was the Apollonian of the pair—in Friedrich Nietzsche's terminology, a personality favoring intellectual rigor over sensuality and emotion. In Webern's sparse, haiku-like compositions, every note carefully selected and meticulously placed, the textures are exceedingly transparent. Yet constantly shifting registers, timbres, and dynamics often make the musical thread difficult to follow. Recognizing this, the composer cautioned performers about his unusual arrangement of a section from Bach's *Musical Offering* in 1938, where the melody bounds from instrument to instrument in short fragments: "The theme throughout must not appear disintegrated." But the task of making melodic splinters seem like a unified whole is easier said than done. The challenge of maintaining the integrity of the musical line under such conditions prompted Webern, after hearing a poor performance of his Symphony, to complain: "A high note, a low note, a note in the middle—like the music of a madman." (Schoenberg faced similar hurdles: "My music is not modern," he once said, "it is only badly played.")

Webern used conventional forms like fugue, sonata, rondo, and variations, but he redefined what a theme could be, allow-

ing three or four notes to become the basis for an entire structure. As he explained of his Variations for Orchestra: "Six
notes are given in a shape determined by the sequence and the
rhythm, and what follows . . . is nothing other than this shape
over and over again!!!" The approach recalls Goethe's studies
of plant life, in which the poet searched for the *Urpflanze,* the
single original plant from which the vegetation of the world
arose. "All shapes," noted Goethe, "are similar and none are the
same," pointing, he claimed, "to a secret law, to a holy riddle."
For Webern, the musical solution to life's eternal riddle was the
pre-established arrangement of notes known as a tone row and
its permutations, the thematic source of everything one might
find in a finished work.

That procedure so permeated his thinking that a Latin magic
word square appears on Webern's tombstone, illustrating the
process of arranging a set of letters into the four possible variations he outlined in his method: the original statement, its
inversion, the retrograde form, and the retrograde-inversion.
The original phrase means: "The sower Arepo holds with care
the wheels." Webern had used it in a 1932 lecture in Vienna,
applying his formulas to create the following rearrangements of
its original letters:

SATOR
AREPO
TENET
OPERA
ROTAS

His death came tragically early, in September 1945, during
the Allied occupation of Austria at the end of World War II.

Forty-five minutes before a curfew was to go into effect, he stepped outside his house to enjoy a cigar without disturbing his sleeping grandchildren, and was shot and killed by an American soldier. In the years that ensued, his influence grew tremendously. Among the composers who followed in his footsteps were such world-renowned figures as Pierre Boulez, Charles Wuorinen (1928–2020), and, as noted earlier, even Stravinsky in his later years.

Berg, who was Dionysus to Webern's Apollo, presented a very different musical vision. Where Webern worked in refined, abstract miniatures, Berg embraced large, boisterous forms, emotionally expansive great oaks rather than delicate bonsais. At the time he was composing his searing opera *Lulu,* about a woman who falls into a downward spiral, hurtling toward prostitution and murder, he wrote: "At last we have come to the realization that sensuality is not a weakness, does not mean surrender to one's own will. Rather it is an immense strength that lies in us—the pivot of all being and thinking."

Berg freely combined tonality and atonality, heart and mind, in works that explored the human condition while mining the complex possibilities in Schoenberg's notions of musical development. He didn't shy away from the intellectual perspectives of his circle. Like them, he was fond of creating webs of hidden codes. His Chamber Concerto, for example, was built on the names of his coterie, selecting the letters that were easily converted into pitches—**ArnolD SCHönBErG, A**nton w**EBE**rn, and **A**l**BA**n **BErG.** His *Lyric Suite* for string quartet contains a secret program based on the initials of the composer and his married lover, Hanna Fuchs-Robettin. That suite contains a symmetrical row, in which the theme is divided into two sections that contain every interval, from half steps to perfect fourths, separated by a pivot tone of an augmented fourth. When he wrote a violin concerto in 1935 to honor the memory of Manon Gropius, the eighteen-year-old daughter of Alma Mahler and Walter Gropius, he connected the music to historical precedent by basing the concluding adagio on Bach's setting of the hymn "Es ist genug" (It is enough) as the final chorale of his cantata "O Ewigkeit, du Donnerwort."

Yet, to a greater extent than his colleagues, Berg was driven by a love of human drama. His first opera, *Wozzeck*, based on Georg Büchner's play *Woyzeck*, was a turning point, personally and professionally. When Berg saw the Vienna premiere of Büchner's play in 1914, he compared himself to the hapless title character, who was an actual impoverished soldier who stabbed to death his faithless mistress. "I have been spending these war years just as dependent on people I hate, have been in chains, sick, captive, resigned, in fact humiliated," he wrote to his wife. And to Webern he further explained his fascination with the subject: "It is not only the fate of this poor man, exploited and tormented by all the world, that touches me so closely, but also the unheard-of intensity of mood of the individual scenes."

His aim was to capture those moods, rather than to unveil, as Webern had, the processes that defined the new "pantonal" (in Schoenberg's preferred terminology) musical terrain. In 1923, when the first and second movements of *Wozzeck* were performed under Webern's direction, Berg regarded it as a measure of his success that "from the moment the curtain parts until it closes for the last time, there is no one in the audience who pays any attention to the various fugues, inventions, suites, sonata movements, variations and passacaglias—no one who heeds anything but the social problems of this opera. . . ."

At *Wozzeck*'s full premiere at the Berlin State Opera in 1925, the right-wing papers reacted with predictable outrage: "Where anarchism in political life will take the nations may be a question of the future for politicians; where it has taken us in art is already manifest. The young talents have had their fling and left us a rubbish dump on which for years henceforth nothing will grow or prosper." The reviewer in the *Deutsche Zeitung* wrote, "As I was leaving the State Opera I had the sensation of having been not in a theater but in an insane asylum. . . . I regard Alban Berg as a musical swindler and a musician dangerous to the community." Yet the opera found great success with audiences; the Berlin premiere was followed by nine more performances.

Berg's second opera, *Lulu,* similarly ended in tragedy, with the heroine, now a streetwalker dying at the hands of Jack the Ripper. Berg died before it could be fully unveiled. He had left behind a mostly completed manuscript, though the orchestration of act 3 wasn't finished until 1979 by composer Friedrich Cerha. Berg's achievements—melding older harmonic traditions with a modern view of dissonance untethered from tonal rules, allowing edgy sounds to float unobstructed through posttonality's intricate, symmetrical patterns—are viewed today as masterpieces.


Schoenberg had always actively supported causes close to his heart, like the Society for Private Musical Performances, which he founded in Vienna in 1918 to promote the work of modern composers. In its three years of existence, the organization gave 353 performances of 154 works, guaranteeing adequate rehearsal time for each. During the first two years, Schoenberg didn't allow any of his own music to be performed. In 1933 he fled the Nazis, first to Paris and then to America. Once abroad, he reclaimed his native religion and made efforts to support German Jews.

Despite a career that had many ups and downs, he remained stoic. When Webern proposed programming Schoenberg's *Music for a Film Sequence* for a concert in Barcelona, where the composer had been living for almost a year, he wryly protested, "I have made many friends here who have never heard my works but who play tennis with me. What will they think of me when they hear my horrible dissonances?" In California, where he had many tennis partners who were also admirers (including George Gershwin), he taught at the University of Southern California and at UCLA, both of which named music buildings after him.

But he often stood in his own way. As a man who at times seemed obsessed by numerical permutations, he had always feared the number thirteen (in his opera *Moses und Aron*, he misspelled "Aaron" to avoid a title with thirteen letters), and worried all his life that he would die in a year that was a multiple of that number. Dreading, for example, his sixty-fifth birthday in 1939, he asked the composer and astrologer Dane Rudhyar to prepare his horoscope. He was told that "the year was dangerous, but not fatal." In a letter dated March 4, 1939, Schoenberg wrote: "Indeed, I am not so well at the moment. I am in my 65th year and you know that 5 times 13 is 65 and 13 is my bad number. But when this five-times-thirteen year has passed, then I have 13 more years."

Unfortunately, the prediction proved unreliable. As his seventy-sixth birthday approached on September 13, 1951, his old friend Oskar Adler warned him that seven plus six equals thirteen. He had not previously considered the number seventy-six ominous, but with Adler's information, he now felt differently, though he said, "I can pull through this year." Adler was right to worry. After staying in bed all day on Friday, July 13, Schoenberg expired near midnight. His wife rushed to his side, to hear his last whispered word: "Harmony."

# CHAPTER 10

# Bebop

Please don't be playing all that Chinese music up there.
—CAB CALLOWAY to Dizzy Gillespie

WHAT MADE James Reese Europe's jazz sounds purely American to the French was his ensemble's sense of freedom. Early jazz was inseparable from dance, and a rhythmic elasticity and snappy buoyancy was the ground on which players would erect their irrepressible improvisations. His musicians, claimed Europe, never fell into "the mechanical quality which is fatal to dancing." In a word, the Harlem Hellfighters could "swing"—a term that is often used but seldom defined.

Composer Gunther Schuller attempted to parse swing's qualities in his monumental book *The Swing Era*. Rhythm, he asserted, "is the most magnetic irresistible force among all the elements of music." When a listener, carried away, inadvertently starts tapping her foot in response to the music, he explained, it is a sure sign of the presence of swing. (Perhaps we call it "swing"

*Portrait of Thelonious Monk at Minton's Playhouse in New York, c. 1947*

because the musical phrases, carried by that elemental push and pull, behave as if riding an imaginary pendulum.) Beyond that, Schuller wrote, the word also connotes something subtle, a kind of equilibrium achieved between the music's horizontal (forward-moving) aspect and its vertical (in-the-moment) quality, the latter an equivalent of "stop-action" photography: "It depends on precisely how a given note is entered, i.e. attacked, and how it is terminated, and how each note is linked to every other succeeding note."

Schuller was aiming for a supple description of "swing" that recognized its organic nature, the sense that things were happening in the right place at just the right time, a state achieved only when innumerable facets of a musical performance—tone, timing, dynamics, and more—all align perfectly. That view explains why vastly different musical personalities and styles (and not just in jazz) can each put a personal stamp on the music and still fulfill what the term "swing" implies.

Eminent critic Nat Hentoff recalled: "John Lewis, pianist, former sideman with Lester Young, Dizzy Gillespie, and Charlie Parker, and longtime musical director of the Modern Jazz Quartet, teaching a class in advanced jazz improvisation at Harvard University, is asked by a student, 'Can swing be written into a score?' 'No,' says Professor Lewis. 'Swing is high musicality. It is like [Rudolf] Serkin playing a Beethoven sonata. He knows all the notes, but he also knows what else is there.'"

Though its meaning was elusive, swing was the prominent feature of jazz throughout its evolution: firing up "hot" ensembles in the 1920s, then gaining a certain suavity in the 1930s, when creamy saxophone sections and mellow brass replaced the bumptious clangor of earlier groups. Large ensembles led by such celebrity bandleaders as Tommy Dorsey, Benny Goodman, Glenn Miller, Duke Ellington, and Paul Whiteman cultivated a smooth, nuanced blend of instrumental sonorities. Their "cool" sounds swept through countless towns and cities even as the country was riled by economic lows and a world war. Throughout the strife, popular taste embraced the soft syncopations and sweet sentimentality of songs like "I'll Be Seeing You" and "We'll Meet Again."

Then a strike by the American Federation of Musicians against the recording industry from 1942 to 1944, and a second one in 1948, helped reshape the dynamics of the music business—ushering in the demise of large ensembles and the proliferation of small groups. By the late 1940s, the homogenous quality of big-band jazz was giving way to more raucously independent musical voices. "With its insistence on individuality of sound (something not sought in symphony players)," explained Ralph Ellison, "and on the capacity to swing with and against one's fellow players, its accents on improvisation and readiness for changes, and its connections with the comedy lanced by tragedy that defines the blues, jazz is a musical language that reminds us what and where we are as U.S. citizens." With the ensuing changes, jazz's independent, rebellious nature came to the fore, and sent a tremor through the culture.

Rhythmic and harmonic sophistication grew by leaps. Along with the increasing complexity, pioneering musicians began to change the sound palette that distinguished their individual contributions, often resulting in a brighter sonority with a cutting edge: reed players gave up the warm, broad vibrato that had characterized the earlier era and instead adopted a lean tone, led in their efforts by saxophonist Lester Young. "Prez [the nickname singer Billie Holiday gave Young] got that soft tone, so different from [Coleman] Hawkins', because that's the way he wanted everything in life," a former sideman told jazz critic Leonard Feather. "I got him a pair of shoes once, and one day I came in and found them in the wastebasket. Then I realized they were hard-soled shoes, and he would always wear moccasins or slippers. It had to be soft and gentle or Prez wanted no part of it." Prez himself, explained Feather, "was soft and gentle, and infinitely lonely."

The transformation could be pegged to the influence of particular musicians. "Most of the tenor players played in the Coleman Hawkins style," remembered saxophonist Al Cohn.

"This was a big, fat sound—large, dark sound. And Prez was so light. To me it was so effortless. . . ." Young had been influenced, he explained, by Orie Frank Trumbauer (1901–1956). "He played the C-melody saxophone. I tried to get the sound of C-melody on a tenor. That's why I don't sound like other people. Trumbauer always told a little story, and I like the way he slurred his notes."

At first, Young's colleagues in the Fletcher Henderson band were unhappy with the sound they were hearing, feeling it lacked body. But at this point, all the instrumental roles were changing: drummers now focused on the cymbal more than on the drumhead; the streams of notes issuing from soloists dramatically increased in velocity. It was music for the few, and for listening rather than for dancing—virtuosic and cerebral, the jazz equivalent of chamber music.

The new musical tack, cultivated by a handful of "insiders," like saxophonist Charlie "Bird" Parker (1920–1955) and trumpeter John Birks "Dizzy" Gillespie (1917–1993), came to be called "bebop," although not by the musicians themselves, who tended to describe it merely as "modern." Exactly where the name arose is a matter of dispute. According to saxophonist Budd Johnson, "When Dizzy would be trying to explain something or show you how to play it, he would hum it to you. And he would say, 'No, no, it goes like this—ump-de-be-de-bop-be-doo-dop-de-de-bop.' So, they would come up to Dizzy and say, 'Hey, play some more of that bebop music,' because he would be scatting like that."

In 1946, *Time* magazine reported on the new sound: "As such things usually do, it began on Manhattan's 52nd Street. A bandleader named John (Dizzy) Gillespie, looking for a way to emphasize the more beautiful notes in 'Swing,' explained:

'When you hum it, you just naturally say bebop, be-de-bop . . .'" But, in a reflection of how the general public was reacting, the magazine added: "What bebop amounts to: hot jazz overheated, with overdose lyrics full of bawdiness, references to narcotics and doubletalk."

Feather attributed the term's genesis to drummer Kenny Clarke, a major contributor to the style's formation. It was in the Teddy Hill band, Clarke remembered, that he began to move away from the steady 4/4 drumming style of swing music: "Diz [another member of the band] was fascinated; it gave him just the right impetus he wanted, and he began to build things around it." As Clarke increasingly used the bass drum for special accents rather than for a regular rhythm—and the top cymbal to maintain the steady four beats—Hill would ask him, "What is that klook-mop stuff you're playing?" That is what the music was called before it became known as bebop, said Hill. In the culture's embrace of onomatopoeia, Clarke himself became known as "Klook."

The search for a proper lexicon to elucidate the music's qualities was often fruitless. In fact, in 1949 *DownBeat* magazine announced a contest offering $1,000 to the person who could coin "a new word to describe the music from Dixieland [the raucous early-jazz style from New Orleans that resembled a free-for-all] through bop; second and third prizes included the services of Charlie Barnet's orchestra and the King Cole Trio for one night in one's own home." Norman Granz, whose Jazz at the Philharmonic tours were successfully bringing jazz to large audiences, offered $400 worth of prizes. Unfortunately, the winning entry was the bland term "crewcut." Alternatives included "freestyle," "mesmerhythm," "bix-e-bop," "blip," and "schmoosic."

Bebop clearly wasn't for everyone, especially since the very idea of it was to exclude the uninitiated. The complex quality of the music set many on edge and left them feeling lost. Yet, remembered Quincy Jones, "there was something about the times then where it was so unhip to be accepted. [Comedian] Sid Caesar used to do this parody of a bebop band—'We got a nine-piece band where the ninth member plays radar to let us know if we get too close to the melody.'"

Yet the very clubbiness of the participants was an asset to the development of the techniques being used. "The most important characteristic of this new style of playing was camaraderie," claimed Clarke, "that was first, because everybody, each musician, just loved the other one." That closeness fostered an approach that was the equivalent of a secret knock used for entrance to a private society. Musicians practiced using alternate harmonies on tunes, so that outsiders would get lost if they tried to join in. Bassist Milt Hinton and Gillespie went to the roof of the Cotton Club during intermissions, for example, to plan new chord changes for "I Got Rhythm." New players who tried to sit in would "eventually put their horns away," reported Hinton, "and we could go on and blow in peace and get our little exercise."

The genre's moment of creation is often traced to a day in 1939 when Parker was practicing in the back room of Dan Wall's Chili House, on Seventh Avenue between 139th and 140th Streets. His early forays into group improvisation had not gone well. In his native Kansas City, Missouri, while attempting to join a jam session at the Reno Club, where legendary drummer Jo Jones was leading the festivities, he had performed a couple of choruses and faltered badly. Jones lifted his cymbal off its stand and threw it at the saxophonist.

Parker was paying his dues. Improvising on chord changes, the standard practice in jazz, involves multiple skills. It requires a player to know the underlying harmonies of a song, and to create, by artfully embellishing them, entirely new melodies, all the while maintaining the rhythmic propulsion and the character embodied in the original. The practice was, in some ways, as old as music itself, though bebop comes perhaps closest to the baroque approach of playing from "figured bass," the harmonic shorthand expressed in numbers that were placed next to the notes of a given bass line. Bach's own sets of variations, using chord arpeggios (harmonies sounded in flurries of individual tones) and melodic figurations over recurring harmonic progressions, resemble bebop lines. The jazz artists who initiated the bebop style crafted fleet, circuitous melodies that wove in and out of a song's basic chord structures with fluid, inventive brilliance, often with little overt reference to the more familiar original. The same could be said of some swing musicians, like Coleman Hawkins, whose recorded improvisation on "Body and Soul," which never quotes the song's actual melody, became an instant sensation. But the flavor of bebop was more aggressive, colorful, and exotic than that of much that characterized swing, resulting from a particular harmonic emphasis.

At Dan Wall's Chili House, recounted Parker, "I'd been getting bored with the stereotyped [chord] changes that were being used at the time, and I kept thinking there's bound to be something else. I could hear it sometimes but I couldn't play it. Well, that night I was working over 'Cherokee'"—a song employing long, held melody notes with shifts of harmony in every bar—"and as I did I found that by using the higher intervals of a chord as a melody line and backing them with appropriately related changes, I could play the thing I'd been hearing.

I came alive." By "higher intervals" he meant "extended" harmonic tones—like the ninth, eleventh, and thirteenth members
of the scale above a root—that had given Debussy's music its
inscrutable quality. That, coupled with an extraordinary level of
virtuosity, helped define the bebop style.

"The first time I heard bebop played on a trumpet . . ."
remembered vibraphonist Lionel Hampton, "was when Dizzy
played 'Hot Mallets' with me." Hampton was amazed: "Here's
a guy on trumpet playing faster than the fastest saxophone
player." It was startling for many other jazz musicians, too.
Bandleader Cab Calloway, though respectful of Dizzy's talent,
found his technically dazzling playing disturbing. "It was really
wild, and it was something that I really had to get used to," he
said. "I used to call him on it. I'd say, 'Man, listen, will you
please don't be playing all that Chinese music up there!' "

In 1944, Norman Granz formed Jazz at the Philharmonic, he
said, to take this music to places where he could "break down
segregation and discrimination, present good jazz and make
bread for myself and for the musicians as well." In many ways,
it represented a socially conscious insurrection. "I don't mean
to be dramatic," he explained, "but I insisted that my musicians
were to be treated with the same respect as Leonard Bernstein or
Heifetz because they were just as good both as men and musicians." Most jazz artists, however, remained perpetual outcasts.

Parker's long apprenticeship involved many hardships,
including a stint as a dishwasher at Jimmy's Chicken Shack in
Harlem, where the phenomenal pianist Art Tatum was in residence. Parker stayed for three months—the length of Tatum's
gig—before moving on. In Chicago, alto saxophonist Goon

Gardner gave Parker clothes and a clarinet, but the instrument was soon in a pawn shop and "Bird" was on a bus to New York. (There are several origin stories about Parker's nickname. One is that while playing with Jay McShann's big band, a car he was riding in hit a chicken, and Parker picked it up, carried it to the boardinghouse where he was staying, and asked to have it cooked—after which other musicians started calling him "Yardbird.") By 1937 he was using drugs, and his first recorded efforts were erratic. Ralph Ellison's probative assessment of Parker's early playing style is insightful: "For all its velocity, brilliance and imagination there is in it a great deal of loneliness, self-depreciation and self-pity," he wrote. "With this there is a quality which seems to issue from its vibratoless tone: a sound of amateurish ineffectuality, as though he could never quite make it."

Of course, Parker's musicality evolved dramatically, but it had to grow on you. Jazz trumpeter Howard McGhee remembered, "When Bird first came on the scene, I asked [Ellington saxophonist] Johnny Hodges, 'What do you think of Charlie Parker?' He said, 'He don't play nothing, he ain't got no sound.' Later when I got a chance to play with Ellington, I asked him again: 'Oh, he was beautiful.' 'But Johnny, you told me he didn't have no sound.' 'Well, I didn't know what I was talking about.'"

The recorded evidence is overwhelming in its brilliance: the saxophonist's reformulations of standard songs into bebop showpieces—like his explosive, lightning-fast "Ko-Ko," based on "Cherokee," and the intricate "Ornithology," based on "How High the Moon"—became historic milestones. But socially he remained undeveloped. Pianist Earl Hines boasted to McShann that he could "make a man of him [Parker]." Yet within a couple of months he was complaining that Bird owed money to everyone in the band, and kept missing shows. Parker was the picture of irresponsibility: he fell asleep while smoking and set fire to his mattress, then wandered naked into his hotel lobby. He was jailed for drug possession.

Despite it all, his impact was undeniable. As Ellington trumpeter Cootie Williams put it, "Louis Armstrong changed all the brass players around, but after Bird, all of the instruments had to change—drums, piano, bass, trombones, trumpets, saxophones, everything."

As Ellison once wrote of the blues, "Their attraction lies in this, that they at once express both the agony of life and the possibility of conquering it through sheer toughness of spirit." Parker's life was the blues writ large, though his conquests were painfully temporary. On March 9, 1955, while scheduled to play at Storyville in Boston, he went instead to the Stanhope Hotel to visit Baroness Pannonica de Koenigswarter, a Rothschild heiress and a patron of jazz musicians. Three nights later he died in her rooms while watching jugglers on Tommy Dorsey's television show. With his passing, Parker's legacy only strengthened. Almost immediately, the scrawl "Bird Lives" began appearing on Greenwich Village walls, and for jazz aficionados it remains true to this day.

Bird crossed paths with Dizzy Gillespie constantly, though their trajectories were significantly different. Dizzy's spiritual life remained a core foundation for him, preventing his descent into physical self-destruction. Both ended up performing with a who's who of the jazz world, and developing individual, recognizable styles. It was Bird, in fact, who had nudged the trumpeter toward a unique approach when the two were performing together. Dizzy was imitating trumpeter Roy Eldridge at the time, to the point where he was accused of becoming a carbon copy. "Say, man, why don't you play your own shit?" remarked Parker.

Miles Davis eventually took special pride in his own originality, but early on even he was stringently imitative of the bebop lines he had heard around him, at times executing the exact same solo on numerous recorded takes of a tune. Dizzy sidestepped such easy comparisons in part because of the surprisingly wide span of his tessitura—the notes he was most comfortable producing, which included those at the highest reaches of the trumpet's capacities. When Miles asked him, "Why can't I play like you?" he replied, "You can, you do. You just play in a low register the same thing I play in a high register."

Gillespie's physical presence could garner as much attention as the music he produced: in addition to the trademark Beat-style beret and goatee he sported—Thelonious Monk similarly had a distinguishing costume, which included dark sunglasses—there was the odd shape of his trumpet horn, bent permanently at a forty-five-degree angle, and the way his cheeks puffed out like helium balloons when he blew. "I didn't get any physical pain from it, but all of a sudden, I looked like a frog whenever I played," he explained. "Dr. Richard J. Compton of NASA wanted to x-ray my cheeks in 1969 to find out why they expand when I play the trumpet. He called my condition 'Gillespie's Pouches.' I told Lorraine [his wife] this and she told her friend Dewilla, 'Guess what? Dizzy's gonna have a disease named after him.' I missed my appointment with Dr. Compton and the reason for my jaws expanding is still unknown."

His instrument had been reshaped by accident, he explained.

"Actually, I left my horn on a trumpet stand and someone kicked it over, and instead of just falling, the horn bent. I was playing at Snookie's on Forty-Fifth Street, on a Monday night, January 6, 1953. . . . Stump 'n' Stumpy [the dance/comedy duo of James Cross and Harold J. Cromer] had been fooling around on the bandstand, and one had pushed the other, and he'd fallen back onto my horn. . . . I played it, and I liked the sound. The sound had been changed and it could be played softly, very softly, not blarey. . . . I contacted the Martin Company. I told them, 'I want a horn like this.' 'You're crazy!' they said. 'O.K.,' I said, 'I'm crazy, but I want a horn like this.'"

As Parker had done with "Cherokee," Dizzy and Monk would spend the afternoon together at the Harlem jazz club Minton's, trying "to work out some complex variations on chords and the like, and we used them at night to scare away the no-talents," said Gillespie, experimenting on tunes like "Nice Work If You Can Get It," "Body and Soul," and "Melancholy Baby." Such collaborative efforts between members of the bebop crowd were fertile ground. Even Monk's singular tunes—strange in the extreme, unlike anyone else's, filled with jarring dissonance and angular leaps—could result from interactions with his comrades. His jaunty, signature "Epistrophy" was written with Kenny Clarke, who said he came up with the tune after guitarist Charlie Christian showed him a fingering while fooling around with a friend's ukulele. And Monk's immortal ballad "'Round Midnight," now a revered standard, began life as a pop song called "I Need You So." Written when he was longing for his future wife, Nellie, it took final shape only after additional contributions from Dizzy and trumpeter Cootie Williams.

. . .

Even in a world of odd, adventurous characters, Thelonious (the name is based on a Latinized version of St. Tillo, a Benedictine monk renowned for his missionary work in France in the seventh century) was unique. He grew up in the San Juan Hill neighborhood of New York, rife with battling ethnic groups: southern Blacks, West Indians, Italians, Irish. He began piano lessons at age eleven, studying first with Simon Wolf, a classically trained Austrian-born Jew, and then with Alberta Simmons, a ragtime and stride player who belonged to the Clef Club. Pianist Herman Chittison became a major influence. Before long Monk's stride piano playing was strong enough to win several contests at the legendary Apollo Theater's Amateur Night. But Monk never finished high school, deciding instead to go on the road for two years as a rhythm- and-blues musician, touring the Southwest with a Pentecostal healer named Reverend Graham, a woman also known as "the Texas Warhorse."

"She preached and healed and we played," he told Nat Hentoff years later. Pianist Mary Lou Williams saw him in action in Kansas City in 1935 and reported, "While Monk was in Kacee he jammed every night, really used to blow on piano, employing a lot more technique than he does today. . . . He was one of the original modernists all right, playing pretty much the same harmonies then that he's playing now."

He probably had not yet fully developed the style for which he became known, undermining listeners' expectations with peculiar chordal clashes, craggy rhythms, and an unusual approach to silence, rendering it as tangible as "negative space" in an abstract painting. Early on, he was technically slick. But as a fully formed artist, his signature piano tone became blunt, even unbeautiful. Nellie Monk described the combination of disruptive rhythms and highly percussive attacks as "Melodious

Thunk." His left-hand harmonies were bare, a series of caustic dissonances. Most pianists embedded those kinds of harmonic clashes in a blanket of additional chord tones, creating a soothing blend. With Monk, they were shockingly exposed.

His radical assault on the norm brings to mind Pablo Picasso's turn to primitivism, which, in his case, was spurred by an exhibit of African masks. His 1907 encounter with those primitive pieces was a revelation that taught him, he said, "what painting really meant. It's not an aesthetic process; it's a form of magic that interposes itself between us and the hostile universe, a means of seizing power by imposing a form on our terrors as well as on our desires. The day I understood that, I had found my path." Picasso's descriptive terms—"magic," "power," "terrors," and "desires"—also conjure the raw experience of Monk's sonic world.

Despite his musical idiosyncrasies and notoriously bizarre behavior (which sometimes included falling asleep at the piano or dancing in circles in the midst of a performance), the pianist was embraced by the greatest musicians of his era. As saxophonist and jazz icon John Coltrane remembered, "I felt I learned from him in every way—through the senses, theoretically, technically. I would talk to Monk about musical problems, and he would sit at the piano and show me the answers just by playing them. I could watch him play and find out the things I wanted to know."

Monk appeared on the cover of *Time* magazine in 1964 and later received a posthumous Pulitzer Prize Special Citation, but the music, like the man, was a study in erratic behavior. When Miles Davis performed Monk's "'Round Midnight" at the 1955 Newport Jazz Festival in a pouring rainstorm, he fended off the hearty congratulations that followed by declaring that the pianist "didn't know the [chord] changes." This despite Miles's assertion that at the time he was attending the Juilliard School of Music, Monk taught him more than anyone else. In any case, the pianist easily swept listeners up into his own, compelling realm. Lorraine Gordon, owner of New York's Village Vanguard, dubbed him "the High Priest of Bebop."

The pianist's worldview and his image became associated with some of the unconventional venues in which he flourished. The Five Spot Café, a bar at 5 Cooper Square in New York's Bowery owned by brothers Joe and Iggy Termini, became a regular outlet. It had been a gathering place for abstract expressionists and Beat Generation literati: patrons included painters Willem de Kooning, Franz Kline, and Larry Rivers and writers Jack Kerouac, Gregory Corso, Allen Ginsberg, and Frank O'Hara. The Terminis had initially hired jazz avant-gardist Cecil Taylor for entertainment; he nearly wrecked the place's cheap piano, sending hammers flying in all directions. Monk began a six-month stay there on July 4, 1957, coinciding with the restoration of his cabaret card—the state-issued license to perform in establishments serving liquor—which had been revoked in 1948 following an arrest for marijuana possession and again in 1951 when he was caught up in the drug bust of pianist Bud Powell, a friend.

The two men were, in a way, musical opposites. Powell's bebop playing was a model of melodic invention, executed at breathtaking tempos. His elegant hornlike musical lines were the focus of this style, his sparse left-hand accompaniments almost an afterthought. Pianist Bill Evans once paid tribute to Powell's artfulness by citing his "artistic integrity . . . incomparable originality, and the grandeur of his work." If he had to choose a single musician as emblematic of these traits, said Evans, it would have to be Powell. Powell's classic recordings, such as "Tempus Fugue-It," "Parisian Thoroughfare," "Un Poco Loco," "52nd Street Theme," and "Dance of the Infidels," are a living testament to Evans's assessment. But the pianist's drug dependence and mental instability remained lifelong challenges.

Monk's appearance at the Five Spot coincided with the reissue of his Prestige and Blue Note recordings on twelve-inch LPs as well as the release of the much-heralded album *Brilliant Corners,* recorded in three sessions in late 1956. One of the compositions, "Ba-Lue Bolivar Ba-Lues-Are," was a rendering of Monk's exaggerated pronunciation of "Blue Bolivar Blues," a reference to the Bolivar Hotel on Central Park West, where Pannonica de Koenigswarter resided. Monk had met "Nica" during his first trip to Europe, in 1954, and it was a relationship that would deepen for both.

On July 16, Monk brought his own quartet to the Five Spot, including saxophonist John Coltrane, bassist Wilbur Ware, and drummer Shadow Wilson. The experience had a profound effect on Coltrane, who became known for taking long, extended solos. "[Monk would] leave the stand for a drink or to do his dance," the saxophonist recalled, "and I could just improvise by myself for fifteen or twenty minutes before he returned." Monk could also at times simply wander off. One night, Joe Termini found him a few blocks away, staring at the moon. "Are you lost?" he asked. "No, I ain't lost. I'm here. The Five Spot's lost," Monk replied.

Still, the pianist became an important resource for those who worked with him. "I learned new levels of alertness with Monk," Coltrane said, "because if you didn't keep aware all the time of what was going on, you'd suddenly feel as if you'd stepped into a hole without a bottom to it." Coltrane learned other things as well. "Monk was one of the first to show me how to make two or three notes at one time on tenor," he revealed. "It's done by false fingering and adjusting your lips, and if it's done right you get triads."

As the eccentric pianist continued to lose the ability to manage his life, however, the Baroness Koenigswarter, who protectively supported many jazz musicians who were unable to fend for themselves, brought him to her large estate in Weehawken, New Jersey. Pianist Barry Harris found him unconscious there on February 5, 1982. He died at Englewood Hospital on February 17. The unique sounds he produced continued to remain a lesson in the rugged individualism that lies at the very heart of jazz.

Revolutions look to leaders who stake out innovations, while some have been quietly lurking behind the scenes, pointing the way to the next artistic stage. Trumpeter Miles Dewey Davis III (1926–1991)—aka "the Prince of Darkness"—transformed his style so often, he might more fittingly be labeled "Jazz's Musical Chameleon." While still an apprentice, a bit wanting in technical prowess, he pursued Dizzy Gillespie and Charlie Parker down the rabbit hole of fiery bebop. Before long, he was piloting the jazz ship, steering along myriad tributaries: taking the art through the subdued, relaxed aesthetic of "cool" jazz, the colorful atmospherics of the album *Kind of Blue,* the hi-tech sizzle of contemporary fusion (for which the trumpeter became, in the words of Nat Hentoff, "the demonic animator of splinters of electronic sound glistening with rock, jazz, blues, and his own horn of spearing loneliness"), and, finally, the panglobal flavors of world music. Wherever the charismatic figure led, others followed. In some ways he was a walking revolution, who defined an era as he went along.

# CHAPTER 11

# Miles Ahead

I think the whole jazz-music business looked to
Miles Davis's innovations to see what direction
jazz music was headed.

—JIMMY COBB, drummer

*Charlie Parker, Tommy Potter, Miles Davis, Duke Jordan, and Max Roach
at the Three Deuces in New York, August 1947*

I N T H E W O R D S O F J A M E S B A L D W I N, he was "a miracu-
lously tough and tender man": handsome, facile, and seductive; socially crude, artistically refined; a masterful bandleader; a
formidable boxer; a junkie who summoned the inner fortitude
to quit his habit cold turkey. His horn playing could shake the
earth with sudden, ferocious torrents of notes or break your
heart with a simple, confessional lament. Miles Davis's practice
of using a Harmon mute with the centerpiece removed on ballads produced a sound so fragile, reported critic Barry Ulanov,
it was like "a man walking on eggshells."

Born in Alton, Illinois, on May 25, 1926, he moved with his
family a year later to East St. Louis, an Illinois town he remembered as a virtual music conservatory. "When I was a kid," he
recalled, "I was fascinated by the musicians, particularly guys
who used to come up from New Orleans and jam all night. . . .
You watched how they hold the horn, how they walk." One of
his neighbors from a nearby town, an early idol, was the trumpeter Clark Terry, who was equally entranced by the musical
sounds around him. "The very first thing I heard in the form of
pulsating beats," said Terry, "was at the Sanctified Church on
the corner. They all played tambourines and there was a certain
beat that was instilled in you right from [the start as] a kid." It
left Terry with an irrepressible rhythmic spark that he would
carry on as he rose to professional maturity.

Miles had his own trumpet by the time he reached the sixth
grade (his mother wanted him to take up the violin instead,
but his father, a dental surgeon, intervened on his behalf). He
studied music with Elwood Buchanan, a teacher at the Crispus
Attucks School (named after the man of African and Native

American descent who is regarded as the first American killed in the Revolutionary War). It was Buchanan who helped forge Miles's very personal sound. "Play without any vibrato," he instructed his young pupil, contrary to the customary fashion, advice Miles carried with him for the rest of his life. "You're gonna get old anyway and start shaking," reasoned the teacher.

At fifteen, Miles, already establishing an impressive reputation, joined a professional band called Eddie Randle's Blue Devils, also known as the Rhumboogie Orchestra. By the age of nineteen, he was playing in singer Billy Eckstine's touring big band, featuring Dizzy Gillespie and Charlie Parker—a destiny-changing moment. This group, wrote Dizzy, was like no other, a virtual training ground for musicians developing bebop. "The greatest feeling I ever had in my life—with my clothes on—was when I first heard Diz and Bird together in St. Louis, Missouri," Miles later recounted. For an impressionable young jazz aspirant, flying so close to the light of these artistic luminaries sparked a lifelong undertaking.

Following high school, Miles headed to New York, purportedly to study at the Juilliard School, but with another agenda in mind. After the high adventure of sharing the bandstand with jazz geniuses, school was little more than a distraction, and he spent his first weeks in the city mostly "looking for Bird and Dizzy." Despite his best efforts, Parker proved particularly difficult to find. Then, "one day I saw in the paper where Bird was scheduled to play in a jam session at a club called the Heatwave, on 145th Street in Harlem," Miles explained. "I remember asking Bean [Coleman Hawkins] if he thought Bird would show up there, and Bean just kind of smiled that slick, sly smile of his and said, 'I'll bet Bird doesn't even know if he'll really be there or not.' " Nevertheless, while standing on the street outside the club, Miles suddenly sensed someone behind him. He turned, and came face to face with Parker. "I heard you've been looking for me," the saxophonist said. And the rest is history.

He roomed with Parker for a while, ended up recording with him ("I wanted to quit every night," he said, "because Bird would leave me on stage"), joined jam sessions as often as possible, checked out scores by contemporary composers like Stravinsky, Berg, Khatchaturian ("the one thing that intrigues me are all those different scales he uses," Miles told Nat Hentoff), and Prokofiev, and continued to find other musicians to learn from and admire, like trumpeter Freddie Webster. "I used to love what he did to a note," said Miles. "He didn't play a lot of notes; he didn't waste any. I used to try to get his sound." Meanwhile, Parker continued to tutor him: "Bird told me, when I was real young, and just getting out of Juilliard, that if you play something that seems to be wrong, play it again, then play the same thing a third time," he once told composer and horn player David Amram. "Then Bird gave a big smile and said, 'Then they'll think that you meant it.'"

He dropped out of Juilliard at the start of his second year, went home, and explained the situation to his father, who once again offered crucial support. "[He] told me something I will never forget," the jazz great later related in his autobiography. "Miles," said his father, "you hear that bird outside our window? He's a mockingbird. He don't have a sound of his own. He copies everybody's sound, and you don't want to do that. You want to be your own man, have your own sound. That's what it's really about." In retrospect, that advice became the driving principle for his life.

.    .    .

Among the influential figures Miles met in New York was composer George Russell, who arrived in 1945 from Cincinnati. Russell was author of *The Lydian Chromatic Concept of Tonal Organization*, a theoretical method designed to foster the kind of impressionistic jazz playing, based on exotic scales (like the octatonic mode, alternating whole steps and half steps), for which the trumpeter would soon become famous. Another pivotal figure was Gil Evans, a former arranger for Claude Thornhill's band, whose sound, said Evans, "hung like a cloud." Evans's basement apartment on West Fifty-Fifth Street became a busy hub for many stellar performing artists. "A very big bed took up a lot of the place; there was one big lamp, and a cat named Becky," remembered Russell. "The linoleum was battered, and there was a little court outside. Inside, it was always dark. The feeling of the room was timelessness. Whenever you got there, you wouldn't care about conditions outside. You couldn't tell whether it was day or night, summer or winter, and it didn't matter." Miles asked Evans to teach him the particular harmonies he had used for Thornhill; their essence became guide rails in the years ahead.

By 1954 he had acquired and then kicked a four-year heroin addiction and was recording with some of the stellar names in modern jazz, like saxophonist Sonny Rollins. "[He] was something else," reported Miles. "Brilliant. He was interested in Africa, so he turned Nigeria backwards and called that tune 'Airegin' for that date. His other tune was 'Doxy.' As a matter of fact, he brought the tunes in and rewrote them right in the studio. He would be tearing off a piece of paper and writing down a bar or a note or a chord. . . . We'd go into a studio and I'd ask Sonny, 'Where's the tune?' And he'd say . . . 'I haven't finished it yet.'" The experience was an education as far from that offered by Juilliard as one could find. "So, I would play what he had and then he might go away in the corner somewhere and write . . . on scraps of paper and come back a little while after that and say, 'Okay, Miles, it's finished.' One tune he wrote like that was 'Oleo' [a tricky, virtuoso jazz standard]. He got the title from oleomargarine, which was a big thing then, a cheap butter substitute."

The drug habit had begun, he said, when he and saxophonist Gene Ammons began experimenting, joining a long list of junkies that included Bird, Monk, Billie Holiday, Stan Getz, John Coltrane, and others. "First, we started snorting it, then we started shooting it. . . . My father bought me a new five-gaited pony. We had 500 acres near St. Louis, in Milstead, Illinois. I stayed out on the farm for about two and a half weeks, until I was straight." In truth it didn't happen that quickly—there were lingering enticements and setbacks for the trumpeter. But once the heroin chains were dissolved, he experienced a surge of creative energy.

With bebop in the rearview mirror, the albums that soon followed—like *Birth of the Cool*, made with contributions by Gil Evans and "cool jazz" pioneers such as baritone saxophonist and arranger Gerry Mulligan and pianist John Lewis (it was released in 1957, but recorded in 1949 and 1950)—helped establish a new, important direction. Like another Evans collaboration released in 1957, *Miles Ahead*, it was quickly heralded as a landmark in "third stream" music—the label given to works that intentionally melded jazz and classical traditions. The contrast between this music and what had come before was stark. "The Meaning of the Blues," from *Miles Ahead*, is a prime example: individual entrances of brass and woodwinds, like a slow-moving fanfare, combine to form stacked, glowing sonorities, over which Miles's soaring flugelhorn gently floats.

*Porgy and Bess* (1959) and *Sketches of Spain* (1960) continued the Davis/Evans collaboration. But the recording that turned the jazz world upside down was *Kind of Blue,* in 1959, the stunningly beautiful, free-flowing epic that became the best-selling jazz album of all time. The approach, like that of the French impressionists a century earlier, reflected the search for the sensuous and ethereal—bringing to life the words of poet Paul Verlaine, who wrote of something "vague in the air and soluble, with nothing heavy and nothing at rest." The evocative sounds that underpinned the music—seemingly suspended without roots—created what pianist Herbie Hancock called "a doorway": like a portal to a hidden realm. Miles took to its entrancing atmosphere like a fish to water.

A number of influences had converged to create the historic recording. One was a performance Miles had witnessed of the Ballet Africaine from Guinea, whose folk strains made a lasting impression. Another was the sense of spaciousness he had admired in the conceptions of pianist Ahmad Jamal. "Listen to the way Jamal uses space," Miles told Nat Hentoff in *The Jazz Review* a year before *Kind of Blue.* "He lets it go so that you can feel the rhythm section and the rhythm section can feel you. It's not crowded." Then there was the trumpeter's move away from complex chord changes—what had been the essence of bebop style—and toward coloristic scales, lending the music a sense of unlimited potential and mystery. Chords are clusters of tones that, as fixed entities, become benchmarks for the directions an improvised melody can take. "When Gil [Evans] wrote the arrangement of 'I Loves You, Porgy,' he only wrote a scale for me. No chords," Miles explained in 1958. "And that . . . gives you a lot more freedom and space to hear things."

As John Coltrane reported of his participation in the *Miles Ahead* album, "I found Miles in the midst of another stage of his musical development. There was one time in his past that he devoted to multi-chordal structures. He was interested in chords for their own sake. But now it seemed that he was moving in the opposite direction to the use of fewer and fewer chord changes in songs. He used tunes with free-flowing lines and chordal direction. This allowed the soloist the choice of playing chordally (vertically) or melodically (horizontally)."

Coltrane as a sideman facilitated the change. The saxophonist, whose virtuosic forays through webs of tones would be labeled "sheets of sound," offered a perfect textural contrast to the direct simplicity and openness of the trumpeter. As critic Whitney Balliett noted, "Trane" had a "dry, unplaned tone that sets Davis off, like a rough mounting for a fine stone." Both men had been increasingly drawn to the exoticism of melodic improvisation based on scales with unique characteristics. "In fact," said Coltrane, "due to the direct and free-flowing lines in [Miles's] music, I found it easy to apply the harmonic ideas that I had. I could stack up chords. . . . I could play three chords on one. Miles's music gave me plenty of freedom."

The sextet on *Kind of Blue* included Coltrane on tenor saxophone, with the phenomenally gifted Julian "Cannonball" Adderley on alto sax and a superb rhythm section of pianist Bill Evans (whose rich harmonic approach was deeply influenced by the music of Maurice Ravel), bassist Paul Chambers, and drummer Jimmy Cobb. An additional pianist, the blues-oriented Wynton Kelly, appeared on one track. By 1962, sales had soared to eighty-seven thousand; in 1997 the figure reached a million. In 2019, the album was certified Quintuple Platinum by the Recording Industry Association of America, designating sales of five million copies.

With *Sketches of Spain,* released in 1960, Miles once again broke new artistic ground. Joaquín Rodrigo's 1939 *Concierto de Aranjuez* for guitar and orchestra, with the guitar solo now assigned to trumpet, became the centerpiece of the album. Gil Evans's brilliant rearrangement was paired with his take on music from Manuel de Falla's ballet *El amor brujo,* along with additional material. "We got a folklore record of Peruvian Indian music, and took a vamp from that," said Miles. "This was 'The Pan Piper' on the album. Then we took the Spanish march 'Saeta,' which they do in Spain on Fridays when they march and testify by singing." Miles's playing, like an anguished town crier, calls out to the listener's heart with unimpeded passion.

The challenge of realizing the project was considerable, said Miles, "because you've got all those Arabic musical scales up in there. . . . And they modulate and bend and twist and snake and move around." He did his best, he claimed, to get the classical musicians on the recording session to loosen up, but that was difficult. In the end, Rodrigo said he actually didn't like the record, "and he—his composition—was the reason I did *Sketches of Spain* in the first place," said Miles, who conjectured that the composer would change his mind once the royalties started flowing. Given all the intricacies, the recording had taken fifteen three-hour sessions to complete. In the end, it was worth the trouble.

Drummer Chico Hamilton summed up the effect the trumpeter had on the jazz world: "Miles Davis is a sound . . . the whole earth singing!" Indeed, by this point, nearly every musician in the business was emulating the harmonies and echoing the tunes set out in Miles's newly recorded legacy. And the jazz icon's crusty persona only added to the seriousness with which his output was received. As critic Ralph Gleason reported in 1960, "He eschews the spotlight; never smiles, makes no announcements. Many people are annoyed when, at the close of his solo, Davis walks off the stage." Yet there was hardly a soul who wasn't paying attention.

In 1963, Miles was facing health problems and multiple lawsuits for failing to show up or canceling on short notice. He began to reshuffle his band members, ultimately forming the group that contained perhaps the most accomplished jazz musicians of their time. Drummer Tony Williams was just seventeen; his intense performing style, an explosion of complex rhythmic interplay between drums and cymbals, left listeners with the impression that he had twelve arms. The impeccable bassist Ron Carter, with never a note out of place, was twenty-six; pianist Herbie Hancock, fresh from achieving a surprise hit with his tune "Watermelon Man," was twenty-three. Lyrical saxophonist George Coleman was twenty-eight. The chemistry between these players, under Miles's direction, spurred each to go beyond what he had previously accomplished, and with the substitution of saxophonist Wayne Shorter (who had been convinced to join by Hancock and Williams), the core group stayed intact for six years, continuously advancing the art to new heights. "It wasn't the bish-bash, sock-em-dead routine we had with [drummer Art] Blakey," recalled Shorter, "with every solo a climax. With Miles, I felt like a cello, I felt viola, I felt liquid, dot-dash . . . and colors started really coming. And then a lot of people started calling me, 'Can you be on my record date?' It was six years of that."

"If I was the inspiration and wisdom and the link for this band," said Miles, "Tony was the fire, the creative spark; Wayne was the idea person, the conceptualizer of a whole lot of musical ideas we did; and Ron and Herbie were the anchors." The trumpeter became the navigator. He used the studio to facilitate the process—first recording, then listening to various takes while making decisions on the fly about form and style. And as the band rose to its place in the pantheon of jazz greats, Miles boasted that he paid his musicians not to practice. The statement was typically provocative, but it was anything but frivolous. Miles, as the reigning wizard of spontaneity, like a musical Zen master, was simply declaring his aesthetic credo—he wanted to preserve the creative freshness of the moment, a state that can evaporate when an artist spends long hours engaged in routine drills, in the hope of achieving technical perfection. It worked: the group developed an almost extrasensory skill in collaborative performance (thus the title of one of their albums, *E.S.P.*, recorded in 1965). Their combined efforts became a study in constant surprise.

Hancock recounted, for example, one extraordinary moment in Stockholm in 1967, during a performance by the quintet. "This night was magical," he remembered. "We were communicating almost telepathically, playing 'So What'"—one of the group's signature pieces. "Wayne had taken his solo. Miles was playing and building and building, and then I played the wrong chord. It was so, so wrong. In an instant, time stood still and I felt totally shattered. Miles took a breath. And then he played this phrase that made my chord right. It didn't seem possible. I still don't know how he did it. But Miles hadn't heard it as a wrong chord—he took it as an unexpected chord. He didn't judge what I played. To use a Buddhist turn of phrase, he turned poison into medicine."

And that fine-tuned responsiveness made it possible to cast aside more and more rules. "By the time we got to *E.S.P.*, Miles said, 'I don't want to play chords anymore,'" reported Hancock. "Here's how I look at it. . . . Now I don't know if this is the way Miles looks at it, but a composition is an example of a conception, so Miles, rather than play the composition, he wants to play the conception that the composition came from. . . . That's why you hear melody fragments and you kind of hear the momentum and the sound of the tune somewhere . . . but maybe the chords are not there."

Tapes of the recording sessions made between 1966 and 1968—during the making of the albums *Miles Smiles, Sorcerer, Miles in the Sky, Nefertiti,* and *Water Babies*—reveal the intimate, pliable dynamics at play. Miles instructs Hancock at one point to use only his right hand, freeing the music from reliance on particular harmonies. In another moment, he gives oblique directions that work only because the collaborators know one another so well: "Hey, Herbie, don't play nothin' until you get ready to play," he instructs. Sometimes a kind of insider shorthand emerges, as when Williams responds to a suggestion by mentioning stylistic options, citing the names of several iconic drummers to make his points. Exchanges between Davis and the drummer lie somewhere between precise and enigmatic: "Don't do nothin' like that," Miles instructs Williams in response to one effort, adding, "Should say babadabada-ba-ba-krchchh." One of the most powerful outcomes arrives in the form of "Nefertiti," a haunting tune by Shorter, in which the musicians forgo the usual improvised solos and instead simply repeat the melody, over and over: an exercise in pure musical minimalism, with intermittent variety provided by Williams's exquisite polyrhythmic interjections on the drums. The result is mesmerizing, and unlike anything else in jazz.

But Miles was soon ready for something new: "I have to change," he once said. "It's like a curse." Although he had introduced electric instruments with the albums *Miles in the Sky* and *Filles de Kilimanjaro* (both recorded in 1968), the 1969 album *In a Silent Way* brought a new phase: pervasive electronic technology, rock-suffused rhythms, and multilayered instrumental filigree, along with a solo guitar—planting the seeds of what would soon be called "jazz fusion." The development was swiftly rejected by most jazz purists. Nevertheless, as *Rolling Stone* writer Lester Bangs asserted, it represented "a transcendental new music which flushes categories away and, while using musical devices from all styles and cultures, is defined mainly by its deep emotion and unaffected originality."

Assembling the personnel for the recording, Miles turned to his then-current players—Wayne Shorter on soprano sax, Chick Corea on electric piano, Dave Holland on bass, and Jack DeJohnette on drums—then added drummer Tony Williams, Herbie Hancock on electric piano, Josef Zawinul on organ, and guitarist John McLaughlin. Miles had cultivated a way of directing his ensembles simply by means of a mere stare or grimace, or a quick musical utterance from his horn; but as their size increased, and his embrace of open-ended forms made that task more difficult, he turned increasingly to studio technology as a way of controlling the outcome, transforming his role of bandleader into one of postproduction arranger. The task now became one of distilling the spontaneous recorded moments of inspiration, or confusion—musical gestures as fleeting as ice crystals formed in the sun—into a tapestry of incantatory power. In the case of *In a Silent Way*, the man who actually assembled the final product was producer Teo Macero, who taped everything, constructing the album from excerpts, splices, and constructed tape loops.

In steering the musicians at this point, Miles was driven by a poetic vision beyond the normal parameters. His instruction to McLaughlin was to play his instrument as if he were a novice. When drummer Lenny White first joined the group, Miles brought no music to a rehearsal, but instead gave White a simple instruction: think of the group as a large stew, he said, "and you are the salt."

Now, the individual technical virtuosity so prized earlier in his career was replaced by a vision of shifting textures and sometimes coincidental instrumental clashes. Miles was ever on the lookout for different sonorities, experimenting in the recording studio with diverse sources, from wah-wah pedals to an Indian sitar player.

His million-selling 1970 record, *Bitches Brew*, brought the approach of *In a Silent Way* to its zenith. "What we did on *Bitches Brew* you couldn't ever write down for an orchestra to play," Miles explained. "That's why I didn't write it all out, not because I didn't know what I wanted, [but because] I knew that what I wanted would come out of a process and not some prearranged stuff." That album's sessions began the day after guitarist Jimi Hendrix performed his shrieking psychedelic version of "The Star-Spangled Banner" at Woodstock, and Miles, who soon formed a friendship with Hendrix, hoped for a collaboration with him—a plan that was cut short by the guitarist's early death. Miles was now under the spell of pop idols, including Sly Stone and James Brown.

As his sidemen spawned bands of their own, the jazz world discovered myriad new shades of contemporary music: Herbie Hancock's Mwandishi Sextet, later replaced by his Headhunters, extended his unique free-form sensibility, combined with elements of jazz-funk and African-induced rhythms; Chick Corea's *Return to Forever* brought his Spanish-inflected lyricism and harmonic elegance into new directions; Wayne Shorter and Joe Zawinul formed the influential jazz-fusion band Weather Report.

With the release of *Bitches Brew,* Miles began to perform as the opener for rock and pop acts, including Blood, Sweat & Tears, the Band, and Laura Nyro. At the 1970 Isle of Wight Festival, he played for an audience of six hundred thousand. He had become a different sort of musician, but retained his vibrancy as a pioneer. He was now drawing on sources from across the musical spectrum: American, European, Asian, classical, and pop. At the time of the album *On the Corner* (1972), Miles was listening to classical avant-gardist Karlheinz Stockhausen, reported cellist Paul Buckmaster: "There would be a bass figure, a drum rhythm that was notated, tabla and conga rhythm and a couple of keyboard figures. . . . [The musicians] played them more or less accurately to begin with and then transformed them in the Stockhausen sense—making them more unrecognizable until they became something else."

Reviewing a 1974 concert in *The Washington Post,* critic Gene Williams observed Miles "leading his exploratory party through a dense electronic rain forest. Sensing a clearing, Davis extends his fingers in a signal and his group halts motionless as a soprano sax or electric guitar or even the leader's trumpet slips ahead alone, reporting what he sees. The leader listens, choosing a path. He arches his body, nodding his head to the desired pulse, beckoning the rhythm guitar, and his group falls in, resuming their journey. Echoing, reverberatingly, electronically shaped notes and phrase form the strange beautiful foliage and strong life rhythms of Davis's musical world." At the time of his death in 1991, he was still searching.

Miles Davis's turn toward minimalism—simplifying phrases, slowing the pace of harmonic change, accentuating repetition—was unusual in jazz, but it mirrored the rise of this genre in the wider culture. In the art world, the label denoted a stripped-down, no-frills approach, giving rise to its own school. In music, it was most often applied to the compositional practice that features short musical fragments obstinately reiterated—like the relentless stuttering of a phonograph needle stuck on a scratched record—generating a hypnotic effect. The style served as a contrast (and relief) against thornier schools of composition—in New York, it represented "downtown" art, as opposed to that of such complex "uptown" composers as Elliott Carter and Milton Babbitt. The label, attributed to composer Michael Nyman, was often rejected by those who actually practiced the technique. Nevertheless, it completely revolutionized the music scene.

# CHAPTER 12

# Process Music

What song would please that is frequently or oft
repeated? Would not such uniformity disgust?
It surely would, for novelty is more delightful.
　　—PHILOSOPHER NICOLE ORESME (C. 1320–1382)

L EADING AMERICAN COMPOSERS Steve Reich (b. 1936) and
Philip Glass (b. 1937) first engaged in the then-fledgling
minimalist approach to musical composition while exploring
the culture of Northern California during the 1970s. Before
long the style had become well established, and traveled around
the world to places like the hills of Estonia, home of the wildly
popular composer Arvo Pärt (b. 1935), who carved out a special stylistic niche with his "mystical" meditative works. The
phenomenon eventually took off commercially, flourishing
on concert stages and in recordings and film scores. "In terms
of reach," wrote *New York Times* critic Corinna da Fonseca-
Wollheim about Pärt—whose music, she said, has the "languorous ferocity of lava"—"no other living composer can match
his rock star status."

Though it radically and permanently changed the direction of classical music, the minimalist idea had historical forebears, as we've already seen. French composer Erik Satie introduced the notion of a kind of "furniture music" in the 1890s, sounds meant simply to hang in the air like fixtures, and his one-page study *Vexations* instructs the performer to repeat the piece 840 times. It was likely intended by Satie as a joke, and was ignored for generations, before finally being presented in 1963 by a relay team of ten pianists at New York's Pocket Theater, an old vaudeville house. The performance took eighteen hours and forty minutes, during which time the event's organizer, composer John Cage, rested on a mattress backstage. But in 2020, esteemed Russian-German pianist Igor Levit played the work singlehandedly in fifteen hours, live-streaming it from his apartment in Berlin and creating an Internet sensation.

The repetitive treatment of musical cells as an overriding technique was promulgated early on by Reich, who arrived in San Francisco from New York in September 1961, drawn there by the allure the town had always held for poets and free spirits—people Jack Kerouac called "the mad ones": people who were "mad to live, mad to talk, mad to be saved, desirous of everything at the same time," and burning "like fabulous yellow roman candles." Kerouac's "Beat Generation" put its stamp on the town in the 1950s, but his description rang just as true in the 1960s, when it became a virtual countercultural playground.

The signs were everywhere. R. G. Davis, founder of the San Francisco Mime Troupe, described the milieu as "good weather, light drugs, a friendly atmosphere, and a bunch of interesting young people." It inspired him to stage street-theater events in the manner of sixteenth-century commedia dell'arte, along with assorted spontaneous "happenings" around the city.

Davis's productions drew the kind of audience that Reich said he "had always wanted to get to," in contrast to those he usually attracted, of insular music-school students "attending Composers Forum at four in the afternoon."

It was a time of intense experimentalism. In the opening years of the decade, California musician Terry Riley, who would later become a minimalist icon, performed—dressed in a tuxedo, a stocking cap, and dark glasses—Richard Maxfield's Piano Concerto, which required him to pour marbles into a piano. Ramón Sender, founder of the San Francisco Tape Music Center, composed a *Tropical Fish Opera,* featuring a fish tank with musical staves drawn along its four sides: as the fish swam across the staves, performers read them as notes.

In dance, avant-garde artists like Anna Halprin (1920–2021) titillated and affronted audiences, and in the same tradition, Davis and Judy (Rosenberg) Goldhaft offered experimental compositions such as *Event II,* in which they stood naked in a mirrored closet, mimicking each other's movements to the accompaniment of scatological commentary. Halprin's disciple Simone Forti created *Huddle*, a work in which the dancers first crowded together and then climbed atop one another; her postmodern "dance constructions" included one in which the audience watched an onion sprouting in a jar.

Distilling things down to a theoretical essence—as in Forti's constructions—was another side of the minimalist impulse, and it emerged in musical works as well, by composers like La Monte Young (b. 1935), who based his early music on the childhood experience of listening to the wind, train whistles, and humming telephone wires. His "Second Dream of the High-Tension Line Stepdown Transformer" (1962), for string instruments, consists simply of sustained tones selected from what he called his "dream chord"—a set of sounds he found emanating from telephone poles in the countryside. Much of his attention was focused on the trancelike state that can be induced through the sustained, serene resonances generated by pure tunings (created through simple harmonic ratios, like those discovered by Pythagoras). Michael Harrison (b. 1958), a composer in the same mold, was mentored by Young, and today similarly creates a shimmering, radiant sonic universe by using specific tunings designed to exploit the clashes that arise when some tones established through pure harmonic proportions rub up against others similarly generated. As mentioned in the chapter on Bach, the mathematical formula that produces the major third of do to mi, for example (tones whose frequencies are in the ratio 5:4), creates a different version of the note mi than that found by stacking perfect fifths from do to mi (that is, do-sol-re-la-mi, tones whose relative frequencies are in the ratio 3:2); they can't gel. What's more, their overtones (the ever-present soft, naturally-occurring multiples of the principal tone) will sometimes reinforce and sometimes fight each other. Harrison exploits and highlights the conflict. The results are often wondrous. In the midst of clouds of dense clusters rapidly drummed in the low or mid end of the instrument, an astute listener can perceive in Harrison's music high ghost tones— sometimes bell-like, at other times vaporous—as if a choir of angels were singing along.

Yet another musical icon with a minimalist bent was Morton Feldman (1926–1967), the thoroughly original, provocative, often enchanting, sometimes boring anarchist of a composer. Feldman was a veteran of that moment in New York when such colleagues as John Cage and Jackson Pollock sent shock waves through the culture, raising questions about just what was possible in art. Like writer Samuel Beckett, with whom Feldman collaborated on an avant-garde opera, the composer rejected modernism's trendy formalities, seeking instead to create a language virtually free of grammar. For Feldman, this meant writing works that unfurled over extended periods of time with little contrast or discernible form, like his six-hour String Quartet no. 2.

But it was infectious rhythm, not heady abstractions, that thrilled Reich. "For a long time during the 1960s," he later complained, "one would go to the dance concert where nobody danced, followed by the party where everyone danced. This was not a healthy situation." Of course, the mantra of the day was "freedom." Painters were "joining rock and roll bands, forgetting paintings and sculpture to become filmmakers," noted Robert Nelson, an artist who became a filmmaker, "everyone moving 'outside' of the prescribed frames that they had been taught in established institutions." Steve Reich was one of them.

Reich had grown impatient with the constraints of the musical academy while studying at Juilliard in New York. That school's atmosphere had seemed stale to him, a refuge for composers steeped in old routines. He left without graduating. One of the musical approaches considered obligatory there for any young composer was the austere twelve-tone serialist method first promulgated by Arnold Schoenberg. "The experience of writing twelve-tone music," Reich would eventually conclude, "was an important and valuable one for me in that it showed me what I had to do—which was to stop writing it." Nevertheless, his decision to begin graduate studies at Mills College in Oakland, California, was prompted by the presence there of famed Italian composer Luciano Berio, a master of the twelve-tone school.

Berio was a commanding but avuncular presence, who often

spoke to his students about subjects other than music, such as science, phonology, or architecture. That multidisciplinary openness was at the center of Berio's interest in the concept of transformation, such as converting the spoken word into musical thought. "We often find . . . more music in speech and noise than in conventional musical sounds," he avowed. His compositions, which could ignore the meaning of words while retaining their aural gestures, were notable especially for a sense of lyricism, theatricality, and humor. Reich described studying with Berio for three semesters as "enormously exciting, like being at the scene of the crime with one of the major criminals."

Yet he eagerly stepped beyond atonality's strict rules to embrace wider possibilities. He had long been attracted to jazz's exciting edge, for instance—to the excitement conveyed by live improvisers. Much of his education, he recalled, had taken place in smoky jazz clubs. "In San Francisco, I was spending the days at Mills College and the nights at the Jazz Workshop," he recalled, citing a popular jazz venue on Broadway Street in North Beach. The difference between them was striking. "The opposition between people writing enormously complicated pieces which [almost] nobody could play—pieces I wasn't even sure they could hear in their heads—and a man who simply got onstage and played his instrument, was almost irresistible."

He soaked up the artistry of saxophonist John Coltrane, who increasingly improvised over harmonies that simply lingered like clouds in a windless sky, while the pace at which chords changed was brought to a near-standstill. If the earlier bebop virtuosos resembled graceful long-distance swimmers navigating complex harmony changes, Coltrane was more like a man energetically treading water. His 1961 album *Africa/Brass* "was essentially a half hour on E," Reich explained. "Coltrane's melodic invention kept it from being boring. I took it as an object lesson: if you have rhythmic invention, timbral variety, and melodic invention, you can stay on E as long as you like. These things went into my ear and my head."

It was a natural step for him to form his own improvisational ensemble, using violin, cello, saxophone, and piano, with the composer on drums. But the musicians in this group followed no particular rules, relying instead on "spur-of-the-moment reactions," and though they met to rehearse once a week for about six months, the results were disappointing. Frustrated, Reich created "pitch charts" as roadmaps, graphic guides that limited the choice of tones. The outcome nevertheless remained, in the estimation of Terry Riley, "self-indulgent." At the group's performance at the San Francisco Mime Troupe's abandoned church in the autumn of 1964, Riley walked out. "There was a lot of loud percussion," he recalled, "and it wasn't good enough for me to stay around and see what the second half would be like."

The next day Reich walked over to Riley's studio. "I was living down the street from Steve," remembered Riley, "and I had my piano in the garage. He came and knocked on my garage door, and said, 'How come you walked out on my concert last night?' I hadn't ever met him yet. After the initial shock was over with, he sat down and we started talking, and I enjoyed meeting him a lot." One of the things Riley shared with Reich that day was a piece he had just written called *In C*—a modest-looking single page of manuscript. It would soon change the shape of modern music.

Terry Riley's *In C* begins with a hiccup, a short "grace note" on C, hit and released as fast as possible, that immediately leaps upward to an E, forming a phrase that repeats as if in an endless loop. That two-tone gesture becomes the heartbeat of the work. After it is set in motion, a group of instrumentalists—thirty-five is the suggested ideal—unfurls a catalog of fifty-three varied melodic and rhythmic fragments, or "modules," that ride atop the pulse. As musicians move from one figure to the next at their own discretion, the separate musical strands—short, long, lyrical, or jazzily angular, all anchored by the insistent pulse—alternately link together, chase one another, or collide like particles in a cloud chamber.

The exchange that afternoon ignited a conspiratorial spark. Reich helped put together an ensemble of different instruments to rehearse *In C*, and when the group had difficulty at rehearsals staying in sync, he contributed the idea of having a single musician keep time by repeatedly playing the note C, effectively becoming a chiming metronome and acting as a glue while the figures from the other players danced around freely. At the premiere in November 1964 at the San Francisco Tape Music Center, fourteen musicians took part, including such celebrated new-music figures as Reich, Pauline Oliveros, and Morton Subotnick.

Each musician was instructed to play a module for "as long as desired and then move on." The combination of steady anchors and bouncy rhythmic strands, in many instrumental timbres and colliding in an endless sonic tapestry, suggested a kind of eternal machine, like the invisible gears of the swirling universe. The review in the *San Francisco Chronicle* perfectly summed up the effect: "This primitivistic music goes on and on," it said. "At times you feel you have never done anything all your life long but listen to this music and as if that is all there is or ever will be." *In C* became a benchmark, the most famous emblem of musical minimalism, and the 1968 recording by Columbia is still treasured by music aficionados.

Reich's own *Music for Two or More Pianos or Piano and Tape* was a logical outgrowth of such ideas. The composer's attention was next focused on a relatively new medium that Berio had already used to great effect. When the Italian master asked his wife, singer Cathy Berberian, to read from James Joyce's *Ulysses,* "you could hardly understand [it] as it is written," noted Reich. "Then he took the recording and edited it into small pieces." This multilanguage, sliced-up, and rearranged version of the "Sirens" chapter of the complex novel became *Thema (Omaggio a Joyce),* considered the first composition to feature an electronically enhanced human voice.

"That was interesting to me," said Reich. "Then one day, [Berio] wanted to play two pieces for me by Stockhausen": *Electronic Studies* (1953–1954), generated completely electronically, and *Gesang der Jünglinge*, "which attracts the ear immediately." Reich realized he wasn't very interested in the electronics. "I was interested in speech," he said.

In Reich's view, a voice is as revealing as a photograph, and he felt increasingly driven to investigate its compositional possibilities. An opportunity to do so came in 1963 with a commission to create music for Robert Nelson's experimental film *Plastic Haircut.* As Ramón Sender of the Tape Music Center put it at the time, while it was once said that all composers had to come to terms with Schoenberg's twelve-tone method, "today the composer cannot afford to ignore the experience of working with tape."

For *Plastic Haircut*, Reich made a sound collage using an old LP record called *The Greatest Moments in Sports,* which captured the voices of Babe Ruth, Jack Dempsey, and other famous athletes. Eventually, he overlaid the sound patterns on top of one another, transferring the material to tape loops—long strips of tape in which the beginning and end were joined to form an uninterrupted circle—and observing the different rhythmic results of using varying lengths of tape. "This was right about the time when I discovered A. M. Jones's book on African music," he added.

In 1962, Berio had taken his class to hear a lecture by composer Gunther Schuller on early jazz. Schuller had mentioned the Jones book, and when Reich found a copy, "it was like looking at a blueprint for something completely unknown. Here was music with repeating patterns (similar to the tape loop material I was beginning to fool around with) which were superimposed so that the downbeats did not coincide." It was an enticing avenue to pursue.

So, with a Uher portable tape recorder and a microphone, he turned the Yellow Cab he had been driving into a staging area for the next musical work. "The material is a quick-cut collage, all analog sound, mostly of speech, sometimes of slamming doors or sirens. I called it *Livelihood*," he explained. The piece after that became his breakthrough creation. It was spurred by a street preacher who gave sermons every Sunday—alerting folks to a coming apocalypse—in Union Square Park, a magnet for soapbox orators dispensing political revelations, religious speeches, and ominous portents. Among them, Pentacostal preacher Brother Walter was a star. He had a way of beginning slowly and building up steam as he went along, holding a Bible in his right hand and gesturing with his left. As he paced back and forth, his voice gained in urgency, taking on a compelling lilt and rising in pitch until, at climactic moments, a loud wheeze emerged with every sharp intake of his breath. His admonition about a world in disorder and headed for annihilation used the story of Noah and the Ark as his paradigm. The preacher's reiteration of the biblical warning "It's gonna rain" seemed an apt metaphor, both for the world situation and for the personal anxiety Reich was experiencing in his life. Two years before, the Cuban Missile Crisis had brought the United States and the Soviet Union to the brink, and the impact had lingered in the public consciousness. At the time, Reich thought, "We might be going up in so much radioactive smoke." He decided that Brother Walter was well worth taping. The man's passionate inflections and the pitches of his words already seemed like music.

"He [Noah] began to warn the people," Walter chanted. "He said: 'After a while, it's gonna rain. After a while,' he repeated, 'for forty days and for forty nights.' And the people didn't believe him. And they began to laugh at him. And they begin to mock him, and they begin to say, 'It ain't gonna rain!' "

Reich focused on the slogan "It's gonna rain," chanted with a single pitch on the first three syllables of the phrase, then rising up a major third to reach "rain" (do to mi). It became the melodic germ of the new work. This raw material was put through a rigorous acoustical process. Reich created two loops out of the signature phrase and played them simultaneously on two machines. They started out in perfect unison, but tape recorders, especially old models, tend to run at slightly different speeds. As one tape fell farther behind or crept farther ahead, the repetitions of fragments like "gon' rain, gon' rain" began to shimmer against each other, as tones on a piano do when the vibrating strings are close in pitch but not exactly the same. The two tapes moved further and further out of sync. Before long, the words, now suffused with aural ghosts and shadows, became reorganized into odd rhythmic groups. The composer had discovered a technique that would become central to his compositions going forward: he called it phasing.

As he listened to the two sources pulling apart and drawing closer again through earphones, Reich's reaction was visceral. "The sensation I had in my head," he recalled, "was that the sound moved over to my left ear, moved down to my left shoulder, down my left arm, down my leg, out across the floor to the left, and finally began to reverberate and shake," and eventually "came back together in the center of my head." By artfully shaping the phase relationships, Reich had turned the original speech into a musical form.

Reich created a two-part work out of Brother Walter's speech, but at its debut on January 27, 1965, at the San Francisco Tape Music Center, he shared only the first section, based entirely on that single sentence about the coming rain. There were perhaps seventy-five people at the premiere; yet this work would establish Reich as a formidable musical presence. Eventually, he would bring together both parts of *It's Gonna Rain*, and record it for Columbia in 1969.

In New York Reich had enjoyed relationships with several members of the downtown minimalist art scene, including Sol LeWitt and Richard Serra—he even owned a Serra sculpture (obtained in exchange for a Reich score)—but he insisted that his music was not so much "minimal" as it was a "gradual process," like "placing your feet in the sand by the ocean's edge and watching, feeling, and listening to the waves gradually bury them."

A key to understanding the "minimalist" perspective can be found in the work of Reich's colleagues in the visual arts: for example, Chuck Close (1940–2021), whose paintings, drawings, and prints emphasized not so much the subject as the specific processes and materials used to make them. In the 1970s, Close began to translate his photographic sources into pixilated images filled with a variety of colors and tones that would cohere into photographic images when viewed from a distance. The focus of the work was no longer the person being photographed, but rather the system used to transform the original image into something new. The musical equivalent similarly brought the *process* a theme underwent to center stage—making obvious the formula employed in its transformation.

After returning to New York City in 1965, Reich was soon gaining adherents. In 1971, Michael Tilson Thomas, associate conductor of the Boston Symphony, was scouting for material for a new music series aimed at attracting young audiences when he first heard a Steve Reich work. The composer had been performing his original brand of music in unconventional venues—mostly small art galleries and museums—so when Tilson Thomas reached out to him he was taken aback: what could he possibly offer the Boston Symphony? Yet the conductor found Reich's pieces refreshing and original, unlike so much contemporary music, which fell into what he called "predictable stylistic puddles," most of it dissonant and rhythmically scattered—art to be admired rather than enjoyed. Reich's work, he felt, managed to "engage and provoke" at the same time. And in choosing it to attract younger audiences, he was onto something.

So Tilson Thomas asked him for an orchestral piece. Reich didn't have one, and offered instead a work written for four Farfisa portable electric organs—the kind used by many rock groups—with an additional player shaking maracas to keep time. He had already premiered it with his ensemble, Steve Reich and Musicians, at the Guggenheim Museum without much incident. So, under Tilson Thomas's direction, *Four Organs* was performed for a Boston audience in 1971. "In Boston, it went over," remembered Tilson Thomas. But when the conductor decided to present it again at New York's Carnegie Hall on January 18, 1973, the response it unleashed was ferocious.

The performance started calmly enough. The organists, sitting across from each other, two by two, with a fifth musician sitting to the side with maracas in hand, begin in lockstep, repeating a single harmony in unison. At the beginning the music asserts itself rhythmically from moment to moment like a military march, but soon it begins subtly to stretch out, as if shifting into slow motion, as individual players start to hold on to some notes a tad longer, or slightly contract the silence between chordal attacks. These small changes persist and slowly become more pronounced, until, after twenty minutes, the delineation between chordal strikes has disappeared altogether, leaving behind a dense aural blanket of pulsating organ tones.

The chord featured in *Four Organs* works against the laws of musical gravity by combining tones from both sides of the usual harmonic transaction, posing both the symbolic question and its answer together. "It contains the direction in which it wants to go and the arrival point simultaneously," said the composer. "It has the driving force of 'I've gotta move' in the bass, and the soprano voice doubled at the octave saying, 'I'm already there!'" Given the lack of a harmonic narrative, the piece simply ends in a sudden outbreak of stillness.

At Carnegie Hall, within minutes of the opening sound, an elderly lady was banging her shoe on the stage and demanding that the group stop. Another audience member ran down the aisle, shouting, "All right, I confess!" *The New York Times*'s chief music critic, Harold Schonberg, reported that concertgoers behaved "as though red-hot needles were being inserted under fingernails." Yells for the music to stop mixed with applause to hasten the end of the piece, along with lusty boos.

"The audience was expecting this elegant, gorgeously upholstered, traditional music," the conductor remembered. "And instead they got this piece for amplified rock organs." The complainers quickly began to drown out the performers. At the height of the din, Tilson Thomas had to shout out the numbers of the beats to the musicians. Finally, as they left the stage, Reich was ashen. Tilson Thomas told him to cheer up, that this moment was history in the making—the kind of thing you read about in history books, like the premiere of *The Rite of Spring*. "Whatever some members of the audience think about your piece," he said, "you can bet by tomorrow everyone in the United States will have heard about you and your work and will be hugely intrigued to hear it for themselves."

He was right. In the years since, Reich fashioned compositions tinged with political themes, explored the depths of human tragedy, increasingly engaged with technology, and created instrumental explorations of shimmering beauty. Reich's stylistic evolution, as witnessed by his lengthy catalog of works, was itself a kind of gradual process, shaped by a lifetime of experiences. As *The New Grove Dictionary of Music and Musicians* put it, over the years Reich's "repetitive, pulse-driven figures have remained a characteristic, but so have the slips and leaps of a lively mind." The capacious range of his creativity is evidenced by such works as the hauntingly lyrical 1995 setting of a sentence by philosopher Ludwig Wittgenstein—"How small a thought it takes to fill a whole life!"—titled *Proverb*, and written in imitation of the medieval composer Pérotin.

Along the way, he garnered myriad high-level prizes, including the Pulitzer Prize for Music (2009); the Polar Music Prize (shared with jazz saxophonist Sonny Rollins, 2007); the Frontiers of Knowledge Award (2013), worth $400,000; the Praemium Imperiale of the Japan Art Association (2006), worth over $131,000; and the Leone d'Oro (Golden Lion) for lifetime achievement from the Venice Biennale (2014). He has over thirty recordings, resulting in two Grammy Awards. And the assignments continue to this day. One recent work, commissioned in 2019 by The Shed in New York, was a collaboration involving the composer in a film by renowned artist Gerhard Richter. His influence has permeated the pop world as well. Revered Broadway composer Stephen Sondheim announced, "Stealing ideas from him is one of the more satisfying pleasures that I've had."

An important direction Reich has continued to pursue interweaves his art with his religious life. The course was stirred by a realization he had as a result of his exploration of West African drumming. When he visited Ghana in 1970 to study its music, he worked closely with a member of the Ewe tribe. On returning, he composed *Drumming,* which was considered his first masterpiece, a ninety-minute work that received its premiere at the Museum of Modern Art in 1971. But Ghana came to mean much more to him than mere musical techniques. He was struck by the sense of community and continuing heritage he found there.

"When I came home," the composer said, "one of the things I thought about was, This is incredible. Here's a tradition that's been handed down from father to son, from mother to daughter, for hundreds and hundreds and hundreds of years. Don't I have anything like that? And I began thinking, I'm a member of the oldest existent group that has still remained somewhat cohesive, going on for 3,500 years, and I don't know *anything* about it. So, I thought, Maybe I ought to go looking in my own backyard, and dig up the crabgrass, and see what's there!" His childhood education about his faith had been minimal. Like many assimilated Jews, his parents had little interest in the ritual aspects of the religion, and his bar mitzvah had been a matter of learning the obligatory text by rote, with no understanding of its meaning or history.

"I grew up with no knowledge of Hebrew, the Torah, the commentaries, the law derived from it, or the mysticism that surrounds the law. It was paradoxically the study of West African and Balinese music that awakened my curiosity about my own cultural background. So I began studying biblical Hebrew and Torah at a modern Orthodox synagogue in New York City and then studied Hebrew cantillation with a cantor, which led to a trip to Israel where I met older men from Yemen, Kurdistan, Iraq, and Cochin, India, to listen to and to record how they chanted the opening of Genesis in Hebrew."

Reich's newly found interest in traditional Judaism led him to set a Hebrew text, *Tehillim* (Psalms, 1981), for which he carefully selected written material that would be accessible to anyone, Jew or non-Jew. Meanwhile, his exploration of Hebrew cantillation also resulted in purely instrumental works like the gorgeous, colorful Octet (1979).

He found a life partner, videographer Beyrl Korot, who shared similar goals, and the groundbreaking work that grew from the husband-and-wife team effort was *The Cave* (1993). Five years to complete, this video opera centered on the Cave of Machpelah in the West Bank city of Hebron, supposedly the burial place of biblical patriarchs and matriarchs, a site sacred to Jews, Muslims, and Christians. Husband and wife conducted hundreds of hours of interviews with members of each of the groups claiming a spiritual affinity with the cave. The composition, based on speech melodies taken from the recorded interviews, is scored for thirteen instruments and four singers, and it presented the composer, he said, with more challenges than anything he had ever attempted before.

Like Reich, Philip Glass was an early proponent of the minimalist style, and though the two invite comparisons, they are dissimilar in important ways. As students, both enrolled at Juilliard, and later on joined forces to form a company called Chelsea Light Moving, carting furniture in and out of apartments in New York's downtown neighborhoods. The men had initially pursued divergent musical paths (though Glass was apparently influenced by a concert by Reich in March 1967 that included his important early piece *Piano Phase*). Reich came to feel that Glass was taking his ideas without giving him proper credit, and they became estranged; their business venture, like the friendship that quickly turned into a rivalry, was short-lived.

Reich's comparison of his musical process to grains of sand shifting beneath his feet stands in contrast to Glass's lapidary style, which features abrupt transitions—blocks of shifting repeating patterns that lengthen and shorten in a simple additive process. The composer was a student of Indian singer Pandit Pran Nath, and the technique is related to Indian cyclic rhythms known as tal, along with aggressively rippling arpeggios. It's a conception that lent itself well to the composer's most successful media: opera and film scores, three of which were nominated for Academy Awards. The open-ended, emotionally neutral nature of this music provided a blank slate on which viewers could project their own dramatic narratives, filling in the details of the stories with their own imaginations. The ambiguous nature of the dramatic action was part of the secret of Glass's success. The composer once quipped that any time a fan proposed an explanation of the action onstage, regardless of what it was, he simply affirmed that interpretation as the correct one. Musically, the works were relentless. Though critic Justin Davidson of *New York* magazine drolly observed that "Glass never had a good idea he didn't flog to death," it was a winning formula.

Glass's operas have shaken the foundations of that world. Beginning in 1976, with *Einstein on the Beach,* a collaboration with Robert Wilson (for which Glass rented New York's Metropolitan Opera House and lost a huge amount of money in the process), followed by *Satyagraha,* based on the life of Gandhi, in 1980, and *Akhnaten,* an Egyptian tale, in 1984, he has come to be seen as the most successful opera composer alive. Ironically, when the Metropolitan Opera commissioned him to compose *The Voyage* for the five hundredth anniversary of Columbus's sailing to the Americas, they paid Glass, who barely managed to scrape together the money for his initial appearance there with *Einstein on the Beach,* the highest fee ever for a new opera. His film scores, including one for the 2002 drama *The Hours,* based on Michael Cunningham's novel, are stunning and memorable. He continues to compose and perform, often with his own ensemble.

A crop of younger composers, like John Adams (b. 1947), whose operas and orchestral works have ridden Glass's coattails, have by now rendered the once-controversial minimalist style a secure part of the mainstream. The approach has continued to evolve in the hands of artists like John Luther Adams (b. 1953), an environmentalist who searches for musical equivalents to solitary landscapes like the Alaskan tundra or the arid deserts of the American Southwest. He describes his nature-based inspirations in a memoir, *Silences So Deep: Music, Solitude, Alaska:* "the glassy tones of candle ice swirling in whirlpools, the intricate arpeggios of meltwater dripping, and the ominous rumbling and grinding of icebergs." The result, he explains, is vibration that "aspires to the condition of place."

In the end, this music recalls on a broad scale the "shimmerings, iridescences, glimmerings, ripplings, and shudderings" of impressionism, as that movement was described by French critic Émile Vuillermoz. John Luther Adams's orchestral works harbor shifting tides and natural collisions, reflecting a world in continuous process. His *Become Ocean,* wrote da Fonseca-Wollheim, "burgeons and recedes, with different instrumental groups sometimes at odds with each other, sometimes in sync. When the crests align, a giant swell is created that registers somehow as both comforting and vertiginous." For her, listening to it became all-consuming. "When the final notes receded," she wrote, "they left me with a stark craving for more, for a return into the amniotic embrace of sound."

Over time, such individual styles have blossomed and faded, leaving a rich legacy, yet one aspect of the music tradition remained an unfortunate fixture for centuries. Women—from Mendelssohn's sister Fanny in the nineteenth century (whose early pieces were sometimes published under the name of her more famous brother) to jazz pianist Hazel Scott in the twentieth—have been consistently marginalized. Only recently has a quiet revolution granted the fair sex a fairer status.

# CHAPTER 13

# A Question of Sex

If a woman, from youth on, dedicates herself to the
same scholarship, why should she not reap the rewards
of it, like the male of the species does?

—CHRISTIANE MARIANE VON ZIEGLER,
librettist for J. S. Bach

*Yuja Wang in performance*

Growing up in the Sugar Hill section of New York's Harlem with her father, George, a Black intellectual, and her mother, Josephine, a blond, onetime Mack Sennett bathing beauty, Philippa Schuyler (1931–1967) gave her first public piano recital at age four. Two years later, venerated critic Deems Taylor was asked to interview her on a radio program and initially balked, asserting that "only by a miracle could a six-year-old possess the emotional and intellectual depth of a mature artist." Hearing Philippa convinced him otherwise. Even the notoriously demanding critic Virgil Thomson, who heard Schuyler at age thirteen, compared her favorably to the young Mozart. But the promise was never entirely fulfilled.

Her parents had believed that mixed race would produce extraordinary offspring, and their confidence seemed justified. It was little surprise to them that Philippa exhibited stellar abilities as a musician, journalist, and novelist, and that she was also stunningly beautiful. Josephine raised her daughter with the guidance of John Broadus Watson of Johns Hopkins University, a disciple of Russian physiologist Ivan Pavlov. The behaviorist's cold, mechanistic view of child rearing yielded early results: at four, Philippa won a spelling competition, with the word "pneumonoultramicroscopicsilicovolcanoconiosis." But her training, which had included recurrent whippings to instill discipline, left psychological scars. And as she grew, societal obstacles remained formidable, because of both her gender and her race.

Her early musical accomplishments included the premiere of her original composition *Manhattan Nocturne* at a New York Philharmonic-Symphony Young People's Concert under conductor Rudolph Ganz in 1945. *The New York Times* called it "truly poetic, the expression of genuine feeling, a gentle, soft beauty and imagination." Yet her long-held hope of being recognized as a major compositional talent failed to materialize. She felt boxed in on all sides, and her life was anguished. While a teen, she contemplated suicide.

The opportunity for female talent had not changed greatly from the time of Mozart, who recognized the abilities of his underappreciated sister, Nannerl, and marveled at the blind glass harmonica player Marianne Kirchgessner, whom he heard in Vienna (the instrument uses glass bowls vibrated by means of friction). Neither woman had been given the advantages commonly granted to male performers. There were others. Mozart's piano maker, Johann Andreas Stein, asked him to give keyboard lessons to his eight-year-old daughter, Nannette (1769–1833), and the composer, while amused at the way she flung her body around, rolled her eyes, and grimaced as she played, still found her a "real talent." But she remained a craftsperson, out of the limelight (though her career of building pianos, as Nannette Streicher, intrigued even the great Beethoven).

In that restrictive time there was actually no dearth of female talent. Another Mozart student, Rose Cannabich (1764–1839), so impressed the master that he dedicated his Piano Sonata no. 7 (K. 309) to her. In the same generation, violin prodigy Gertrud Mara (1749–1833) became a celebrated performer, supported by the Queen of England, who convinced her to become a singer instead, because the violin was "unfeminine." The star virtuoso Paganini gave violin lessons to Caterina Calcagno, born in Genoa in 1797, who at the age of fifteen astounded Italy by the boldness of her style. Yet despite such successes, an implacable glass ceiling hovered over the heads of most women artists.

In her twenties, Philippa Schuyler did enjoy a moderate degree of acknowledgment. She toured South and Central America and Africa, producing a travelogue titled *Adventures in Black and White* and a novel whose protagonist (a black-haired and amber-eyed concert pianist) was a thinly disguised alter ego of the author, who had yearned for a romantic relationship of her own. In Philippa's story, she falls hard for a mysterious man: "Powerful vibrations of icy disdain, intellect and pride emanated from him, and attracted me like a magnet," reports the heroine. Sadly, in real life, Schuyler was as unlucky in love as she was in gaining the musical respect in full that she so richly deserved.

Despite the social headwinds, she garnered occasional rave notices. In June 1962 critic Herbert Roussel in *The Houston Post* described her as "one of the most uncannily beautiful players of this instrument it has been this reviewer's pleasure to encounter in forty years of attendance at concerts." Nevertheless, obstacles remained, especially as she encountered unrelenting racial prejudice. In 1959, in an effort to turn the tide, she began to list herself as "white" on entry forms when she traveled, attempting to "pass" as such, and she eventually applied for a passport with a new name altogether: Felipa Monterro y Schuyler. The new identity suggested she was Iberian-American rather than Black. It didn't help much.

In the spring of 1966, Henry Cabot Lodge, then United States ambassador to South Vietnam, invited her to perform for wounded soldiers. At the same time, William Loeb, owner of the *Manchester* (New Hampshire) *Union Leader*, engaged her as a foreign correspondent. She willingly accepted both opportunities, but on arrival discovered conditions she found horrendous: from Saigon, she reported, "Everyone around here must have done something wrong in their last reincarnation and is getting punished for it now. . . . The Viet Cong are AWFUL, CRUEL; the Americans are AWFUL, CRUDE; and the South Vietnamese are AWFUL, CORRUPT. Take your choice."

On April 15, 1967, she gave a piano concert on South Vietnamese television. The program included her own composition *Normandie*, based on a fifteenth-century tune; transcriptions of Gershwin's *Rhapsody in Blue* and *An American in Paris;* and Aaron Copland's early piano study "The Cat and the Mouse." Summing up her impressions of the war-torn country, she reported, "Hue was romantic, Saigon raucous, Da Nang infinitely sad."

Things would soon become even more tragic. While engaged in evacuation attempts to move young children from an orphanage, she was in the midst of preparing a return to America, but postponed the journey home because of an astrologer's cryptic prediction that on the evening of May 9 she would "emerge from the mouth of the dragon." On that very date, while transporting children to Da Nang, her helicopter crashed. Most of the passengers survived. Philippa did not.

As a Black woman, Philippa Schuyler was doubly encumbered. Yet many female musicians of all ethnic backgrounds, especially composers, had similar experiences. The New York Symphony, a predecessor of the New York Philharmonic, apparently programmed only a single work by a woman, Cécile Chaminade's "Chanson slave," which was performed on February 20, 1891. It wasn't until 2020 that the Philharmonic's administration opened its doors wide to female composers by launching Project 19, a multiyear initiative celebrating the centennial of the

Nineteenth Amendment to the American constitution, the law that gave women the right to vote. In recognition of the occasion, the venture commissioned nineteen women to write new works.

The path to success had been somewhat easier for instrumentalists and vocalists, especially by the end of the nineteenth century. Several women began to enjoy recognition at this time, especially the singers. There was Adelina Patti, who between the ages of seven and nine performed three hundred times in the United States, Cuba, and Mexico (by all accounts she was spoiled, selfish, and egotistical). Opera diva Pauline Viardot (1821–1910), a friend of Chopin's, developed a vast social network, entertaining a virtual who's who of nineteenth-century icons at her weekly salons in Paris, including composers Rossini, Liszt, and Schumann and novelists Victor Hugo and Ivan Turgenev.

Other female artists of note, though often not rewarded as well as their male counterparts, were also recognized. They included Arabella Goddard (1836–1922), who as a child played for Chopin and his mistress, George Sand, and later gave the English premiere of Beethoven's difficult *Hammerklavier* Sonata; she became one of the first teachers at the Royal College of Music in London. Another was Venezuelan pianist Teresa Carreño (1853–1917), called "the second Arabella Goddard" by George Bernard Shaw. For much of her career she was also known as "the Valkyrie of the Piano." She performed at the White House for Abraham Lincoln at the age of ten, and was promoted by then-renowned virtuoso Louis Moreau Gottschalk. Carreño played under the baton of such eminent conductors as Hans von Bülow and Gustav Mahler.

Then there were Franz Liszt's many students, each of whom

hoped to steal a bit of the master's incandescence, including German composer and pianist Adele aus der Ohe (1861–1937), who made her debut at age ten performing Beethoven's Piano Concerto no. 2. She toured Russia and America and appeared during Carnegie Hall's opening week, playing Tchaikovsky's First Piano Concerto under his baton. She was a favorite soloist of the Chicago Symphony and the Boston Symphony, playing Liszt's First Concerto and Brahms's Second as well as the Tchaikovsky. Other celebrated Liszt protégées included Russian Vera Timanova (1855–1942), who gave her final concert at age eighty-two and died of hunger during the siege of Leningrad, and German virtuoso Sophie Menter (1846–1918), whom Liszt described as his "only piano daughter." Some women even succeeded in becoming legendary superstars.

Clara Wieck (1819–1896), the eventual wife of Robert Schumann, was a renowned piano prodigy, touring Europe even as a youngster—in Vienna, restaurants served torte à la Wieck, a delicate pastry layered with whipped cream and featuring swirls and rosettes, in her honor. Clara had her own disciples, today little remembered, including pianists Adelina de Lara (1872–1961) and Fanny Davies (1861–1934), an early proponent of the music of Debussy and Scriabin.

Like her husband, Clara also composed on a high level. But unlike him, she felt compelled to downplay those gifts. "I once believed that I possessed creative talent," she acknowledged, "but I have given up this idea; a woman must not desire to compose—there has never yet been one able to do it. Should I expect to be the one?" She was, of course, unjustifiably lacking in confidence and somewhat misinformed on the subject of female composers. There were female success stories even in the Middle Ages: Hildegard of Bingen, in the twelfth century, became one of the best-known composers of sacred monophony; her chants are more widely performed than those of any other composer of her time. And in Clara's day, compositional talents like the French Louise Farrenc (1804–1875), though never fully appreciated, managed to make important contributions. Still, Clara's trepidation about the ability of women to compose stemmed from deeply entrenched beliefs, long cemented into Western culture.

Some attributed the male hierarchy in creative endeavors to God's natural order. Eighteenth-century theorist Georg Andreas Sorge explained it in terms of music theory: "Just as in this universe there has always been created a creature more splendid and perfect than the others of God," he claimed, "we observe exactly this also in musical harmony. Thus, we find after the major triad another, the minor triad, which is indeed not as complete as the first, but also lovely and pleasant to hear. The first can be likened to the male, the second to the female sex."

The origins of these convictions are a complicated matter. Pathbreaking psychologist Karen Horney suggested a kind of "womb envy" at work—a term that encapsulates the sense of awe and jealousy felt by men in the face of a woman's ability to bear children, prompting in them the need to make up for the deficiency through artistic efforts. It was a plausible explanation for the societal dynamic at the time: since women hold an incontestable monopoly in the realm of biological creation, men, in response, could well attempt to corner the market in acts of creative imagination.

At the same time, sexual anxieties—revealed in generations of tales found in the Bible, Greek mythology, and medieval literature—encouraged a distrust of feminine "wiles," further bolstering the desire to keep women in their places. Musical instruction became a means to that end, a moral training ground on which to accomplish this. Thus, the entry in Diderot's *Encyclopédie* (1751–72) for "instrumental skill" described it as "one of the primary ornaments in the education of women." The piano, observed the Reverend H. R. Haweis in the nineteenth century, "makes a girl sit upright and pay attention to details." As for her emotions: "A good play at the piano has not infrequently taken the place of a good cry upstairs," he contended. As A. C. Wheeler, critic of the *New York World*, put it in 1875, the piano can become a young girl's "companion, her confidant, her lover. It tells her what no one else dare utter. It responds to her passion, her playfulness, her vagaries, as nothing else can."

The piano as the instrument of choice for women had other advantages. As writer John Essex put it in *The Young Ladies Conduct: or, Rules for Education, under Several Heads; with Instructions upon Dress, Both Before and After Marriage. And Advice to Young Wives* (1722): some instruments were "unbecoming the Fair Sex; as the Flute, Violin and Hautboy [oboe]; the last of which is too Manlike, and would look indecent in a Woman's Mouth; and the Flute is very improper, as taking away too much of the Juices, which are otherwise more necessarily employ'd to promote the Appetite, and assist Digestion."

The power imbalance that relegated female musicians to a lesser role was in evidence in the other arts as well. An organization founded in 2009, Advancing Women Artists, identified and restored hundreds of paintings created by Italian women from the sixteenth to the twentieth centuries, including *The Last Supper* by Plautilla Nelli (1524–1588), one of the few female painters mentioned in Giorgio Vasari's *Lives of the Artists*. She was a nun by age fourteen, entering the Dominican convent of Santa Caterina da Siena in 1538, and created an artist's studio within the monastery. Like Artemisia Gentileschi (1593–1653), who achieved recognition in the Medici court and became the first woman member of the Accademia delle Arti del Disegno in Florence, her work is little remembered. She developed a style that celebrated powerful mythological heroines. Florentine painter and poet Irene Parenti Duclos (1754–1795) has "hidden" works in the Uffizi Galleries, including self-portraits kept in storage. She became known as a teacher of other women.

Women were stymied in multiple ways. In Padua in 1678, Elena Lucrezia Cornaro Piscopia became the first woman to earn a doctor of philosophy degree. Then it took a half century before another female, Laura Maria Caterina Bassi, obtained a doctorate, this one from the University of Bologna. Females enjoyed few of the opportunities afforded men until relatively modern times.

Nevertheless, in the music world, as the cultural climate shifted into a more modern sensibility, many more women emerged as stars, especially those who cultivated a special expertise. Olga Samaroff (1880–1948), whose given name was Lucy Hickenlooper (she took the stage name for obvious reasons), was only the second pianist in history to perform all thirty-two of Beethoven's piano sonatas in public. She was also the first woman to self-produce a concert at Carnegie Hall, and established a reputation as a renowned teacher, becoming perhaps the most celebrated of her generation.

Just as in the male-dominated world, women found that one of the surest ways to stir interest was through celebrated rivalries. Perhaps the most striking was between Wanda Landowska

(1879–1959) and Rosalyn Tureck (1913–2003), each woman claiming to have special insights into proper Bach performance. (Landowska quipped to Pablo Casals that he could play Bach his way, but she would play it Bach's way, a remark often mistakenly thought to have been aimed at Tureck.) Known as a stellar harpsichordist as well as a pianist, Landowska established a center for baroque music at her home in Saint-Leu-la-Forêt, France, before World War II, and was the first to record Bach's *Goldberg Variations* on the harpsichord, in 1933. Her recordings are filled with authority and passion.

Tureck, who became known as "the High Priestess of Bach," had interests that went well beyond that label, championing contemporary composers like Charles Ives, William Schuman, and David Diamond. In 1952 she presented the first concert in the United States of tape and electronic music. At seventeen she made her Carnegie Hall debut playing the theremin. She was also one of the first to experiment with the Moog synthesizer, collaborating with inventor Robert Moog in 1964. While teaching at various institutions, including Juilliard, the Mannes School, and Columbia University, she was made a life fellow of St. Hilda's College, Oxford, and a visiting fellow of Wolfson College, also at Oxford. Her own educational foundation, the Tureck Bach Research Institute, held annual symposia, in which experts from various fields, such as science and the plastic arts, addressed topics like embellishment, structure, and style.

Tureck's plunge into the possibilities offered by the Moog synthesizer continued in the work of transgender artist Wendy Carlos (b. 1939, as Walter). Carlos's takes on Bach popularized the device among young audiences, winning three Grammy Awards in the process. Carlos went on to score films, including two by director Stanley Kubrick—*A Clockwork Orange* (1971) and *The Shining* (1980)—as well as the Walt Disney sci-fi feature *Tron* (1982).

Carlos was on the cutting edge of another radical change. Even as women performers found cracks in the wall of resistance to equal acceptance, any dramatic violations of accepted gender roles—artists following an inner compulsion to embrace life with a sexual identity other than the one with which they were biologically endowed—stoked continued outrage. Often the changes were simply outward artistic expressions, like styles of dress and behavior (as in Chopin's romantic partner, the cigar-smoking, pants-wearing George Sand), but sometimes the aim was calculated to disguise what was beneath. Jazz pianist and bandleader Billy Tipton (1914–1989) was born Dorothy Lucille Tipton but identified as a man, and his romantic partners went along with the deception; friends were shocked to learn the truth after his death.

Pianist David Buechner (b. 1964), a Juilliard-trained, award-winning musician, went through a period of agonizing "gender dysphoria"—a dissonance between his sex assigned at birth and gender identity—culminating in a decision, in his mid-thirties, to undergo what was called at the time "gender reassignment surgery," announcing her identity as Sara Davis Buechner. The change spelled disaster for the pianist's career: "Conductors who once routinely engaged me stopped returning calls," she recounted, "prestigious teaching offers were withdrawn, and concert opportunities vanished. Changing managers did not help. I recall one particularly low point as the time I received a check from a Florida recital presenter several weeks before my appearance—having booked David Buechner, they paid Sara not to come."

She seized on an opportunity to move to Canada, accepting a teaching post in Vancouver from 2003 to 2016, where performing opportunities again opened up, though it felt to her like a period of exile. After several years of rebuilding a career slowly, the concert dates and recording credits returned, even in the United States. Today, the extraordinarily gifted pianist is a member of the keyboard faculty of Temple University's Boyer College of Music and Dance in Philadelphia, and a bold (and marvelously entertaining) spokesperson for the transgender community.

The twentieth century marked a turning point. As the era began, critics still judged women by different standards than they did their male counterparts. Slightly earlier, violinist Camilla Urso (1840–1902) was admitted to the Paris Conservatory at age seven as its first-ever female candidate, and left at age ten, first in her class. But a reviewer was struck mostly by her face, "so solemn and unchanging in its expression that it seemed as if a smile had never visited it." In like fashion, *The New York Times* used the occasion of a concert review to cite the physical features of Italian-born violinist Teresina Tua (1866–1956), who had won the Paris Conservatory's highest prize on her instrument. "She has a face that will be music to the unmusical," the paper declared in 1887, "and an unfailing knowledge of the value of her delightful smiles, which she rained down on the front rows in a manner calculated to diminish whatever soundless judgment the young men in that neighborhood possessed when they entered the hall." So much for professional music reporting.

Women organists have faced similar situations, in particular because of attitudes in the church, where female performers were not welcome in the organ lofts. Jeanne Demessieux (1921–1968) was criticized for wearing high heels, or, as *The Boston*

*Globe* put it in 1953, for being "too young and attractivce to be an organist of the first rank." And Henriette Puig-Roget (1910–1992) felt compelled to submit her name as Monsieur Roget and cross-dress, in order to substitute for Charles Tournemire at Ste.-Clotilde. Yet, Marie-Claire Alain (1926–2013) made three hundred recordings, including three on organs of different periods for the complete organ works of J. S. Bach. Joséphine Boulay (1869–1925), blind from the age of three, became the first woman to win first prize in organ at the Paris Conservatory in 1888.

Some women found champions in male musicians. For example, Marie Soldat (1863–1955) became Brahms's favorite violinist (he discovered her when she was fifteen). She formed two all-female string quartets, and both achieved significant success in the concert world. By the middle of the twentieth century, real equity remained elusive, yet a new level of respect was often shown. One recipient of the change was the legendary Spanish pianist Alicia de Larrocha (1923–2009). Another was violinist Ida Haendel, the Polish-born prodigy (1928–2020), who during the dark days of World War II had joined British pianist Myra Hess (1890–1965) in presenting morale-boosting concerts in London. Today the situation is notably improved, and living violinists of great repute include Anne-Sophie Mutter (b. 1963) and Leila Josefowicz (b. 1977), a champion of contemporary music and winner of a prestigious MacArthur Fellowship (known popularly as the Genius Grant). However, the discrepancy in opportunities for female artists today is still striking, especially in the realm of music composition. An orchestral survey in 2014–2015 revealed that in the programs of the twenty-one largest American orchestras, women composers accounted for a mere 1.8 percent of the season.

Talented women composers could make their mark in other ways: France's Nadia Boulanger (1887–1979), who had set out to be a composer, as had her talented sister, Lili (1893–1918), became one of the most celebrated musical pedagogues of all time, teaching such renowned talents as Aaron Copland, Virgil Thomson, Elliott Carter, Philip Glass, and Astor Piazzolla. They all trekked to Paris to work with her. As Thomson once quipped, she was "a one-woman graduate school so powerful and so permeating that legend credits every U.S. town with two things: a five-and-dime, and a Boulanger pupil."

Nevertheless, in the twentieth century adventurous female composers and performers increasingly made an impact on the development of serious music. They included Julia Wolfe

*Nadia Boulanger and her class, Paris, 1923.*
*From left to right: Eyvind Hesselberg; unidentified; Robert Delaney;*
*unidentified; Boulanger; Aaron Copland; Mario Braggiotti;*
*Melville Smith; unidentified; Armand Marquint*

(b. 1958), the ultra-modernist and folk music specialist Ruth Crawford Seeger (1901–1963), and Pauline Oliveros (1932–2016), the accordionist and composer who explored free improvisation with Terry Riley; she was an integral member of the San Francisco Tape Music Center in the 1960s and when it moved to Mills College and became the Center for Contemporary Music, she served as its director. Many other women were attracted to the world of electronic composition, like Daphne Oram (1925–2003), who co-founded the BBC's influential Radiophonic Workshop. She and her many colleagues, including Suzanne Ciani, Laurie Spiegel, and Éliane Radigue, are featured in the 2021 documentary created by Lisa Rovner, *Sisters with Transistors: Electronic Music's Unsung Heroines.*

Among other formidable musicians in the twenty-first century, flutist Claire Chase (b. 1978), another MacArthur Fellow, has left an indelible mark, championing contemporary music and creating the much-heralded International Contemporary Ensemble in 2001. At the time of this writing, she is teaching at Harvard University. In New York, pianist Wu Han co-directs the Chamber Music Society of Lincoln Center, along with her husband, the impressive cellist David Finckel.

In the jazz world, stars emerged who nevertheless remained in the shadows of history: Viola Smith (1912–2020), billed as the "fastest girl drummer in the world," wrote a widely read essay during World War II advocating for big bands to hire female musicians in place of the males who had been drafted. "There are many girl trumpet players, girl saxophonists and girl drummers who can stand the grind of long tours and exacting one-night stands," she argued. Among these were pianist Lovie

Austin (1887–1972), who accompanied and composed for some of the greatest singers of the early recording era, including Ma Rainey and Ethel Waters; she was also a tremendous influence on other women talents, like the formidable pianist and composer Mary Lou Williams (1910–1981), who confessed that her "entire concept" was based on the few times she was around Austin. Lil Hardin Armstrong (1898–1971) met her future husband, Louis Armstrong, when she joined King Oliver's famed Creole Jazz Band as the group's pianist. Valaida Snow (1904–1956) was a trumpet virtuoso who also played a dozen other instruments; saxophonist Peggy Gilbert (1905–2007) led many small ensembles; pianist Dorothy Donegan (1922–1998), a unique voice with a blazing, two-fisted technique, was the first Black instrumentalist to give a concert at Orchestra Hall in Chicago.

Women guitarists have also made their mark in rock. Joan Jett, Lita Ford, Nancy Wilson, Carrie Brownstein, and the Great Kat (trained at Juilliard as a violinist) are among the virtuosic players who mesmerized audiences with flying fingers and wailing solos. Superstar Carlos Santana enthusiastically endorsed the Australian newcomer Orianthi: "If I was going to pass the baton to someone," he said, "she would be my first choice."

Women conductors have faced perhaps the steepest climb, since that role requires a commanding sense of authority toward the orchestral players—and the players' willingness to accede to it. In the United States, less than 10 percent of the orchestras are directed by women. But even here, there is some progress. In 2007, Marin Alsop (b. 1956) became the first woman music director of an American orchestra, the Baltimore Symphony. She recently retired from her Baltimore position, but is busy as chief conductor of the ORF Vienna Radio Symphony and chief conductor and curator of Chicago's Ravinia Festival, among other activities.

"When I started [conducting], I assumed there were going to be a lot of women doing it pretty soon," said Alsop. "Five years went by, then ten, and very little changed. It's very difficult to escape deeply engrained social norms." In 2013, Vasily Petrenko, then chief conductor of the Oslo Philharmonic and the Royal Liverpool Philharmonic, explained the traditional view that orchestras "react better when they have a man in front of them," while "a cute girl on a podium means that musicians think about other things." It resulted in calls for his resignation.

In 2021, Nathalie Stutzmann (b. 1965) was appointed music director of the Atlanta Symphony, becoming only the second woman to lead a major American orchestra. The position was clearly earned. Already principal guest conductor of the Philadelphia Orchestra and chief conductor of Norway's Kristiansand Symphony Orchestra, Stutzmann is also a respected contralto, with more than eighty recordings to her credit, and was named Chevalier de la Légion d'Honneur, France's highest honor. "Nathalie is the real thing," stated Sir Simon Rattle, who mentored her. "So much love, intensity and sheer technique. We need more conductors like her."

Also in 2021, Eun Sun Kim (b. 1980), from South Korea, became the first woman to serve as music director of one of America's largest opera companies, the San Francisco Opera. Yet other women have been recognized in the ranks of outstanding maestros, including JoAnn Falletta (b. 1954), named by *The New York Times* as "one of the finest conductors of her generation"; Finland's Susanna Mälkki (b. 1969), chief conductor of the Helsinki Philharmonic; and Canadian Barbara Hannigan (b. 1971), an extraordinarily virtuosic soprano and commanding music director. Ukrainian Oksana Lyniv (b. 1978) became the first woman ever to conduct at the Bayreuth Festival in 2021, and Lithuanian Mirga Gražinytė-Tyla (b. 1986) has served as Music Director of the City of Birmingham Symphony Orchestra in the U.K.

Yet the battle is not over. In the view of Falletta, an upset male conductor inspires players to practice, while an upset woman on the podium "conveys the impression that the person is out of control, because of how we view women's anger." At Juilliard, where she studied conducting with Jorge Mester in the 1970s, these incongruities were part of the conversation. As the only woman in the class, she had to consider how to address an orchestra, and noticed how often she was apologizing when asking the oboe to play softer, and how she had developed an unconscious tendency to look at her score instead of directly at a musician when offering a critique.

"Jorge helped me realize that as a conductor it wasn't really my right to ask for things, it was my responsibility," says Falletta. "This is the job. I had to make things better, and to make things better, I had to identify what needed to be changed and improved upon. And if I couldn't do that, I couldn't be in that position." These issues continue to plague aspiring women in the music world, of course.

Still, in some respects, the tradition has simply marched on, especially in regard to the long parade of women pianists, from France's Marguerite Long (1874–1966), Romanian Clara Haskil (1895–1960), Lithuanian-American Nadia Reisenberg (1904–1983), and Greece's Gina Bachauer (1913–1976) to the next generation of artists, like Argentina's Martha Argerich (b. 1941) and including Americans like Ruth Laredo (1937–2005), whose recordings included the ten sonatas of Alexander Scriabin and the compete solo works of Rachmaninoff (though resistance from music critics continued to haunt her), and Barbara Nissman (b. 1944), known especially for her performances of music by Alberto Ginastera and Sergei Prokofiev. American Ursula Oppens (b. 1944) has demonstrated a command in the complex music of modernists like Elliott Carter; Japan's Mitsuko Uchida (b. 1948) is an eloquent interpreter of Mozart and Schoenberg; the French Labèque sisters, Katia (b. 1950) and Marielle (b. 1952), form an eloquent duo piano team. American Gloria Cheng is a contemporary specialist who has put a spotlight on film composers; Venezuelan-American Gabriela Montero (b. 1970) is a pianist of impeccable classical sensibilities who also improvises brilliantly; and there is the incredibly virtuosic, Beijing-born Yuja Wang, who stirs nearly as much reaction with her short, tight-fitting outfits as she does with her flashy technique and deep musicality.

In a video promotion for fashion designer Giorgio Armani, she is shown playing Liszt's arrangement of Schubert's *Gretchen at the Spinning Wheel,* the work's dark, dulcet tones swirling against a dimly lit backdrop of piano and pianist as the music gently weaves a spell of soulful mystery. The performance, technically impeccable and full of subdued passion, is intercut with images of the pianist in a variety of tasteful poses.

In a *New York Times* Arts and Leisure feature, the diminutive pianist was shown seated at the keyboard, adorned in five-inch heels, arms outstretched as if ready to take flight, head extended to the sky, her graceful right leg extending to the sustain pedal. It could have been a study by the elegant sculptor Constantin Brancusi. The caption noted her "power and poetry." There was a time when all this would have raised eyebrows, along with protestations about classical music's chaste role in a world full of commercial taint. Welcome to the twenty-first century, when women play the piano as well as men, and feel free to flaunt their natural beauty as well.

Wang, a prodigy who studied from the age of seven at Beijing's Central Conservatory of Music, emigrated to America at the tender age of twelve, where she settled first at Canada's Music Bridge International Music Festival, and then, at fifteen, went on to work with revered pianists Gary Graffman and Leon Fleisher at Philadelphia's Curtis Institute of Music. Today she is perhaps the most celebrated of classical music's new crop of superstars.

In the pop domain, women composers have long made an impact. Carrie Jacobs-Bond (1862–1946), who wrote "I Love You Truly," was the first to sell a million copies of a song; among her colleagues Dana Suesse (1911–1987) was known as "the female Gershwin." Women songwriters and entertainers are certainly as celebrated as their male counterparts. But today, in a new wrinkle, classical composers, among them Amy Beach (1867–1944), Florence Price (1887–1953), Sofia Gubaidulina (b. 1931), and Kaija Saariaho (b. 1952), are finally appearing on concert programs around the world in truly significant numbers. In the twenty-first century, classical music has finally begun to shed some of its sexist bent. To casual observers of the newest generation, the change may seem sudden; for dozens of deserving talents, it has been a slow, steep climb.

A similar trajectory has been traced in the seemingly sudden popularity of Western classical music in China, a phenomenon that actually emerged through a long and difficult history.

· CHAPTER 14 ·

# Mozart Among the Lotus Blossoms

If one should desire to know whether a kingdom is well
governed, if its morals are good or bad, the quality of its
music will furnish the answer.

—CONFUCIUS

*The China National Center for the Performing Arts Orchestra
at Shenzhen Concert Hall in Guangdong, on April 16, 2021,
during its 2021 National Tour. Music Director Lü Jia conducted.*

As Copernicus suggested, the notion of revolution includes a return to beginnings. In China, that history includes Western musical elements, once championed, then rejected, and finally rediscovered. The rejection was a particularly painful period, illustrated by the turmoil that swept into Moying Li's village one day in 1966, a force as destructive and unpredictable as the sudden gales that toppled ships in the East China Sea. Until that moment, life had been pleasantly monotonous for Moying, a schoolgirl living on the outskirts of Beijing, whose free time was normally spent either toiling in the family's garden—a small patch of earth redolent with the fragrance of pale jasmine and chrysanthemums—or teasing out melodies from the bamboo lute her uncle had given her. Everything changed when the thugs took over.

The aggressors were mere children themselves, high-school students intoxicated by the calls of Chairman Mao Zedong to rally against the poison of Western influence. Marching around town in green outfits, with large bands on their sleeves announcing membership in the Red Guard, they wielded placards with slogans such as "Confess your crime!" But mere demonstrations were felt to be not enough, and before long, the search was on for suspected enemies.

Within days a crowd had gathered in front of the office of Li Ping, the headmaster of Moying's school. She watched with rising panic as the mob surrounded the respected scholar, his glasses soon smashed on the ground, his clothes disheveled, and his nose bleeding. Not long after, she heard the news: Li had hanged himself from a tree, a letter protesting his innocence tucked into his pocket.

The scene was replicated in villages across China as the Cultural Revolution took root. Overnight, artists and intellectuals faced prison, re-education in forced-labor camps, or death. Musicians became a special target. Fearful members of the educated class began burying their instruments, destroying music books, and melting down their vinyl records. Chinese composers were forced to devote their efforts to imitations of traditional folk songs, or to Communist propagandist works in the mold of the *Yellow River Cantata,* written during the second Sino-Japanese War in 1939. Pianos and violins took a backseat to the bowed two-stringed erhu or the plucked pipa. And the skills needed to appreciate and perform sophisticated Western music began to wither.

Today, some of the brightest young classical superstars on the world stage are Chinese-born; the piano is no longer shunned, and thirty-eight million Chinese students are currently taking lessons. China is embracing Western culture as never before, and the West is proving a willing partner. The turnabout seems stunning, though surveying the history of Western involvement in Chinese culture reveals a longstanding, durable entanglement.

Western inroads into Chinese culture began back on January 24, 1601, when the Italian missionary Matteo Ricci arrived in Beijing bearing a cache of gifts he had spent years assembling, a treasure trove gathered in the hope of obtaining an audience with the elusive Wanli Emperor. Though turned away twice before, Ricci was nevertheless determined somehow to convert Chinese heathens to his idea of "the true way," and meeting the emperor was an essential first step. "The time at which we now find ourselves in China," he told a childhood friend in 1599, "is not yet that of the harvest, nor even of sowing, but rather of opening up the wild woods and fighting with the wild beasts and poisonous snakes that lurk within."

Zhu Yijun, the fourteenth emperor of the Ming dynasty, found the timing of Ricci's arrival less than opportune. The royal court was in disarray, and the emperor, who had occupied the throne from the age of ten, was now, at twenty-nine, an exile in his own palace. Zhu had abandoned his official obligations following the death of an important official, and neglected governmental meetings, where councillors, in his absence, entered and bowed to an empty room. It marked the beginning of Zhu's, and the empire's, long decline.

Yet Ricci's third attempt on behalf of civilized Christendom to breach the seemingly impenetrable wall around Chinese culture won the emperor's agreement that he could be welcomed. Among the items he had brought to induce the Chinese leader's cooperation were such European curiosities as paintings, maps, mechanical clocks, religious objects, and a clavichord. The clavichord traditionally engendered an aura of intimacy, and the European masters who played it—ranging from J. S. Bach to Mozart—had a variety of subtle effects at their fingertips. Once a note has been produced, for instance, the clavichord could create a tiny expressive vibrato—a small wavering of pitch—as a musician pushed and relaxed the metal tangent (which served as a hammer) against the vibrating string. In Europe, this was a prized quality, emotionally charged. To the Chinese, it was new.

"Musical instruments are quite common and of many varieties [in China]," Ricci wrote, "but the use of the organ and the clavichord is unknown, and the Chinese possess no instrument of the keyboard type." Indeed, though China in the 1600s had numerous rich musical traditions that employed both domestic and imported instruments, it had nothing resembling the stringed instrument that Ricci possessed. That's why the priest brought it, hoping to excite the emperor's curiosity. Ricci's elaborate plan both to win the emperor's attention, and ultimately to convert his entire nation to Christianity, of course was largely ineffective: the emperor was indeed intrigued by the strange instrument, and he ultimately sent four eunuchs from the College of Musicians to learn how to play it, but Ricci achieved little more.

Some Chinese instruments offered similar effects to the clavichord's, including both its subdued volume and its wide timbral palette. None was more cherished than the qin, a seven-stringed zither with a sound reminiscent of a plucked cello, regarded as "the instrument of the sages." The qin was said to have been played by Confucius, and by the Yellow Emperor, the legendary sovereign regarded as divine (2698–2598 BCE), and its sounds were forever associated with deep philosophical principles.

Qin technique could draw from the instrument a spectacular range of colorful qualities. There was, for example, a kind of vibrato called *yin* that was said to imitate "a cold cicada bemoaning the coming of autumn," and one known as *changyin*, which was long and drawn out like "the cry of a dove announcing rain." Another, *yuyin*, brought to mind "fallen blossoms floating down with the stream." And then there was the subtlest vibrato of all, requiring a player to keep his hand still while allowing the timbre of the instrument to be controlled by the faint pulsation of blood moving to the fingertips. By the early thirteenth century, Chinese composers were including rubbing, tapping, and sliding fingers to their bag of performing techniques.

But the sensibilities of East and West were completely different. Ricci found Chinese music to be hideous. At one performance, he saw an ensemble using bronze bells, "basin shaped vessels, some made of stone, with skins over them like drums, stringed instruments like the lute, bone flutes and organs played by blowing into them with the mouth rather than with bellows. They had other instruments also shaped like animals, holding reeds in their teeth." When all these sounded simultaneously, he reported, the result "can be readily imagined, as it was nothing other than a lack of concord, a discord of discords." (The impression Chinese music made on Western ears had still not changed in 1852 when Hector Berlioz found that it was comprised of "nasal, guttural, moaning, hideous tones, which I may without too much exaggeration compare to the sounds a dog makes when after a long sleep it stretches its limbs and yawns.")

The music of the West similarly had less of a positive impact on the Chinese than Ricci had hoped. The musical vocabularies of Europe and China were entirely different. Nevertheless, after being forced to cool his heels for nearly a year, the priest was finally invited to display his self-ringing clocks to the imperial eunuchs and, later, to demonstrate to them the clavichord. Ricci was not a musician, but he had brought along another Jesuit priest, Diego Pantoja, who taught the emperor's eunuchs four songs for which Ricci wrote lyrics infused with Christian theology. Pantoja's lessons lasted a month, after which the eunuchs presumably gave a recital, although Ricci was not invited to hear it, and he never got to meet, let alone convert, the emperor. However, while his gift failed to turn China into a nation of Christians, it did start the country on the path to becoming what it is today: a nation of pianists, piano makers, piano students, and piano lovers.

At first, the classical repertoire for which the clavichord was designed made no inroads on Chinese culture, though some of Ricci's original songs on the subjects of virtue and ethics remained popular at the palace: "O shepherd boy, shepherd boy," went one ditty, "how can you expect to transform yourself by changing your dwelling place? If you move away, can you leave yourself behind? Sorrow and joy sprout in the heart. If the heart is peaceful, you'll be happy everywhere."

In the end, the clavichord's novelty was ephemeral. On his deathbed, however, Ricci remained hopeful. "I am leaving you on the threshold of an open door that leads to a great reward," he claimed, "but only after labors endured and dangers encountered." He had no idea how many centuries would pass before his prediction came true.

Jesuit missionaries continued to present China's monarchs with keyboard instruments. The Kangxi Emperor (1654–1722) even took the time to learn a few tunes on the harpsichord, and required several of his sons to play it, too. The musical tradition continued with the eventual introduction of the piano, which was invented in Italy around 1700. As "Princess" Der Ling (1885–1944), the Western-educated daughter of a Qing diplomat (who was given her title while serving as the first lady-in-waiting for Empress Dowager Cixi), wrote of the Guangxu Emperor (1871–1908): "He was a born musician and could play any instrument without studying. He loved the piano, and was always after me to teach him. There were several beautiful grand pianos at the Audience Hall."

Katharine Carl, an American artist who in 1903 spent several months living in the imperial palaces, described those instruments:

> In the back of the hall were three pianos, two upright and a new Grand piano, which had but lately arrived at the Palace. Her Majesty wished us to try the Grand piano . . . [she] thought the piano a curious sort of instrument, but

lacking in volume and tone for so large an instrument. Keyboard instruments spread outside the palace too, starting in churches, where the early missionaries installed organs, and then spreading rapidly after the Opium War [1839–1842]. Protestant missionaries began to enter China in large numbers at this time, and they established schools in which pianos (or, in more remote areas, harmoniums [small reed organs with bellows that were pumped]) became standard teaching tools.

By the 1850s, keyboards were everywhere. In the 1870s, Sydenham Moutrie from London established a shop in Shanghai to import, sell, and repair them. China's first homegrown piano factories arose soon after, often inhabited by men who had worked at Moutrie's, many of whom hailed from the port city of Ningbo, along the Silk Road, a town renowned for the skill of its woodworkers.

The Moutrie piano-building operation emulated similar operations in Europe and America. Its two-story factory on Nanking Road used the bottom floor for storing wood and metal parts and for tuning finished instruments. Types of lumber included beech from Japan, teak from Bangkok, and fir and spruce from Vancouver. The second floor was a spacious warehouse, where the wood was seasoned for two years, then cut, and heated for three months to become completely dry before being finally stored on the roof. The assembled instruments were strung with amalgam-plated steel wires and copper-covered bass strings. The result rivaled the quality of Western models.

By the end of the century, the piano had thoroughly permeated the culture at all levels, from the lowest to the highest. In October 1898, *The New York Times* reported that Moutrie had been called to Beijing to repair the emperor's piano. "The keys were filthy," he reported, "and had various Chinese hieroglyphics stamped on them, while the instrument had not been tuned for years." He tuned it and cleaned off the writing— only to be told by the emperor that the characters should be replaced (perhaps because they were used as a guide for playing the instrument).

It's little surprise that music should play so important a role in Chinese society. As Confucius put it in the *Analects*, "Personal cultivation begins with poetry, is made firm by rules of ceremonials, and is perfected by music." But there was an inherent tension provoked by the piano itself, which represented an alien invasion of sorts. Its foreignness was intriguing, but also dangerous, difficult to fathom, a bit subversive. Nonetheless, learning to play the piano was by now being seen as a necessary part of a proper education, particularly for young women. This replicated the British and European experience. In 1847, critic Henri-Louis Blanchard in France wrote that "cultivating the piano is something that has become as essential, as necessary, to social harmony as the cultivation of the potato is to the existence of the people."

Many of the early teachers were of course Westerners, among them, Italian conductor and pianist Mario Paci (1878–1946), who sailed into Shanghai in the winter of 1918 along with his Steinway grand piano. His instrument was damaged by water in the hull of the P&O steamer, and Paci himself took ill; he had to be brought to Shanghai General Hospital to recuperate, while the Steinway was carried off to Moutrie's for repair. Paci recovered, and became a fixture, and a cultural influencer.

In 1919, when Paci took over the reins of the Shanghai Symphony Orchestra, originally known as the Shanghai Public

Band, he actively recruited Italian musicians for the ensemble, which he subsequently led for twenty-three years, during which time it was transformed from an organization whose purpose was simply to entertain Europeans—the ensemble was comprised mostly of Filipinos—to one more integrated into Chinese society. It was not until 1923 that Chinese musicians joined the organization. Five years later, the group's summer outdoor concerts were finally opened to Chinese audiences.

By then, the local orchestra had performed compositions by Weber, Schubert, Liszt, and Beethoven—the last finding a special place in the hearts of Chinese listeners. As in Europe, Beethoven's character loomed large, though questions arose over whether this esteemed Western composer should serve as a model: did his music reflect bourgeois decadence, or revolutionary fervor? In 1907, the Chinese Buddhist monk Li Shutong had authored a short essay about Beethoven, entitled "The Sage of Music," focusing on Beethoven's life and his persistent struggles with impending deafness, declaring the composer "the guiding spirit for young men and women, driven by a love of their country, who were determined to seize fate by the throat and build a China of social equality and dignity." His music sparked more admiration than hostility, at least for a while: in 1925, at the funeral of Sun Yat-sen, the first president of the Republic of China, mourners heard the second movement of Beethoven's *Eroica* Symphony. (When the People's Republic of China celebrated its tenth anniversary in 1959, the Central Philharmonic Orchestra performed Beethoven's Ninth Symphony, with Schiller's "Ode to Joy" translated into Mandarin. But not long after, this composer's work would be banned.)

The Western classical tradition continued to make inroads when Xiao Youmei established what is now the Shanghai Conservatory in 1927, inviting a number of foreign piano teachers to join the faculty. Among the most influential were Boris Zakharoff and Alexander Tcherepnin. Zakharoff, a graduate of the St. Petersburg Conservatory and a student of Leopold Godowsky's, headed the school's piano department and taught such pianists as Ding Shande (who also composed and would later become president of the Shanghai Conservatory). Tcherepnin, a composer of some repute, wrote the first piano primer based on the pentatonic scale (found by playing the black keys of the piano, and used extensively in traditional Chinese music) and encouraged Chinese composers to create music that sounded Chinese, rather than Russian or European; composer He Luting's popular piece "Buffalo Boy's Flute" was written for a contest organized by Tcherepnin.

But classical music was not the only influential style making inroads at this time. Shanghai, with a reputation as "the Paris of the East," was becoming a jazz mecca when trumpeter Buck Clayton arrived in 1935. As James Reese Europe found in France, the foreign environment enabled American musicians to find the respect they craved. Clayton and his colleagues— billed as "the Harlem Gentlemen" even though they hailed from Los Angeles—lived, the bandleader remembered, "like we were millionaires." China's "first lady," Madame Chiang Kai-shek, attended the group's first performance at the Canidrome ballroom with one of her sisters, who also took tap-dancing lessons from trombone player Duke Upshaw. The problem, as James Europe discovered in France, was other American expatriates with racist leanings, making life difficult.

But Western music, classical or popular, was clearly a draw, live and on phonograph records. By 1949, the piano was so commonplace that Chairman Mao—whose wife, Jiang Qing, took piano lessons in her youth—used it as a metaphor for a well-run society, in a speech that was later included in his Little Red Book. "Learn to 'play the piano,'" Mao told his followers. "In playing the piano, all ten fingers are in motion; it will not do to move some fingers only and not others. However, if all ten fingers press down at once, there is no melody. To produce good music, the ten fingers should move rhythmically and in co-ordination."

As pianos and piano teachers, who were mostly imported from the Soviet Union, proliferated, the bond between the two great Communist powers, China and Russia, had been on solid ground. But by the 1960s an ideological rift was growing. In the view of the Chinese authorities, after Stalin's death the Soviets had become guilty of "counterrevolutionary trends," especially in their more open stance toward the United States. As the political atmosphere heated up, on June 14, 1963, an official Chinese statement declared that for true believers in Communist ideals "peaceful coexistence" with the West was simply impossible. The Soviets showed increasing interest in joining and influencing the world community, while the Chinese were tending toward insularity, and the divide continued to deepen.

In the 1950s, however, China, not yet completely committed to isolationism, had begun to send young pianists who played exceptionally well to overseas competitions. Among them was Fou Ts'ong (1904–2020), a former student of Mario Paci's, who placed third (just behind Vladimir Ashkenazy, who came in second) at the 1955 Chopin Competition in Poland. The son of a leading scholar who translated Romain Rolland's ten-volume,

Nobel Prize–winning novel, *Jean-Christophe,* into Chinese, Fou enjoyed the advantages of a classical education at a time when China still embraced a wide world of intellectual exploration. His father, he remembered, had taught the works of Lao-tse and Confucius side by side with Aristotle, Plato, and Voltaire. His translation of *Jean-Christophe* was done in that spirit, and became "an enormous influence in China," Fou told British journalist Jessica Duchen. "I think that was because it represented the liberation of the individual." Such thinking was, of course, now anathema to the state.

Following his success at the Chopin Competition, teachers and supporters in Poland were able to secure for Fou an invitation to London, and pianist Julius Katchen lent him the airfare to make his escape possible. A nonexistent "farewell" concert was announced to throw watchful Chinese authorities off the track, a deceit that worked. Once in the West, he flourished as both a performer and a teacher; his parents, though, caught in the Cultural Revolution back home, both committed suicide.

The line of formidable Chinese pianists continued to grow, however, with Liu Shikun (b. 1939), who shared second prize at the 1958 Tchaikovsky Piano Competition in Moscow. Liu's story, like that of Fou, encapsulated China's entry into a dark period, when it struggled to balance nationalist fervor against the pursuit of artistic excellence. The Tchaikovsky Competition had been created to tout Russia's artistic preeminence on the world stage, at a time when China was pulling back from the fellowship in the community of nations, so Liu's triumph in Moscow, which followed his third-place finish at the Liszt Competition in Budapest, was not welcomed. In Hungary, "After each of my performances, the jury—which included such great pianists as Emil Gilels, Alexander Goldenweiser, and Annie Fischer—stood up" in a show of respect, Liu recalled. He insisted that Lev Vlassenko had won the Liszt contest for purely political reasons. At the Tchaikovsky, Liu and Vlassenko tied for second place, and the gold medal was awarded to American Van Cliburn.

"But when I returned to China after the Tchaikovsky Competition," said Liu, "the culture had changed. Common labor was valued above art, and I had to engage in physical work for two months to serve as an example. Meanwhile, Mao Zedong was promoting the idea that music and art must be based on folk traditions, and if I wanted to compose I had to follow those principles.

"I thought this wasn't a bad idea. So in 1959 I wrote a piano concerto—it was called *Youth Concerto*, because I was still a teenager—and for the first time China had a piece that utilized both Western and Chinese instruments." He became a professor at the Beijing Conservatory, and performed for both Mao and Zhou Enlai, who criticized his playing as not suited to Chinese audiences. Then the climate continued to worsen. By the time the Cultural Revolution was under way in 1966, he found himself under arrest, and was placed in a variety of prisons.

"There were two reasons," he says, for the punishment. "Officially, I was under suspicion, both because I played classical music and because I had studied in the Soviet Union—China and the Soviets were no longer on good terms. They accused me of being a Soviet spy. But the real reason was that Mao's wife, Jiang Qing, was trying to force me to give false testimony against my father-in-law, who was a man of some political standing."

He cleaned toilets. Guards repeatedly struck his right arm with a military belt, fracturing the bone. In the notorious Qincheng Prison, he was tortured. "In summer and winter, I had only one shirt. There were no showers. For food they gave me some moldy bread and rotten leaves with insects, loaded with lots of salt. I had to spend hours bowing to a portrait of Mao."

When he finally gained release in 1973, he spent months in the hospital before resuming his career as a pianist, now performing such officially sanctioned works as the *Yellow River Concerto* (which he learned by listening to the piece over loudspeakers while in his jail cell). But following Mao's death in 1976, the cloud lifted. In 1990, Liu emigrated to Hong Kong, where he taught piano ten hours a day. After two years, he had gathered enough money to create his first music school. He has now founded over one hundred such schools in more than thirty cities, serving a total of sixty thousand to seventy thousand Chinese students. Today, he is flourishing.

The year of Liu Shikun's release was also a time of monumental political change in Chinese-American dynamics, largely spurred by President Richard Nixon's efforts to normalize relations. Music played an important role. American secretary of state Henry Kissinger scheduled an initial visit in October 1971, and China's premier, Zhou Enlai, suggested that the Central Philharmonic should play Beethoven, because "Kissinger's German." It was not a bad idea in the scheme of things. But when Kissinger was also treated to a performance of Peking opera, he found it "an art form of truly stupefying boredom in which villains were the incarnation of evil and wore black, good guys wore red, and as far as I could make out the girl fell in love with a tractor."

President Nixon made the trip himself a year later, and was similarly feted. "The president and most of his party attended a performance of *The Red Detachment of Women,* a revolutionary ballet," reported American diplomat Nicholas Platt. "Uniformed ballerinas in puttees pirouetted, vigorously pointing their Mauser automatic pistols, uttering piercing denunciations of the Japanese invaders and paeans of praise for Communist heroes, all to the loud accompaniment of gongs, drums, and cymbals." However much this spectacle seemed questionable in advancing the cause of diplomacy, it was a step forward, and the door was opened for a visit to Beijing in 1973 by conductor Eugene Ormandy and the Philadelphia Orchestra. The eminent music director wanted to be the first in this new era to bring Western classical music to the People's Republic.

The visit was fraught. Ambassador Platt mediated between the Chinese authorities and Ormandy, who wanted to perform Beethoven's Fifth Symphony. Jiang Qing, Mao's wife, opposed the selection: that particular symphony, she claimed, was about fate, and Communists don't believe in fate. She wanted to hear Beethoven's Sixth, the *Pastoral,* instead.

Ormandy was aghast. "I hate Beethoven's Sixth," he announced. Platt scrambled. He told Ormandy that Beethoven's pastoral themes represented peasant life, that the Chinese identified the storm in the fourth movement with the struggle the Chinese people had been through, and that the peaceful, triumphant ending called to mind China under Mao's rule. Besides, Platt said, the request had come from Madame Mao herself. "Of course, I made it all up," Platt revealed later. Ormandy, however, was convinced.

The event had strong, positive repercussions. As a young boy, composer Tan Dun, now famous for his Oscar-winning film score for *Crouching Tiger, Hidden Dragon* (2000), heard the orchestra as it was piped into his village's public-address system. He was struck by the instruments of the Philadelphia Orchestra and the artistry of the musicians. It all helped set in motion the wheels of a Western music resurgence.

Following the death of Mao in 1976, there was a rush to buy pianos, which were still in short supply. Only ten thousand were manufactured in China in 1980. By 1990, China was producing 10 percent of the world's pianos, which grew to almost 80 percent, or 376,000 pianos (mostly uprights), in 2013, a year in which the nation also imported one hundred thousand pianos. It began to produce top pianists such as Lang Lang, known to virtually anyone with a passing knowledge of contemporary classical performance, and Yundi Li, the poetic artist with a devoted following who won the International Chopin Piano Competition in Warsaw in 2000, at the age of eighteen.

According to critic Norman Lebrecht, "The number of children learning to play the piano in China varies from forty to sixty million, depending on who you ask. Walk through a tower-block residential area in Shanghai at five in the afternoon and you can hear the clangor of many hands playing scales." But neither Lang Lang nor Yundi Li "was the trigger for China's piano mania," claims Lebrecht. "The man who first got China's fingers moving was the silky French entertainer Richard Clayderman, a Liberace-style merchant of melancholy kitsch who burst upon the Chinese in the mid-1980s with his signature tunes 'Ballade pour Adeline' and 'Les Feuilles mortes.' Some 800 million viewers watched his first China TV appearance in 1987."

The explosion of interest in Western music was also due to the efforts of a generation of trailblazers, men who lived through the difficult times and emerged with a sense of purpose, like conductor Long Yu, described by *The New York Times* as "China's Herbert von Karajan . . . the most powerful figure in

*Long Yu conducting the Guangzhou Symphony Orchestra*

China's Western classical music scene." He has served as music director of the Shanghai Symphony, the China Philharmonic, and the Guangzhou Symphony, principal guest conductor of the Hong Kong Philharmonic, and chairman of the Beijing International Music Festival Arts Council.

A grandson of Ding Shande, recognized as one of China's greatest pianist/composers, Long was born in 1964, two years before the Cultural Revolution began. During that turbulent period his mother, a pianist, and his father, a choreographer, were arrested and sent to a farm for re-education. "I remember standing in fear as the Red Guards came and burned music in our garden," he recounts. Yet Long's connection to music continued. "I took piano lessons," he recalls of his boyhood, "training my fingers by playing revolutionary songs." Eventually, he studied in Europe, before returning home to grab the reins of his orchestras. He remains an important figure.

The musical transition for China has been a long work in

progress. The cultural obstacles were made clear in the 1979 film *From Mao to Mozart*, tracing violinist Isaac Stern's visit with Chinese music students. He found them stiff and wary, unaccustomed to the West's emotional syntax. A teacher at the newly reopened Shanghai Conservatory reported that many of the students who had come through the Cultural Revolution "just play the notes. Everything must be fast, loud, noisy." Stern tried to convey the importance of other qualities: "There must always be life," he explained. "There is not a single casual note in music. Everything has a reason."

The bitter past remained topmost in the minds of many. "I taught people to make violins," recounted one teacher. "I was confined to a closet in the basement of the library. There was a pipe going to the septic tank. I had to stay there for fourteen months. The lack of air caused my legs to swell. The chief reason they did that to all the old teachers was to get rid of us, to get control of the music. I was treated as a prisoner. Ten of our teachers died by suicide because they couldn't stand the humiliation."

More recent official attitudes toward Western music in China are an entirely different matter. In 2010, the China NCPA Orchestra was founded as the resident orchestra of the National Centre for the Performing Arts in Beijing. Since that time, important Western musicians have guest-conducted the ensemble, including Lorin Maazel, Zubin Mehta, Valery Gergiev and Christoph Eschenbach, who declared it "one of the finest orchestras in Asia."

Another sign of expansion has been the recent opening in Tianjin of the famed Juilliard School of music, located about forty-five minutes by train from Beijing. It is the first performing-arts institution in China to confer a United States–

accredited master of music degree, offering a mix of resident artists and visiting faculty from Juilliard in New York and instruction in ensemble performance, woodwinds, brass, percussion, piano, and strings.

There are other indications of the change. Chen Guangzian, director of the China Symphony Development Foundation, reported in *China Daily* that in the four years prior to 2017, the number of professional symphony orchestras in the country had grown from thirty to eighty-two. Clearly, China has rejoined the global music community in a major way.

Even apart from Juilliard, the resurgence has been tied intimately to America. Chinese composers who lived through the Cultural Revolution have found inspiration and refuge in the West. Among the most prominent have been the aforementioned Tan Dun, whose Oscar- and Grammy-winning film music has thrust him into public awareness; Bright Sheng (b. 1955), who was sent as a teenager to a province near Tibet, where he absorbed the region's folk music, and who subsequently became one of the first students to enroll at the Shanghai Conservatory when it reopened, later studied in the United States with Leonard Bernstein, and eventually won a MacArthur Fellowship; and Chen Yi (b. 1953), from a musical family in Guangzhou—the first woman to earn a master's degree in composition in China. Chen is married to Zhou Long (b. 1953), a graduate of both Beijing's Central Conservatory and Columbia University, and the first Chinese American to win the Pulitzer Prize in music.

Despite the historical obstacles, the marriage of East and West now seems irrevocable.

# The Revolutionary Spirit

O N CHRISTMAS DAY in 1989, the Berlin Wall, a cruel artifact of the Communist-imposed division between East and West, had recently been felled, and the entire city was in a celebratory mood. Dozens of musicians now gathered under the baton of conductor Leonard Bernstein in the Schauspielhaus of the former East Berlin for a performance of the final movement of Beethoven's grandiose Ninth Symphony. The orchestra was culled from both sides of the Iron Curtain, including West Germany's Bavarian Radio Symphony Orchestra, members of East Germany's Dresden Staatskapelle, and musicians from orchestras that represented the four countries that had initially partitioned Berlin in 1945: the New York Philharmonic, the London Symphony, the Orchestre de Paris, and the Orchestra of the Kirov Theater (known today as the

Mariinsky). There were vocal soloists as well, and three choirs: the Bavarian Radio Chorus; members of the radio chorus of what had been East Berlin; and the large children's choir of the Dresden Philharmonie.

Symphonies are normally written for instruments, not singers, but Beethoven was determined to include the poem by Friedrich Schiller known as the "Ode to Joy," promoting universal brotherhood:

> Joy, beautiful spark of Divinity,
> Daughter of Elysium . . .
> All men become brothers,
> Where thy gentle wing abides.

Twenty thousand people witnessed the Berlin concert via five-by-ten-meter screens along one of the busiest streets in Berlin. Beethoven's sweeping strains, in a dramatic, emotional, and deeply personal proclamation harnessed by an extraordinary level of musical craftsmanship, spurred one deeply inspired observer to tell the *Los Angeles Times* that the performance was "about freedom, peace and justice in the entire world."

The poem and the symphony had by this point become iconic. Performed at the opening of the 1936 Berlin Olympics and thereafter a mainstay of modern Olympic ceremonies, over time it resonated across multiple cultures, coming to represent a universal yearning for liberty. In 1972 it was adopted as the "Anthem of Europe." And its influence spread well beyond Europe. Six months before the Berlin Wall concert, as protesting Chinese students poured into Tiananmen Square, the "Ode to Joy" blared over their loudspeakers.

It wasn't merely the poem's noble sentiment that drew acolytes. Hundreds of other works expressing similar ideas could have conveyed the same message with little or no impact. Beethoven's powerful symphony stood apart, mainly because anyone experiencing its majestic framework could sense the deep revolutionary spirit behind it. Bernstein made one change to Schiller's text: he substituted *Freiheit* (freedom) for *Freude* (joy). But the power of the work went beyond subtleties of political messaging.

Nevertheless, the Ninth Symphony stands as a cautionary tale for would-be musical revolutionaries. After its London premiere in 1825—the Philharmonic Society in London had commissioned it—the piece was trashed by musical authorities. (It had fared better a year earlier in Vienna, where the composer was a hometown hero.) Posterity often rewards daring with a future place of honor; yet in the short term, giving in to revolutionary impulses like that advanced by Beethoven can be a perilous endeavor.

"It is to be remembered," declared one London critic covering the London premiere, proposing an excuse for the work's "want of perfection," "that the great composer is afflicted with an incurable disorder (deafness). . . . May not this disturb a mind gifted with such extraordinary genius?" The Ninth Symphony is "bizarre," reported the *Allgemeine musikalische Zeitung.* For one thing, there is the music's extraordinary duration, which left the critic squirming in his seat. "It embodies enough of original matter, of beautiful effects and skillful contrivances, to form an admirable symphony of ordinary duration. . . . Unfortunately, the author has spun it out to so unusual a length, that he has 'drawn out the thread of his verbosity finer than the staple of his argument,' and what would have been delightful had it been contained within moderate limits, he has rendered wearying by expansion, and diluted his subjects till they became weak and vapid. When we add that the time which it is calculated this composition will take in performing cannot be much less than an hour and twenty minutes, our readers, though they have not heard it, may almost judge for themselves of its inadequacy to fix the attention of any audience, or to produce such an effect as the admirers of Beethoven must earnestly wish."

Besides, there was the strangeness of the singing in the final movement. What justification could there possibly be for this violation of tradition? To nineteenth-century ears, it made no sense. "Though there is much vocal beauty in parts of it," opined the critic, "yet it does not, and no habit will ever make it, mix up with the three first movements. This chorus is a hymn to joy, commencing with a recitative, and relieved by many solo passages. What relation it bears to the symphony we could not make out; and here, as well as in other parts, the want of intelligible design is too apparent."

Time has borne out Beethoven's conception. Yet, as always, the revolutionary impulse carries risks. As I have tried to demonstrate, however, artistic daring like Beethoven's has often led to greatness. The human spirit is, in the end, irrepressible. And the revolution continues.

# Acknowledgments

Jonathan Segal, my editor at Knopf, has been an enthusiastic supporter of my work for over twenty years. I value his expertise and skill, and his friendship, more than I can say. Thanks are also due to his generous assistant, Sarah Perrin.

No words would be adequate to express my gratitude to my wife, Adrienne, and to my daughters, Nora and Rachel. Their encouragement and care were unflagging, especially as I faced health challenges while completing this book,

In the process I drew on the kindness of many friends, musicians and music-industry professionals, including pianist Steven Lubin; the late Noah Creshevsky (who convinced me of the necessity of including chapter two) and his partner, David Sachs; Steve Sidorsky; Nicholas Platt; Michael Harrison; Steve Reich; Sara Davis Buechner; Bill Charlap; Long Yu; Roberto Prosseda; Carol Ann Cheung of Boosey & Hawkes; Wei Zhou of Weiber Consulting; Patricia Price and Julianne Zahl of 8VA Music Consultancy; graphic designer Mason Phillips; Ruth Rando of the Closter Public Library; and Laura Kuhn of the John Cage Trust.

# Bibliography

ARTICLES

[n.a.] "History of the Public Lighting of Paris," *Nature*, 132 (1933)

Beardsley, Eleanor, "Women Conductors Are the Rule, Not the Exception, at a New Classical Event," *Billboard*, October 2, 2020

Chandler, Arthur, "Revolution: The Paris *Exposition Universelle*, 1889," revised and expanded from *World's Fair* magazine 7, no. 1 (1986).

Cole, Ross, "Fun, Yes, but Music? Steve Reich and the San Francisco Bay Area's Cultural Nexus, 1962–65," *Journal of the Society for American Music* 6, no. 3 (2012)

Duchen, Jessica, "Fou Ts'ong," jessicamusic.blogspot.com

Dupree, Mary Herron, "Jazz, the Critics, and American Art Music in the 1920s," *American Music* 4, no. 3 (Autumn 1986)

Eliot, T. S., "London Letter," *The Dial* 71, October 1921

Fawcett-Lothson, Amanda, "The Florentine Camerata and Their Influence on the Beginnings of Opera," *IU South Bend Undergraduate Research Journal* 9 (2009)

Fonseca-Wollheim, Corinna da, "Making Music Visible: Singing in Sign," *The Wall Street Journal*, April 9, 2021

Gillett, Rachel, "Jazz and the Evolution of Black American Cosmopolitanism in Interwar Paris," *Journal of World History* 21, no. 3 (September 2010)

Gopinath, Sumanth, "Reich in Blackface: *Oh Dem Watermelons* and Radical Minstrelsy in the 1960s," *Journal of the Society for American Music* 5, no. 2 (May 2011)

Hentoff, Nat, "An Afternoon with Miles Davis," *The Jazz Review* 1, no. 2 (December 1958)

Isacoff, Stuart, review of Miles Davis Quintet, *Freedom Jazz Dance*, The Bootleg Series, vol. 5, *The Wall Street Journal*, November 7, 2016

Jackson, Timothy L, "The Schenker Controversy," *Quillette*, December 20, 2021

Johnson, James H. III, "The Myth of Venice in Nineteenth-Century Opera," *Journal of Interdisciplinary History* 36, no. 3 (Winter 2006)

Kenney, William H. III, "The Assimilation of American Jazz in France, 1917–1940," *American Studies* 25, no. 1 (Spring 1984)

Kotnik, Vlado, "The Adaptability of Opera: When Different Social Agents Come to Common Ground," *International Review of the Aesthetics and Sociology of Music* 44, no. 2 (December 2013)

LaGrave, Katherine, "Talk About the Slow Road to Equality," *Billboard*, December 9, 2019

Lebrecht, Norman, "The Chinese Are Coming," *The Spectator*, November 25, 2017

MacFarquhar, Roderick, "How Mao Molded Communism to Create a New China," *The New York Times,* October 23, 2017

Muir, Edward, "Why Venice? Venetian Society and the Success of Early Opera," *Journal of Interdisciplinary History* 36, no. 3 (Winter 2006)

Orledge, Robert, "Satie and America," *American Music* 18, no. 1 (Spring 2000)

Parker, James, "The Electric Surge of Miles Davis," *The Atlantic*, July/August 2016

Smith, Christopher, "A Sense of the Possible: Miles Davis and the Semiotics of Improvised Performance," *The Drama Review* 39, no. 3 (Autumn 1995)

Sternfeld, Frederick W., "Orpheus, Ovid and Opera," *Journal of the Royal Musical Association* 113, no. 2 (1988)

Zoladz, Lindsay, "Amplifying the Women Who Pushed Synthesizers into the Future," *The New York Times,* April 21, 2021

MEDIA

*From Mao to Mozart: Isaac Stern in China*, dir. Murray Lerner, Hopewell Foundation, 1979

BOOKS

Albert, Richard M., ed., *From Blues to Bop: A Collection of Jazz Fiction*, New York: Anchor Books, 1992

Antheil, George, *Bad Boy of Music*, New York: Doubleday, 1945

Archer-Straw, Petrine, *Negrophilia: Avant-Garde Paris and Black Culture in the 1920s,* New York: Thames & Hudson, 2000

Auner, Joseph, ed., *A Schoenberg Reader*, New Haven: Yale University Press, 2003

Badger, Reid, *A Life in Ragtime: A Biography of James Reese Europe*, New York: Oxford University Press, 1995

Baker, Jean-Claude, and Chris Chase, *Josephine: The Hungry Heart*, New York: Random House, 1993

Bernstein, David W., ed., *The San Francisco Tape Music Center: 1960s Counterculture and the Avant-Garde*, Berkeley: University of California Press, 2008

Busoni, Ferruccio, *Sketch of a New Esthetic of Music*, trans. Theodore Baker, New York: G. Schirmer, 1911

Cage, John, *Empty Words: Writings '73–'78*, Middletown, CT: Wesleyan University Press, 1981

Cai, Jindong, and Sheila Melvin, *Beethoven in China*, Melbourne: Penguin Random House Australia, 2015

————, *Rhapsody in Red: How Western Classical Music Became Chinese,* New York: Algora Publishing, 2004

Carr, Ian, *Miles Davis: A Biography*, New York: Quill, 1984

Carter, Marva Griffin, *Swing Along: The Musical Life of Will Marion Cook*, New York: Oxford University Press, 2008

Cohen, J. Bernard, *Revolution in Science*, Cambridge, MA: Harvard University Press, 1985

Cowell, Henry, *Essential Cowell,* ed. Dick Higgins, Kingston, NY: McPherson & Co., 2002

David, Hans T., and Arthur Mendel, eds., *The New Bach Reader: A Life of Johann Sebastian Bach in Letters and Documents*, revised and expanded by Christoph Wolff, New York: W. W. Norton & Company, 1998

Davis, Miles, with Quincy Troupe, *Miles: The Autobiography*, New York: Simon & Schuster, 1989

Davis, Ronald G., *The San Francisco Mime Troupe: The First Ten Years*, Palo Alto, CA: Ramparts Press, 1975

Dreyfus, Laurence, *Bach and the Patterns of Invention*, Cambridge, MA.: Harvard University Press, 2004

Duffy, Eamon, *Saints & Sinners: A History of the Popes*, New Haven: Yale University Press, 1997

Durant, Will and Ariel, *The Age of Reason Begins*, New York: Simon & Schuster, 1961

Eidam, Klaus, *The True Life of J. S. Bach*, trans. Hoyt Rogers, New York: Basic Books, 2001

Ellison, Ralph, *Living with Music*, New York: Modern Library, 2002

Erickson, Raymond, ed., *The Worlds of Johann Sebastian Bach*, New York: Amadeus Press, 2009

Fauser, Annegret, *Musical Encounters at the 1889 Paris World's Fair*, Rochester, NY: University of Rochester Press, 2009

Feather, Leonard, *From Satchmo to Miles*, New York: Stein and Day, 1972

Fétis, François-Joseph, *Nicolo Paganini, with an Analysis of His Compositions and a Sketch of the History of the Violin*, introduction by Stewart Pollens, Mineola, NY: Dover Publications, 2013

Flanner, Janet (Genêt), *Paris Was Yesterday, 1925–1939*, New York: Viking Press, 1972

Fried, Johannes, *Charlemagne*, Cambridge, MA: Harvard University Press, 2016

Gammond, Peter, *Scott Joplin and the Ragtime Era*, New York: St. Martin's Press, 1975

Ganz, David, trans. and ed., *Two Lives of Charlemagne: Erhard and Notker the Stammerer*, New York: Penguin Classics, 2008

Gardiner, John Eliot, *Bach: Music in the Castle of Heaven*, New York: Alfred A. Knopf, 2013

Gaunt, Simon, and Karen Pratt, trans., *The Song of Roland*, New York: Oxford University Press, 2016

Gelly, Dave, *Being Prez: The Life and Music of Lester Young*, New York: Oxford University Press, 2007

Giddens, Gary, *Celebrating Bird: The Triumph of Charlie Parker*, New York: William Morrow, 1987

Gillespie, Dizzy, with Al Fraser, *To Be or Not to Bop*, New York: Doubleday, 1979

Giroud, Vincent, *French Opera: A Short History*, New Haven: Yale University Press, 2010

Glover, Jane, *Mozart's Women: His Family, His Friends, His Music*, New York: HarperCollins, 2005

Golden, Eve, *Vernon and Irene Castle's Ragtime Revolution*, Lexington: University Press of Kentucky, 2007

Guido, *Micrologus (Little Treatise)*, 1028

Guido d'Arezzo's *"Regule rithmice," "Prologus in antiphonarium," and "Epistola ad Michahelem," a Critical Text and Translation*, with an introduction, annotations, indices, and new manuscript inventories by Dolores Pesce, *Musicological Studies*, vol. 73, Ottawa: Institute of Mediaeval Music, 1999

Hartenberger, Russell, *Performance Practice in the Music of Steve Reich*, Cambridge, UK: Cambridge University Press, 2016

Haster, Cate, *Passionate Spirit: The Life of Alma Mahler*, New York: Basic Books, 2019

Hemingway, Ernest, *A Moveable Feast*, New York: Scribner, 1964

Hentoff, Nat, *Jazz Is*, New York: Random House, 1976

Isacoff, Stuart, *A Natural History of the Piano*, New York: Vintage, 2012

———, *When the World Stopped to Listen*, New York: Alfred A. Knopf, 2017

———, *Temperament: How Music Became a Battleground for the Great Minds of Western Civilization,* New York: Vintage, 2003

Johnson, James Weldon, *Black Manhattan,* New York: Alfred A. Knopf, 1930

Jones, Andrew F., *Yellow Music: Media Culture and Colonial Modernity in the Chinese Jazz Age,* Durham, NC: Duke University Press, 2001

Kahn, Ashley, *Kind of Blue: The Making of the Miles Davis Masterpiece,* New York: Da Capo Press, 2000

Keith, Phil, and Tom Clavin, *All Blood Runs Red: The Legendary Life of Eugene Bullard—Boxer, Pilot, Soldier, Spy,* Toronto: Hanover Square Press, 2019

Kelley, Robin D. G., *Thelonious Monk: The Life and Times of an American Original,* New York: Free Press, 2009

Kenney, William Howland, *Chicago Jazz: A Cultural History, 1904–1930,* New York: Oxford University Press, 1993

Kerr, Ruth Slenczynska, *Forbidden Childhood,* Garden City, NY: Doubleday, 1957

Kostelanetz, Richard, ed., *Writings on Glass,* New York: Schirmer Books, 1997

Lang Lang, with David Ritz, *Journey of a Thousand Miles: My Story,* New York: Spiegel & Grau, 2008

Leibowitz, René, *Schoenberg and His School,* trans. Dika Newlin, New York: Philosophical Library, 1949

Lesh, Phil, *Searching for the Sound: My Life with the Grateful Dead,* New York: Back Bay Books, 2006

Levy, David Benjamin, *Beethoven: The Ninth Symphony,* New Haven: Yale University Press, 2003

Lewis, David Levering, *When Harlem Was in Vogue,* New York: Penguin Books, 1997

Li, Moying, *Snow Falling in Spring: Coming of Age in China During the Cultural Revolution,* New York: Farrar, Straus and Giroux, 2008

Lockspeiser, Edward, *Music and Painting,* New York: Harper and Row, 1973

Maher, Paul, and Michael K. Don, eds., *Miles on Miles,* Chicago: Lawrence Hill Books, 2009

Mason, Susan V., ed., *The San Francisco Mime Troupe Reader,* Ann Arbor: University of Michigan Press, 2005

McAuliffe, Mary, *When Paris Sizzled,* London: Rowman & Littlefield, 2016

Messiaen, Olivier, *The Technique of My Musical Language,* trans. John Satterfield, Paris: Alphonse Leduc, 1956

Milhaud, Darius, *Notes Without Music: An Autobiography,* New York: Alfred A. Knopf, 1953

Myers, Walter Dean, and Bill Miles, *The Harlem Hellfighters: When Pride Met Courage,* New York: HarperCollins, 2006

Nagler, A. M., *Theatre Festivals of the Medici, 1539–1637,* New Haven: Yale University Press, 1964

Neighbour, Oliver, Paul Griffiths, and George Perle, *Second Viennese School: Schoenberg, Webern, Berg,* New York: W. W. Norton, 1983

Owens, Thomas, *Bebop: The Music and the Players,* New York: Oxford University Press, 1995

Palisca, Claude, ed., *Hucbald, Guido, and John on Music: Three Medieval Treatises,* trans. Warren Babb, New Haven: Yale University Press, 1978

Pesic, Peter, *Polyphonic Minds: Music of the Hemispheres,* Cambridge, MA: MIT Press, 2017

Platt, Nicholas, *China Boys: How U.S. Relations with the PRC Began and Grew,* Washington, DC: New Academia Publishing/VELLUM Books, 2010

Potter, Keith, *Four Musical Minimalists,* Cambridge, UK: Cambridge University Press, 2000

Reich, Steve, *Writings on Music, 1965–2000,* New York: Oxford University Press, 2002

Ringer, Alexander L., *Arnold Schoenberg: The Composer as Jew,* New York: Oxford University Press, 1993

Rosand, Ellen, *Opera in Seventeenth-Century Venice: The Creation of a Genre,* Berkeley: University of California Press, 1990

Rose, Michael, *The Birth of an Opera,* New York: W. W. Norton, 2013

Rosen, Charles, *Arnold Schoenberg,* New York: Viking Press, 1975

Sachs, Joel, *Henry Cowell: A Man Made of Music,* New York, Oxford University Press, 2012

Schoenberg, Arnold, *Style and Idea,* New York: Philosophical Library, 1950

Schonberg, Harold C., *The Virtuosi,* New York: Times Books, 1985

Schuller, Gunther, *The Swing Era,* New York: Oxford University Press, 1989

Schwarz, K. Robert, *Minimalists,* London: Phaidon Press, 1996

Shack, William A., *Harlem in Montmartre: A Paris Jazz Story Between the Great Wars,* Berkeley: University of California Press, 2001

Shaw, Arnold, *The Jazz Age: Popular Music in the 1920s,* New York: Oxford University Press, 1987

Shawn, Allen, *Arnold Schoenberg's Journey,* New York: Farrar, Straus and Giroux, 2002

Silverman, Kenneth, *Begin Again: A Biography of John Cage,* New York: Alfred A. Knopf, 2010

Slonimsky, Nicolas, *Lexicon of Musical Invective*, Seattle: University of Washington Press, 1978

Spotts, Frederic, *Bayreuth: A History of the Wagner Festival*, New Haven: Yale University Press, 1994

Strickland, Edward, *Minimalism Origins*, Bloomington: Indiana University Press, 1993

Stubbs, David, *Mars by 1980: The Story of Electronic Music*, London: Faber & Faber, 2018

Stuckenschmidt, H. H., *Twentieth Century Music*, trans. Richard Deveson, New York: McGraw-Hill, 1970

Talalay, Kathryn, *Composition in Black and White: The Tragic Saga of Harlem's Biracial Prodigy*, New York: Oxford University Press, 1995

Taruskin, Richard, *Oxford History of Western Music, vol. 1*, New York: Oxford University Press, 2005

Taruskin, Richard, and Christopher H. Gibbs, *The Oxford History of Western Music*, College Edition, New York: Oxford University Press, 2013

Walker, Alan, *Reflections on Liszt*, Ithaca, NY: Cornell University Press, 2011

Walsh, Stephen, *Debussy: A Painter in Sound*, New York: Alfred A. Knopf, 2018

Wolfe, Tom, *The Electric Kool-Aid Acid Test*, New York: Farrar, Straus and Giroux, 1968

# Index

## ILLUSTRATION CREDITS

A NOTE ABOUT THE AUTHOR

Stuart Isacoff is a pianist and composer and a recipient of the ASCAP Deems Taylor Award for excellence in writing about music and the Cremona Musica Award in the category of Communication. He is a frequent contributor to *The Wall Street Journal* and numerous music periodicals, as well as a lecturer at major venues in the United States and Europe. This is his fourth book for Alfred A. Knopf.

## A NOTE ON THE TYPE

This book was set in Adobe Garamond. Designed for the Adobe Corporation by Robert Slimbach, the fonts are based on types first cut by Claude Garamond (c. 1480–1561). Garamond was a pupil of Geoffroy Tory's and is believed to have followed the Venetian models, although he introduced a number of important differences, and it is to him that we owe the letter we now know as "old style."

*Composed by North Market Street Graphics, Lancaster, Pennsylvania*

*Printed and bound by Berryville Graphics, Berryville, Virginia*

*Design by Maggie Hinders*